EXCEL MODELING AND ESTIMATION
IN CORPORATE FINANCE
Third Edition

CRAIG W. HOLDEN
Max Barney Faculty Fellow and Associate Professor
Kelley School of Business
Indiana University

PEARSON

Prentice
Hall

Upper Saddle River, NJ 07458

To Kathryn, Diana and Jimmy

CIP date on file with the Library of Congress.

Executive Editor: Mark Pfaltzgraff
VP/Editorial Director: Sally Yagan
Product Development Manager: Ashley Santora
Project Manager: Susie Abraham
Editorial Assistant: Vanessa Bain
Marketing Manager: Jodi Bassett
Marketing Assistant: Ian Gold
Senior Managing Editor: Judy Leale
Project Manager: Ana Jankowski
Operations Specialist: Michelle Klein
Cover Design: Jayne Conte
Printer/Binder: Bind-rite Graphic / Robbinsville

Credits and acknowledgments borrowed from other sources and reproduced, with permission, in this textbook appear on appropriate page within text.

Microsoft® and Windows® are registered trademarks of the Microsoft Corporation in the U.S.A. and other countries. Screen shots and icons reprinted with permission from the Microsoft Corporation. This book is not sponsored or endorsed by or affiliated with the Microsoft Corporation.

Pearson Education LTD.
Pearson Education Singapore, Pte. Ltd
Pearson Education, Canada, Ltd
Pearson Education–Japan

Pearson Education Australia PTY, Limited
Pearson Education North Asia Ltd
Pearson Educación de Mexico, S.A. de C.V.
Pearson Education Malaysia, Pte. Ltd.

10 9 8 7 6 5 4 3 2
ISBN-13. 978-0-13-602561-0
ISBN-10: 0-13-602561-7

CONTENTS

PART 4 FINANCIAL PLANNING 106

PART 5 OPTIONS AND CORPORATE FINANCE 140

PART 6 EXCEL SKILLS 188

CONTENTS ON CD

- Readme.txt
- Excel Mod Est in Corp Fin 3.pdf
- Ch 01 Single Cash Flow.xlsx
- Ch 02 Annuity.xlsx
- Ch 03 NPV Constant Discnt.xlsx
- Ch 04 NPV General Discnt.xlsx
- Ch 05 Loan Amortization.xlsx
- Ch 06 Bond Valuation.xlsx
- Ch 07 Cost of Capital.xlsx
- Ch 08 Stock Valuation.xlsx
- Ch 09 Firm and Project Val.xlsx
- Ch 10 The Yield Curve.xlsx
- Ch 11 US Yield Curve Dynam.xlsx
- Ch 12 Project NPV.xlsx
- Ch 13 Cost Reducing Proj.xlsx
- Ch 14 Break Even Analysis.xlsx
- Ch 15 Corp Financial Plan.xlsx
- Ch 16 DuPont Ratio Anal.xlsx
- Ch 17 Life-Cycle Fin Plan.xlsx
- Ch 18 Binomial Option Pric.xlsx
- Ch 19 Real Options.xlsx
- Ch 20 Black Scholes Opt Pr.xlsx
- Ch 21 Debt and Equity Val.xlsx
- Ch 22 International Parity.xlsx
- Files in Excel 97-2003 Format

Preface

For more than 20 years, since the emergence of PCs, Lotus 1-2-3, and Microsoft Excel in the 1980's, spreadsheet models have been the dominant vehicles for finance professionals in the business world to implement their financial knowledge. Yet even today, most Corporate Finance textbooks rely on calculators as the primary tool and have little coverage of how to build and estimate Excel models. This book fills that gap. It teaches students how to build and estimate financial models in Excel. It provides step-by-step instructions so that students can build and estimate models themselves (active learning), rather than being handed already completed spreadsheets (passive learning). It progresses from simple examples to practical, real-world applications. It spans nearly all quantitative models in corporate finance.

My goal is simply to *change finance education from being calculator based to being Excel based*. This change will better prepare students for the 21st century business world. This change will increase student evaluations of teacher performance by enabling more practical, real-world content and by allowing a more hands-on, active learning pedagogy.

Third Edition Changes

New to this edition, the biggest innovation is **Ready-To-Build Spreadsheets on the CD.** The CD provides ready-to-build spreadsheets for every chapter with:

The model setup, such as input values, labels, and graphs

Step-by-step instructions for building and estimating the model on the spreadsheet itself

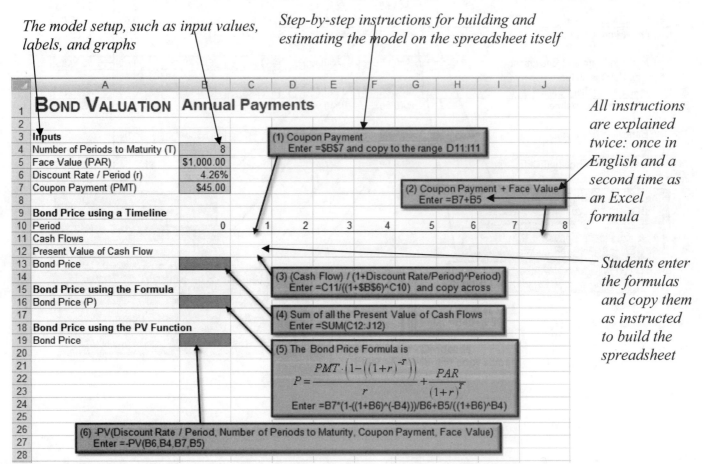

All instructions are explained twice: once in English and a second time as an Excel formula

Students enter the formulas and copy them as instructed to build the spreadsheet

Spin buttons, option buttons, and graphs facilitate visual, interactive learning

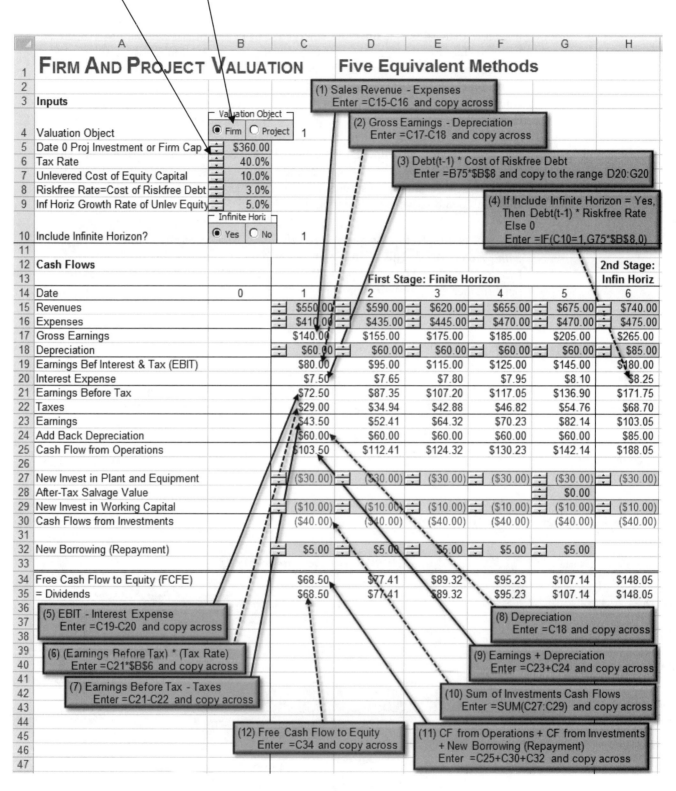

Many spreadsheets use real-world data

	A	B	C	D	E	F	G	H	I	J
1	**CORPORATE FINANCIAL PLANNING**				**Full-Scale Estimation**					
2	**Nike, Inc.**	5/31/2003	5/31/2004	5/31/2005	5/31/2006	5/31/2007	5/31/2008	5/31/2009	Ave. %	
3	**Financial Plan**	Actual	Actual	Actual	Actual	Forecast	Forecast	Forecast	of Sales	
4	**Key Assumptions**									
5	Sales Growth Rate		14.5%	12.1%	8.8%	7.0%	6.0%	5.0%	(1) Forecast key	
6	Tax Rate	44.7%	34.8%	34.9%	35.0%	35.0%	35.0%	35.0%	assumptions	
7	Int Rate on Short-Term Debt	1.0%	2.1%	3.4%	5.1%	4.5%	4.5%	4.5%	Enter forecast	
8	Int Rate on Long-Term Debt	2.3%	3.9%	3.8%	5.1%	5.5%	5.5%	5.5%	values in the	
9	Dividend Payout Rate	29.1%	19.0%	19.5%	20.9%	21.0%	22.0%	23.0%	range F5:H10	
10	Price / Earnings	62.3	39.6	35.4	29.5	30.0	31.0	32.0	(done for you)	
11										
12				(2) Gross Margin - Sum of Expenses						
13	**Income Statement (Mil.$)**			Enter =B16-SUM(B18:B21) and copy across						
14	Sales	$10,697.0	$12,253.1	$13,739.7	$14,954.9	$16,001.7	$16,961.8	$17,809.9		
15	Cost of Goods Sold	$6,072.8	$6,824.0	$7,596.3	$8,190.7	$8,901.8	$9,435.9	$9,907.7		
16	Gross Margin	$4,624.2	$5,429.1	$6,143.4	$6,764.2	$7,100.0	$7,526.0	$7,902.3		
17										
18	Selling, Gen & Adm Expenses	$3,137.6	$3,702.0	$4,221.7	$4,477.8	$4,809.0	$5,097.6	$5,352.5		
19	Other Expense	$79.9	$74.7	$29.1	$4.4	$63.9	$67.8	$71.1		
20	Accounting Change, Net	$266.1	$0.0	$0.0	$0.0	$99.5	$105.5	$110.8		
21	Depreciation	$240.8	$177.4	$28.0	$177.2	$203.5	$215.7	$226.5		
22	EBIT	$899.8	$1,475.0	$1,864.6	$2,104.8	$1,924.0	$2,039.4	$2,141.4		
23										
24	Interest Expense, Net	$42.9	$25.0	$4.8	($36.8)	$24.5	$48.3	$55.8		
25	Taxes	$382.9	$504.4	$648.2	$749.6	$664.8	$696.9	$730.0		
26	Net Income	$474.0	$945.6	$1,211.6	$1,392.0	$1,234.6	$1,294.3	$1,355.6		
27	Shares Outstanding (Millions)	527.2	526.2	522.2	512.0	512.0	512.0	512.0		
28	Earnings Per Share	$0.90	$1.80	$2.32	$2.72	$2.41	$2.53	$2.65		
29										
30	Allocation of Net Income:									
31	Dividends	$137.8	$179.2	$236.7	$290.9	$259.3	$284.7	$311.8		
32	Change in Equity	$336.2	$766.4	$974.9	$1,101.1	$975.4	$1,009.5	$1,043.8		

The Third Edition advances in many ways:

- The new **Ready-To-Build spreadsheets on the CD** are very popular with students. They can open a spreadsheet that is set up and ready to be constructed. Then they can follow the on-spreadsheet instructions to complete the Excel model and don't have to refer back to the book for each step. Once they are done, they can double-check their work against the completed spreadsheet shown in the book. This approach concentrates student time on *implementing financial formulas and estimation*.

- There is great new corporate finance content, including:

    o Estimating firm valuation or project valuation in a two-stage framework using five alternative techniques and demonstrating their equivalence:

        ▪ Free Cash Flow to Equity
        ▪ Free Cash Flow to the Firm
        ▪ Residual Income
        ▪ Dividend Discount Model
        ▪ Adjusted Present Value

    o Estimating the cost of capital using the Static CAPM based on the Fama-MacBeth method, o   Estimating the cost of capital using the APT or Intertemporal CAPM based on the Fama-MacBeth method, including the Fama-French three factor model, and

    o   Four international parity conditions

- There is a new chapter on useful Excel tricks.

    🗀 Files in Excel 97-2003 Format

- The Ready-To-Build spreadsheets on CD and the explanations in the book are based on **Excel 2007** by default. However, the CD also contains a folder with Ready-To-Build spreadsheets based on **Excel 97-2003** format. Also, the book contains "Excel 2003 Equivalent" boxes that explain how to do the equivalent step in Excel 2003 and earlier versions.

> **Excel 2003 Equivalent**
> To call up a Data Table in Excel 2003, click on **Data | Table**

- The instruction boxes on the Ready-To-Build spreadsheets are *bitmapped images* so that the formulas cannot just be copied to the spreadsheet. Both the instruction boxes and arrows are *objects*, so that all of them can be deleted in one step when the spreadsheet is complete and everything else will be left untouched. Click on **Home | Editing | Find & Select down-arrow | Select Objects**, then select all of the instruction boxes and arrows, and press the delete key. Furthermore, any blank rows can be deleted, leaving a clean spreadsheet for future use.

What Is Unique About This Book

There are many features which distinguish this book from any other:

- **Plain Vanilla Excel.** Other books on the market emphasize teaching students programming using Visual Basic for Applications (VBA) or using macros. By contrast, this book does nearly everything in plain vanilla Excel. Although programming is liked by a minority of students, it is seriously disliked by the majority. Plain vanilla Excel has the advantage of being a very intuitive, user-friendly environment that is accessible to all. It is fully capable of handling a wide range of applications, including quite sophisticated ones. Further, your students already know the basics of Excel and nothing more is assumed. Students are assumed to be able to enter formulas in a cell and to copy formulas from one cell to another. All other features of Excel (such as built-in functions, Data Tables, Solver, etc.) are explained as they are used.

- **Build From Simple Examples To Practical, Real-World Applications.** The general approach is to start with a simple example and build up to a practical, real-world application. In many chapters, the previous Excel model is carried forward to the next more complex model. For example, the chapter on binomial option pricing carries forward Excel models as follows: (a.) single-period model with replicating portfolio, (b.) eight-period model with replicating portfolio, (c.) eight-period model with risk-neutral probabilities, (d.) eight-period model with risk-neutral probabilities for American or

European options with discrete dividends, (e.) full-scale, fifty-period model with risk-neutral probabilities for American or European options with discrete dividends using continuous or discrete annualization convention. Whenever possible, this book builds up to full-scale, practical applications using real data. Students are excited to learn practical applications that they can actually use in their future jobs. Employers are excited to hire students with Excel modeling and estimation skills, who can be more productive faster.

- **Supplement For All Popular Corporate Finance Textbooks.** This book is a supplement to be combined with a primary textbook. This means that you can keep using whatever textbook you like best. You don't have to switch. It also means that you can take an incremental approach to incorporating Excel modeling and estimation. You can start modestly and build up from there.

- **A Change In Content Too.** Excel modeling and estimation is not merely a new medium, but an opportunity to cover some unique content items which require computer support to be feasible. For example, the full-scale estimation Excel model in Corporate Financial Planning uses three years of historical 10K data on Nike, Inc. (including every line of their income statement, balance sheet, and cash flow statement), constructs a complete financial system (including linked financial ratios), and projects these financial statements three years into the future. Using 10 years of monthly returns for individual stocks, U.S. portfolios, and country portfolios to estimate the cost of capital using the Static CAPM based on the Fama-MacBeth method and to estimate the cost of capital using the APT or Intertemporal CAPM based on the Fama-MacBeth method. The Excel model to estimate firm valuation or project valuation demonstrates the equivalence of the Free Cash Flow To Equity, Free Cash Flow to the Firm, Residual Income, Dividend Discount Model, and Adjusted Present Value technique, not just in the perpetuity case covered by some textbooks, but for a fully general two-stage project with an arbitrary set of cash flows over an explicit forecast horizon, followed by a infinite horizon growing perpetuity. As a practical matter, all of these sophisticated applications require Excel.

Conventions Used In This Book

This book uses a number of conventions.

- **Time Goes Across The Columns And Variables Go Down The Rows.** When something happens over time, I let each column represent a period of time. For example in life-cycle financial planning, date 0 is in column B, date 1 is in column C, date 2 is in column D, etc. Each row represents a different variable, which is usually a labeled in column A. This manner of organizing Excel models is so common because it is how financial statements are organized.

- **Color Coding.** A standard color scheme is used to clarify the structure of the Excel models. The Ready-To-Build spreadsheets on CD uses: (1) yellow shading for input values, (2) no shading (i.e. white) for throughput formulas, and (3) green shading for final results ("the bottom line"). A few Excel models include choice variables. Choice variables use blue shading. The Constrained Portfolio Optimization spreadsheet includes constraints. Constaints use pink-purple shading.

- **The Time Line Technique.** The most natural technique for discounting cash flows in an Excel model is the time line technique, where each column corresponds to a period of time. As an example, see the section labeled Calculate Bond Price using a Timeline in the figure below.

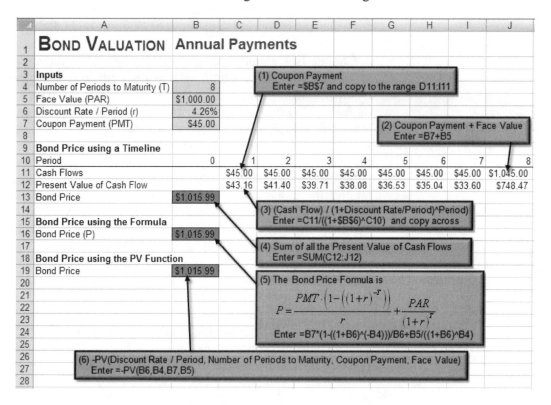

- **Using As Many Different Techniques As Possible.** In the figure above, the bond price is calculated using as many different techniques as possible. Specifically, it is calculated three ways: (1) discounting each cash flow on a time line, (2) using the closed-form formula, and (3) using Excel's PV function. This approach makes the point that all three techniques are equivalent. This approach also develops skill at double-checking these calculations, which is a very important method for avoiding errors in practice.

- **Symbolic Notation is Self-Contained.** Every spreadsheet that contains symbolic notation in the instruction boxes is self-contained (i.e., all symbolic notation is defined on the spreadsheet). Further, I have stopped using symbolic notation for named ranges that was used in prior editions. Therefore, there is no need for alternative notation versions that were provided on the CD in the prior edition and they have been eliminated.

Craig's Challenge

I challenge the readers of this book to dramatically improve your finance education by personally constructing all of the Excel models in this book. This will take you about 10 – 20 hours hours depending on your current Excel modeling skills. Let me assure you that it will be an excellent investment. You will:

- gain a practical understanding of the core concepts of Corporate Finance,
- develop hands-on, Excel modeling skills, and
- build an entire suite of finance applications, which you fully understand.

When you complete this challenge, I invite you to send an e-mail to me at **cholden@indiana.edu** to share the good news. Please tell me your name, school, (prospective) graduation year, and which Excel modeling book you completed. I will add you to a web-based honor roll at:

http://www.excelmodeling.com/honor-roll.htm

We can celebrate together!

The Excel Modeling and Estimation Series

This book is part of a series on **Excel Modeling and Estimation** by Craig W. Holden, published by Pearson / Prentice Hall. The series includes:

- **Excel Modeling and Estimation in Corporate Finance,**
- **Excel Modeling and Estimation in the Fundamentals of Corporate Finance,**
- **Excel Modeling and Estimation in Investments,** and
- **Excel Modeling and Estimation in the Fundamentals of Investments.**

Each book teaches value-added skills in constructing financial models in Excel. Complete information about the **Excel Modeling and Estimation** series is available at my web site:

http://www.excelmodeling.com

All of the **Excel Modeling and Estimation** books can be purchased any time at:

http://www.amazon.com

If you have any suggestions or corrections, please e-mail them to me at **cholden@indiana.edu**. I will consider your suggestions and will implement any corrections in the next edition.

This book provides educational examples of how to estimate financial models from real data. In doing so, this book uses a tiny amount of data that is copyrighted by others. I rely upon the fair use provision of law (Section 107 of the Copyright Act of 1976) as the legal and legitimate basis for doing so.[1]

Suggestions for Faculty Members

There is no single best way to use **Excel Modeling and Estimation in Corporate Finance**. There are as many different techniques as there are different styles and philosophies of teaching. You need to discover what works best for you. Let me highlight several possibilities:

1. **Out-of-class individual projects with help.** This is a technique that I have used and it works well. I require completion of several short Excel modeling projects of every individual student in the class. To provide help, I schedule special "help lab" sessions in a computer lab during which time myself and my graduate assistant are available to answer questions while students do each assignment in about an hour. Typically about half the questions are Excel questions and half are finance questions. I have always graded such projects, but an alternative approach would be to treat them as ungraded homework.

2. **Out-of-class individual projects without help.** Another technique is to assign Excel modeling projects for individual students to do on their own out of class. One instructor assigns seven Excel modeling projects at the beginning of the semester and has individual students turn in all seven completed Excel models for grading at the end of the semester. At the end of each chapter are problems that can be assigned with or without help. Faculty members can download the completed Excel models at **http://www.prenhall.com/holden**. See your local Pearson / Prentice Hall (or Pearson Education) representative to gain access.

3. **Out-of-class group projects.** A technique that I have used for the last fifteen years is to require students to do big Excel modeling projects in groups. I have students write a report to a hypothetical boss, which intuitively explains their method of analysis, key assumptions, and key results.

4. **In-class reinforcement of key concepts.** The class session is scheduled in a computer lab or equivalently students are required to bring their (required) laptop computers to a technology classroom, which has a data jack and a power outlet at every student station. I explain a key concept in words and equations. Then I turn to a 10-15 minute segment in which students open a Ready-To-Build spreadsheet and build the Excel model in real-time in the

---

[1] Consistent with the fair use statute, I make transformative use of the data for teaching purposes, the nature of the data is factual data that is important to the educational purpose, the amount of data used is a tiny, and its use has no significant impact on the potential market for the data.

class. This provides real-time, hands-on reinforcement of a key concept. This technique can be done often throughout the semester.

5. **In-class demonstration of Excel modeling.** The instructor can perform an in-class demonstration of how to build Excel models. Typically, only a small portion of the total Excel model would be demonstrated.

6. **In-class demonstration of key relationships using Spin Buttons, Option Buttons, and Charts.** The instructor can dynamically illustrate comparative statics or dynamic properties over time using visual, interactive elements. For example, one spreadsheet provides a "movie" of 37 years of U.S. term structure dynamics. Another spreadsheet provides an interactive graph of the sensitivity of bond prices to changes in the coupon rate, yield-to-maturity, number of payments / year, and face value.

I'm sure I haven't exhausted the list of potential teaching techniques. Feel free to send an e-mail to **cholden@indiana.edu** to let me know novel ways in which you use this book.

Acknowledgements

I thank Mark Pfaltzgraff, David Alexander, Jackie Aaron, P.J. Boardman, Mickey Cox, Maureen Riopelle, and Paul Donnelly of Pearson / Prentice Hall for their vision, innovativeness, and encouragement of **Excel Modeling and Estimation in Corporate Finance**. I thank Susan Abraham, Kate Murray, Lori Braumberger, Holly Brown, Debbie Clare, Cheryl Clayton, Kevin Hancock, Josh McClary, Bill Minic, Melanie Olsen, Beth Ann Romph, Erika Rusnak, Gladys Soto, and Lauren Tarino of Pearson / Prentice Hall for many useful contributions. I thank Professors Alan Bailey (University of Texas at San Antonio), Zvi Bodie (Boston University), Jack Francis (Baruch College), David Griswold (Boston University), Carl Hudson (Auburn University), Robert Kleiman (Oakland University), Mindy Nitkin (Simmons College), Steve Rich (Baylor University), Tim Smaby (Penn State University), Charles Trzcinka (Indiana University), Sorin Tuluca (Fairleigh Dickinson University), Marilyn Wiley (Florida Atlantic University), and Chad Zutter (University of Pittsburgh) for many thoughtful comments. I thank my graduate students Scott Marolf, Heath Eckert, Ryan Brewer, Ruslan Goyenko, Wendy Liu, and Wannie Park for careful error-checking. I thank Jim Finnegan and many other students for providing helpful comments. I thank my family, Kathryn, Diana, and Jimmy, for their love and support.

About The Author

CRAIG W. HOLDEN

Craig Holden is the Max Barney Faculty Fellow and Associate Professor of Finance at the Kelley School of Business at Indiana University. His M.B.A. and Ph.D. are from the Anderson School at UCLA. He is the winner of many teaching and research awards. His research on security trading and market making ("market microstructure") has been published in leading academic journals. He has written four books on **Excel Modeling and Estimation** in finance, which are published by Pearson / Prentice Hall and Chinese editions are published by China Renmin University Press. He has chaired sixteen dissertations, been a member or chair of 46 dissertations, served on the program committee of the *Western Finance Association* for nine years, and served as an associate editor of the *Journal of Financial Markets* for eleven years. He chaired the department undergraduate committee for eleven years, chaired three different schoolwide committees over six years, and is currently chairing the department doctoral committee. He has lead several major curriculum innovations in the finance department. More information is available at Craig's home page: **www.kelley.iu.edu/cholden**.

PART 1 TIME VALUE OF MONEY

Chapter 1 Single Cash Flow

1.1 Present Value

Problem. A single cash flow of $1,000.00 will be received in 5 periods. For this cash flow, the appropriate discount rate / period is 6.0%. What is the present value of this single cash flow?

Solution Strategy. We will calculate the present value of this single cash flow in three equivalent ways. First, we will calculate the present value using a time line, where each column corresponds to a period of calendar time. Second, we use a formula for the present value. Third, we use Excel's **PV** function for the present value.

FIGURE 1.1 Excel Model for Single Cash Flow - Present Value.

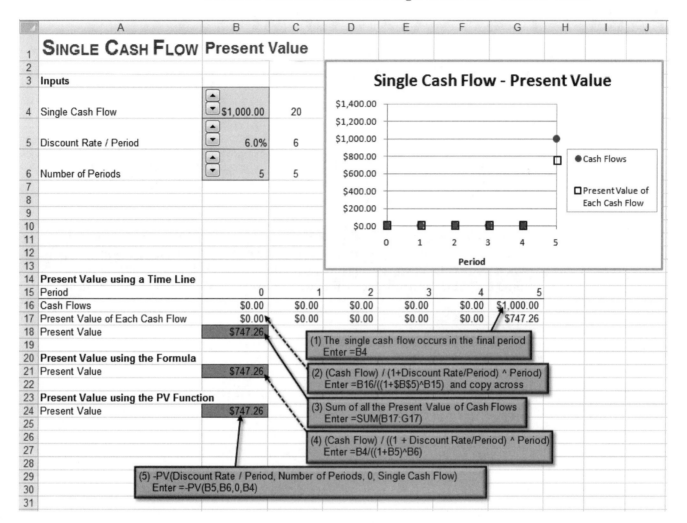

The Present Value of this Single Cash Flow is $747.26. Notice you get the same answer all three ways: using the time line, using the formula, or using the PV function!

1.2 Future Value

Problem. A single cash flow of $747.26 is available now (in period 0). For this cash flow, the appropriate discount rate / period is 6.0%. What is the period 5 future value of this single cash flow?

Solution Strategy. We will calculate the future value of the single cash flow in three equivalent ways. First, we will calculate the future value using a time line, where each column corresponds to a period of calendar time. Second, we use a formula for the future value. Third, we use Excel's **FV** function for the future value.

FIGURE 1.2 Excel Model for Single Cash Flow - Future Value.

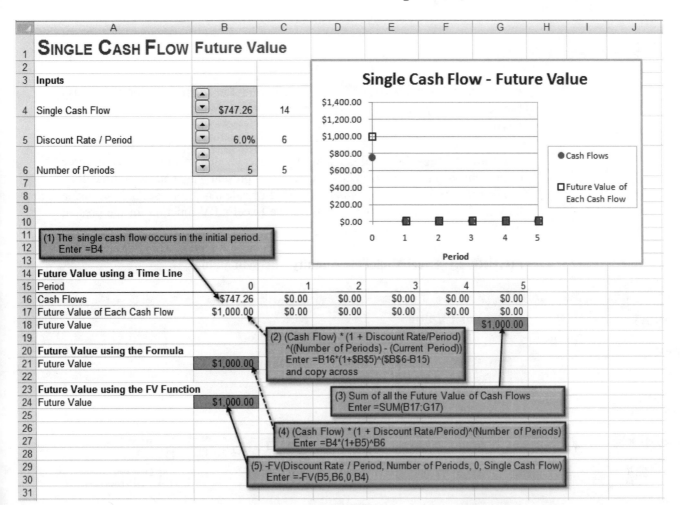

The Future Value of this Single Cash Flow is $1,000.00. Notice you get the same answer all three ways: using the time line, using the formula, or using the FV function!

Comparing Present Value and Future Value, we see that they are opposite operations. That is, one operation "undoes" the other. The Present Value of $1,000.00 in period 5 is $747.26 in period 0. The Future Value of $747.26 in period 0 is $1,000.00 in period 5.

Problems

1. A single cash flow of $1,673.48 will be received in 4 periods. For this cash flow, the appropriate discount rate / period is 7.8%. What is the present value of this single cash flow?

2. A single cash flow of $932.47 is available now (in period 0). For this cash flow, the appropriate discount rate / period is 3.9%. What is the period 4 future value of this single cash flow?

Chapter 2 Annuity

2.1 Present Value

Problem. An annuity pays $80.00 each period for 5 periods. For these cash flows, the appropriate discount rate / period is 6.0%. What is the present value of this annuity?

Solution Strategy. We will calculate the present value of this annuity in three equivalent ways. First, we will calculate the present value using a time line, where each column corresponds to a period of calendar time. Second, we use a formula for the present value. Third, we use Excel's **PV** function for the present value.

FIGURE 2.1 Excel Model for Annuity - Present Value.

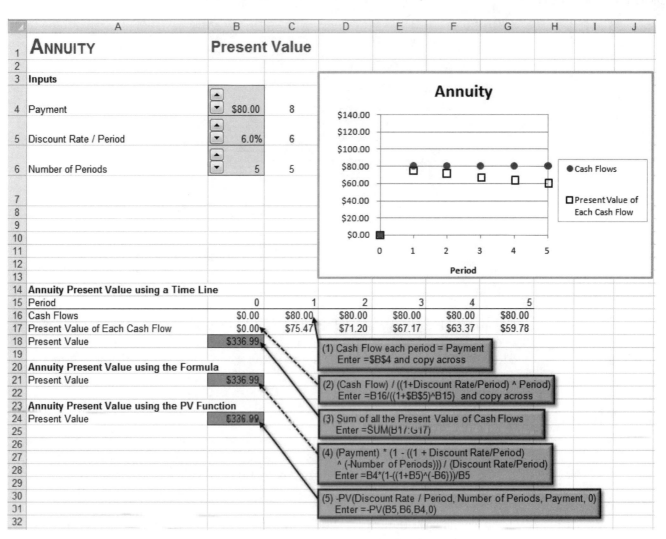

The Present Value of this Annuity is $336.99. Notice you get the same answer all three ways: using the time line, using the formula, or using the PV function.

2.2 Future Value

Problem. An annuity pays $80.00 each period for 5 periods. For these cash flows, the appropriate discount rate / period is 6.0%. What is the period 5 future value of this annuity?

Solution Strategy. We will calculate the future value of this annuity in three equivalent ways. First, we will calculate the future value using a time line, where each column corresponds to a period of calendar time. Second, we use a formula for the future value. Third, we use Excel's **FV** function for the future value.

FIGURE 2.2 Excel Model for Annuity - Future Value.

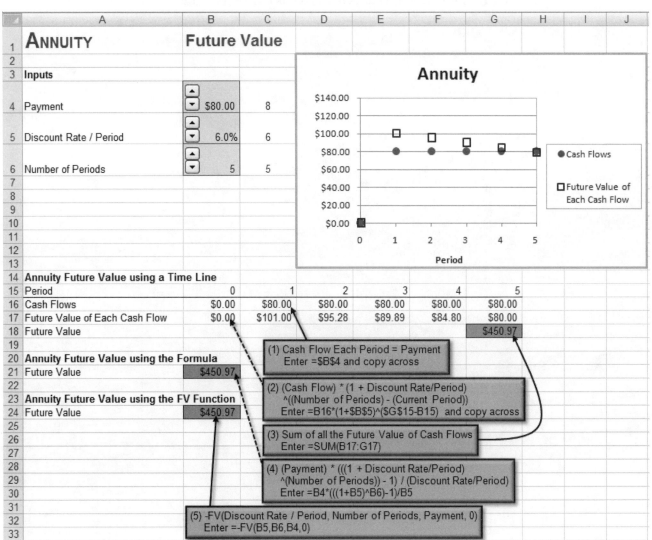

The Future Value of this Annuity is $450.97. Notice you get the same answer all three ways: using the time line, using the formula, or using the FV function.

2.3 System of Four Annuity Variables

Problem. There is a tight connection between all of the inputs and output to annuity valuation. Indeed, they form a system of four annuity variables: (1) Payment, (2) Discount Rate / Period, (3) Number of Periods, and (4) Present Value. Given any three of these variables, find the fourth variable.

Solution Strategy. Given any three of these variable, we will use as many equivalent ways of solving for the fourth variable as possible. The Annuity – Present Value spreadsheet solves for the Present Value, use a Time Line, formula, and the **PV** function. Building on that spreadsheet, add the Payment using the formula and **PMT** function. Then add the Discount Rate / Period using the **RATE** function. Then add the Number of Periods, use the **NPER** function.

FIGURE 2.3 Excel Model for Annuity - System of Four Annuity Variables.

	A	B	C	D	E	F	G	H	I	J
1	ANNUITY	System of Four Annuity Variables								
2										
3	Inputs									
4	Payment	$80.00	8							
5	Discount Rate / Period	6.0%	6							
6	Number of Periods	5	5							
7	Present Value	$336.99	6							
8										
9										
10										
11										
12										
13										
14	Annuity Present Value using a Time Line									
15	Period	0	1	2	3	4	5			
16	Cash Flows	$0.00	$80.00	$80.00	$80.00	$80.00	$80.00			
17	Present Value of Each Cash Flow	$0.00	$75.47	$71.20	$67.17	$63.37	$59.78			
18	Present Value	$336.99								
19										
20	Annuity Present Value using the Formula									
21	Present Value	$336.99								
22										
23	Annuity Present Value using the PV Function									
24	Present Value	$336.99								
25										
26										
27	Payment									
28	Payment using the Formula	$80.00								
29	Payment using the PMT Function	$80.00								
30										
31	Discount Rate / Period									
32	Discount Rate / Per using the RATE Func	6.0%								
33										
34	Number of Periods									
35	Num of Periods using the NPER Function	5								
36										
37										
38										
39										
40										
41										
42										
43										
44										
45										
46										
47										

Annuity chart (Cash Flows; Present Value of Each Cash Flow) plotted against Period 0 through 5.

(6) Payment formula is:
= (Present Value) / ((1 - ((1 + Discount Rate/Period)
^ (-Number of Periods))) / (Discount Rate/Period)).
Enter =B7/((1-((1+B5)^(-B6)))/B5)

(7) Payment function is:
=PMT(Discount Rate / Period, Number of Periods, -Present Value, 0).
Enter =PMT(B5,B6,-B7,0)

(8) Rate function is:
=RATE(Number of Periods, Payment, -Present Value, 0).
Enter =RATE(B6,B4,-B7,0)

(9) Number of Periods function is:
=NPER(Discount Rate / Period, Payment, -Present Value, 0).
Enter =NPER(B5,B4,-B7,0)

We see that the system of four annuity variables is internally consistent. The four outputs in rows **13** through **32** (Present Value = $336.99, Payment = $80.00, Discount Rate / Period = 6.0%, and Number of Periods = 5) are identical to the four inputs in rows **4** through **7**. Thus, any of the four annuity variables can be calculated from the other three in a fully consistent manner.

Problems

1) An annuity pays $142.38 each period for 6 periods. For these cash flows, the appropriate discount rate / period is 4.5%. What is the present value of this annuity?

2) An annuity pays $63.92 each period for 4 periods. For these cash flows, the appropriate discount rate / period is 9.1%. What is the period 5 future value of this annuity?

3) Consider a system of four annuity variables.

   (a) An annuity pays $53.00 each period for 4 periods. For these cash flows, the appropriate discount rate / period is 7.0%. What is the present value of this annuity?

   (b) An annuity pays each period for 10 period, the appropriate discount rate / period is 7.0%, and the present value is $142.38. What is the payment each period?

   (c) An annuity pays $173.00 each period for 13 periods, and the present value is $513.94. What is the discount rate / period of this annuity?

   (d) An annuity pays $40.00 each period, the appropriate discount rate / period is 6.0%, and the present value is $168.49. What is the number of periods?

Chapter 3 NPV Using Constant Discounting

3.1 Nominal Rate

Problem. A project requires a current investment of $100.00 and yields future expected cash flows of $21.00, $34.00, $40.00, $33.00, and $17.00 in periods 1 through 5, respectively. All figures are in thousands of dollars. For these expected cash flows, the appropriate nominal discount rate is 8.0%. What is the net present value of this project?

Solution Strategy. We will calculate the net present value of this project in two equivalent ways. First, we will calculate the net present value using a time line, where each column corresponds to a period of calendar time. Second, we use Excel's **NPV** function for the net present value.

FIGURE 3.1 NPV Using Constant Discounting – Nominal Rate.

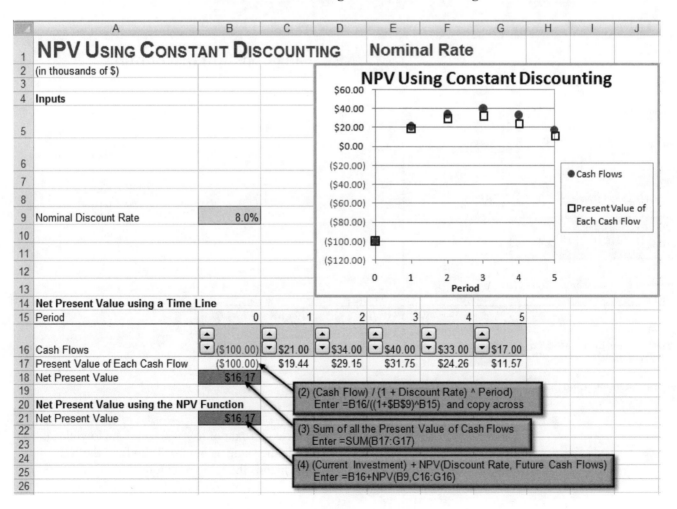

The Net Present Value of this project is $16.17. Notice you get the same answer both ways: using the time line or using the NPV function.

3.2 Real Rate

Problem. A project requires a current investment of $100.00 and yields future expected cash flows of $21.00, $34.00, $40.00, $33.00, and $17.00 in periods 1 through 5, respectively. All figures are in thousands of dollars. The inflation rate is 3.0%. For these expected cash flows, the appropriate Real Discount Rate is 4.854%. What is the net present value of this project?

Solution Strategy. We begin by calculating the (nominal) discount rate from the inflation rate and the real discount rate. The rest of the net present value calculation is the same as the Net Present Value - Constant Discount Rate Excel model.

FIGURE 3.2 NPV Using Constant Discounting – Real Rate.

	A	B	C	D	E	F	G
1	NPV USING CONSTANT DISCOUNTING				Real Rate		
2	(in thousands of $)						
3							
4	Inputs						
5	Inflation Rate	3.0%	3				
6	Real Discount Rate	4.854%	4				
7							
8	Outputs						
9	Nominal Discount Rate	8.0%					
10	(1) (1 + Inflation Rate) * (1+ Real Discount Rate) - 1 Enter =(1+B5)*(1+B6)-1						
11							
12							
13							
14	Net Present Value using a Time Line						
15	Period	0	1	2	3	4	5
16	Cash Flows	($100.00)	$21.00	$34.00	$40.00	$33.00	$17.00
17	Present Value of Each Cash Flow	($100.00)	$19.44	$29.15	$31.75	$24.26	$11.57
18	Net Present Value	$16.17					
19							
20	Net Present Value using the NPV Function						
21	Net Present Value	$16.17					

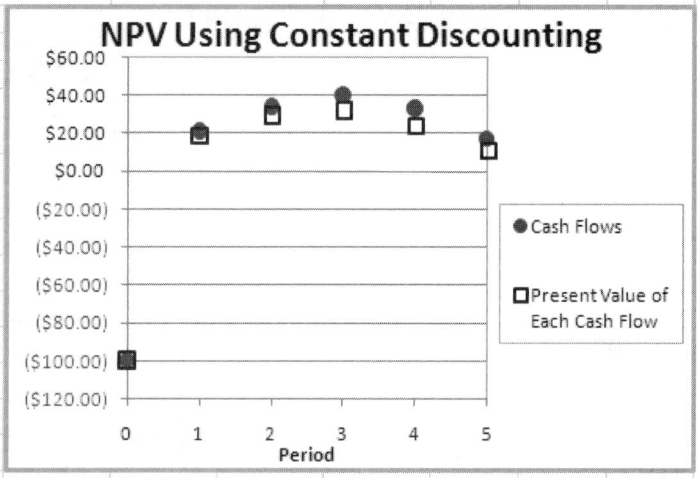

The inflation rate of 3.0% and the real discount rate of 4.854%, combine to yield a nominal discount rate of 8.0%, which is the same as before. Therefore, the Net Present Value of this project is $16.17, which is the same as before.

Problems

1. A project requires a current investment of $189.32 and yields future expected cash flows of $45.19, $73.11, $98,54, $72.83, and $58.21 in periods 1 through 5, respectively. All figures are in thousands of dollars. For these expected cash flows, the appropriate discount rate is 6.3%. What is the net present value of this project?

2. A project requires a current investment of $117.39 and yields future expected cash flows of $38.31, $48.53, $72.80, $96.31, and $52.18 in periods 1 through 5, respectively. All figures are in thousands of dollars. The inflation rate is 2.7%. For these expected cash flows, the appropriate Real Discount Rate is 8.6%. What is the net present value of this project?

Chapter 4 NPV Using General Discounting

4.1 Nominal Rate

Problem. A project requires a current investment of $100.00 and yields future expected cash flows of $21.00, $34.00, $40.00, $33.00, and $17.00 in periods 1 through 5, respectively. All figures are in thousands of dollars. For these expected cash flows, the appropriate nominal discount rates are 8.0% in period 1, 7.6% in period 2, 7.3% in period 3, 7.0% in period 4, and 7.0% in period 5. What is the net present value of this project?

Solution Strategy. We will calculate the Net Present Value of this project using a Time Line. This is the *only* possible way to calculate the project NPV in the general case where the discount rate changes over time. Excel's **NPV** function cannot be used because it is limited to the special case of a constant discount rate. And there is no simple formula for NPV, short of typing in a term for each cash flow.

FIGURE 4.1 NPV Using General Discounting – Nominal Rate.

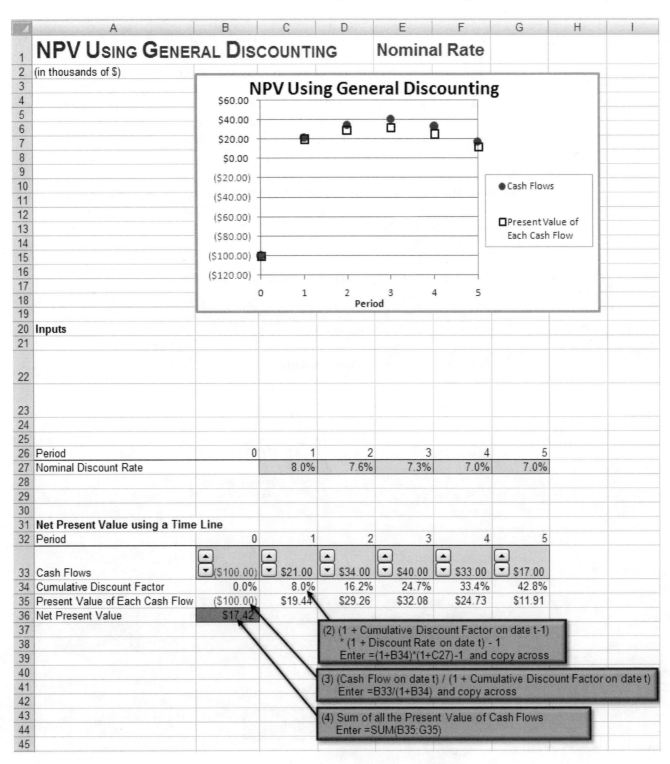

The Net Present Value of this project is $17.42.

4.2 Real Rate

Problem. A project requires a current investment of $100.00 and yields future expected cash flows of $21.00, $34.00, $40.00, $33.00, and $17.00 in periods 1 through 5, respectively. All figures are in thousands of dollars. The forecasted inflation rate is 3.0% in period 1, 2.8% in period 2, 2.5% in period 3, 2.2% in period 4, and 2.0% in period 5. For these expected cash flows, the appropriate REAL discount rate is 4.854% in period 1, 4.669% in period 2, 4.683% in period 3, 4.697% in period 4, and 4.902% in period 5. What is the net present value of this project?

Solution Strategy. We begin by calculating the (nominal) discount rate for each period from the inflation rate in each period and corresponding real discount rate. The rest of the net present value calculation is the same as the Net Present Value - General Discount Rate Excel model.

FIGURE 4.2 NPV Using General Discounting – Real Rate.

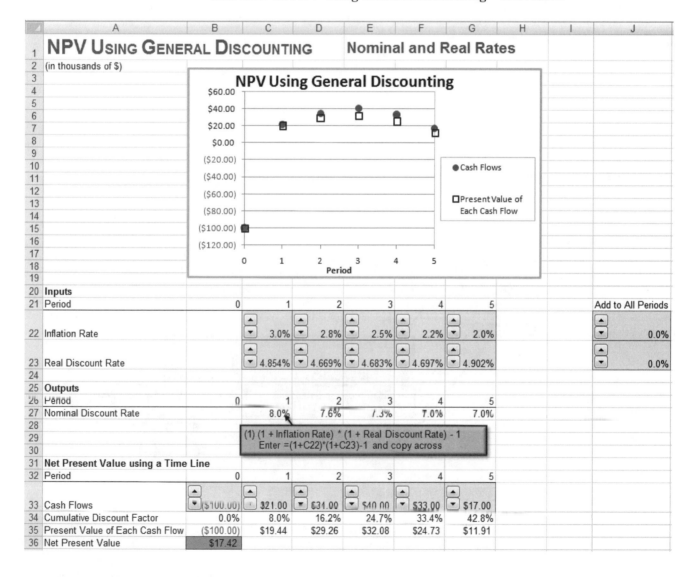

The Net Present Value of this project is $17.42, the same as above.

You can experiment with different inflation rates or real discount rates by clicking the corresponding spin button for each period. Alternative you can raise or lower the inflation rates or real discount rates for *all periods* by click on the spin button in the range **J22:J23**.

This Excel model can handle *any* pattern of discount rates. For example, it can handle the special case of a constant inflation rate at 3.0% and a constant real discount rate at 4.854%.

FIGURE 4.3 NPV Using General Discounting – Real Rate.

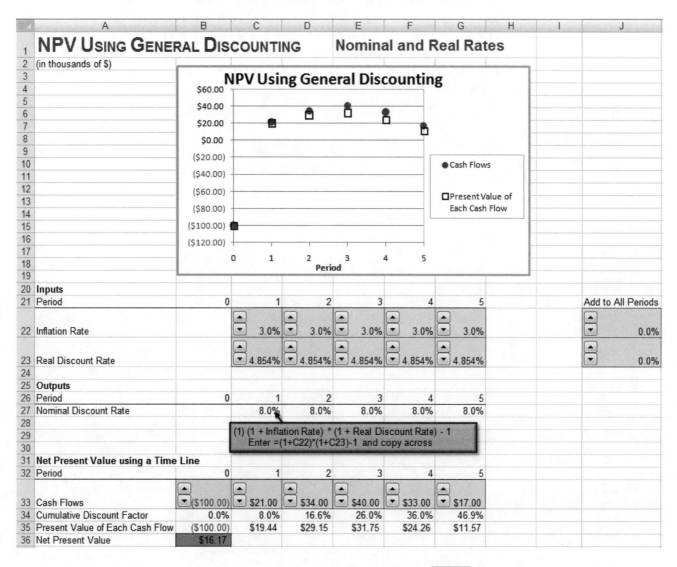

The Net Present Value of this project is $16.17, which is the same answer as the previous chapter on NPV Using Constant Discounting. The general discount rate Excel model is the most general way to do discounting and is the most common approach that we will use in the rest of this book.

Problems

1. A project requires a current investment of $54.39 and yields future expected cash flows of $19.27, $27.33, $34.94, $41.76, and $32.49 in periods 1 through 5, respectively. All figures are in thousands of dollars. For these expected cash flows, the appropriate nominal discount rates are 6.4% in period 1, 6.2% in period 2, 6.0% in period 3, 5.7% in period 4, and 5.4% in period 5. What is the net present value of this project?

3. A project requires a current investment of $328.47 and yields future expected cash flows of $87.39, $134.97, $153.28, $174.99, and $86.41 in periods 1 through 5, respectively. All figures are in thousands of dollars. The forecasted inflation rate is 3.4% in period 1, 3.6% in period 2, 3.9% in period 3, 4.4% in period 4, and 4.7% in period 5. For these expected cash flows, the appropriate REAL discount rate is 7.8% in period 1, 7.1% in period 2, 6.5% in period 3, 6.0% in period 4, and 5.4% in period 5. What is the net present value of this project?

Chapter 5 Loan Amortization

5.1 Basics

Problem. To purchase a house, you take out a 30 year mortgage. The present value (loan amount) of the mortgage is $300,000. The mortgage charges an interest rate / year of 8.00%. What is the annual payment required by this mortgage? How much of each year's payment goes to paying interest and how much reducing the principal balance?

Solution Strategy. First, we use Excel's **PMT** function to calculate the annual payment of a 30 year annuity (mortgage). Then we will use a time line and simple recursive formulas to split out the payment into the interest component and the principal reduction component.

FIGURE 5.1 Excel Model for Loan Amortization - Basics.

	A	B	C	D	E	F	G	H	I	J
1	**LOAN AMORTIZATION**	**Basics**								
3	Inputs									
4	Present value	$300,000		30						
5	Interest rate / year	8.00%		8						
6	Number of years	30		30						
17	Outputs									
18	Year	1	2	3	4	5	6	7	8	9
19	Beg. Principal Balance	$300,000	$297,352	$294,492	$291,403	$288,067	$284,464	$280,573	$276,370	$271,832
20	Payment	$26,648	$26,648	$26,648	$26,648	$26,648	$26,648	$26,648	$26,648	$26,648
21	Interest Component	$24,000	$23,788	$23,559	$23,312	$23,045	$22,757	$22,446	$22,110	$21,747
22	Principal Component	$2,648	$2,860	$3,089	$3,336	$3,603	$3,891	$4,202	$4,539	$4,902

(1) Present Value
Enter =B4

(5) = (Beg. Principal Balance in year t-1) - (Principal Component in year t-1)
Enter =B19-B22 and copy across

(2) PMT(Interest Rate / Year, Number of Years, - Present Value, 0)
Enter =PMT($B$5,$B$6,-$B$4,0) and copy across

(3) (Interest rate/year) * (Beginning Principal Balance in year t)
Enter =$B$5*B19 and copy across

(4) Payment - (Interest Component)
Enter =B20-B21 and copy across

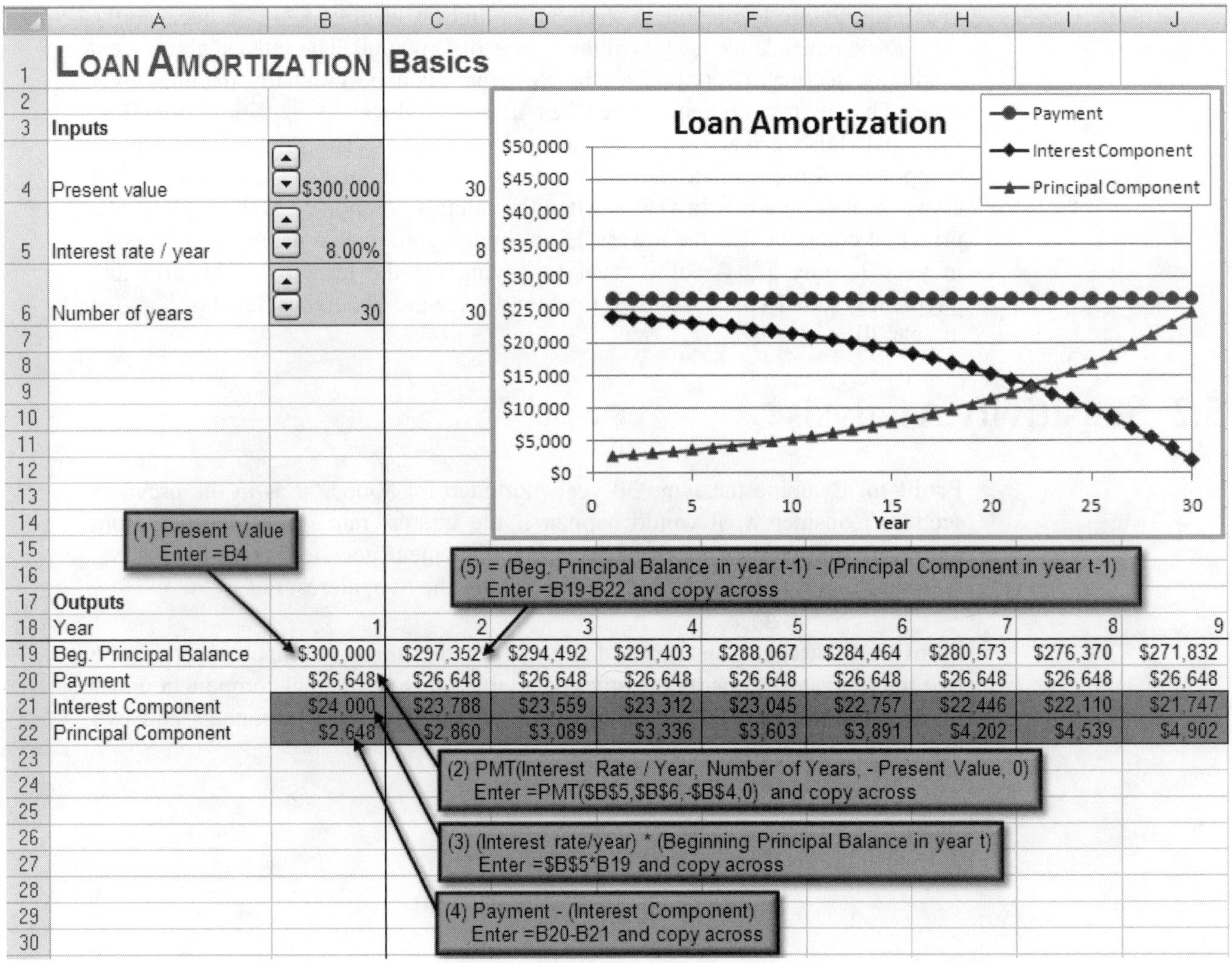

The Annual Payment is $26,648. The figure below shows the final years of the time line for the loan.

FIGURE 5.2 Final Years of the Time Line of Loan Amortization - Basics.

	A	B	Z	AA	AB	AC	AD	AE	AF
17	Outputs								
18	Year	1	25	26	27	28	29	30	31
19	Beg. Principal Balance	$300,000	$123,192	$106,399	$88,262	$68,675	$47,521	$24,674	($0)
20	Payment	$26,648	$26,648	$26,648	$26,648	$26,648	$26,648	$26,648	
21	Interest Component	$24,000	$9,855	$8,512	$7,061	$5,494	$3,802	$1,974	
22	Principal Component	$2,648	$16,793	$18,136	$19,587	$21,154	$22,847	$24,674	

The principal balance drops to zero in year 31 after the final payment is made in year 30. The loan is paid off! It doesn't matter whether the zero amount in cell AF10 displays as positive or negative. The only reason it would display as negative is due to round off error in the eighth decimal or higher, which is irrelevant of our purposes.

The Interest Component depends on the size of the Beg. Principal Balance. In year 1 the interest component starts at its highest level of $24,000 because the Beg. Principal Balance is at its highest level of $300,000. The interest component gradually declines over time as the Principal Balance gradually declines over time. The interest component reaches its lowest level of $1,974 as the Beg. Principal Balance reaches its lowest level of $24,674. The principal repayment component is the residual part of the payment that is left over after the interest component is paid off. In year 1 when the interest component is the highest, the principal component is the lowest. Even though you made a payment of $26,648 in year 1, only $2,648 of it went to paying off the principal! The principal payment gradually increases over time until it reaches its highest level of $24,674 in year 30.

5.2 Sensitivity Analysis

Problem. Examine the same 30 year mortgage for $300,000 as in the previous section. Consider what would happen if the interest rate / year dropped from 8.00% to 7.00%. How much of each year's payment goes to paying interest vs. how much goes to reducing the principal under the two interest rates?

Solution Strategy. Construct a data table for the interest component under the two interest rates. Construct another data table for the principal component under the two interest rates. Create a graph of the two interest components and two principal components.

	A	B	C	D	E	F	G	H	I	J
1	**LOAN AMORTIZATION**		**Sensitivity Analysis**							
17	Outputs									
18	Year	1	2	3	4	5	6	7	8	9

(6) Enter the input values for Interest Rate / Year. Enter 7.0% and 8.0% in the range A44:A45

(7) Enter the output formulas for the Interest Component. Enter =B21 in cell B43 and copy across

(8) Create the interest component Data Table. Select the range A43:AE45, click on Data | Data Tools | What-If Analysis | Data Table, enter B5 in the Column Input Cell, and click on OK.

Data Table
Row input cell:
Column input cell: B5
OK   Cancel

	A	B	C	D	E	F	G	H	I	J
41	Data Table: Sensitivity of the Interest Component to the Interest Rate / Year									
42	Input Values for		Output Formula: Interest Component							
43	Interest rate / year	$24,000	$23,788	$23,559	$23,312	$23,045	$22,757	$22,446	$22,110	$21,747
44	7.00%	$21,000	$20,778	$20,540	$20,285	$20,013	$19,722	$19,410	$19,076	$18,719
45	8.00%	$24,000	$23,788	$23,559	$23,312	$23,045	$22,757	$22,446	$22,110	$21,747

(9) Enter the input values for Interest Rate / Year. Enter 7.0% and 8.0% in the range A58:A59

(10) Enter the output formulas for the Principal Component. Enter =B22 in cell B57 and copy across

(11) Create the principal component Data Table. Select the range A57:AE59, click on Data | Data Tools | What-If Analysis | Data Table, enter B5 in the Column Input Cell, and click on OK.

Data Table
Row input cell:
Column input cell: B5
OK   Cancel

	A	B	C	D	E	F	G	H	I	J
55	Data Table: Sensitivity of the Principal Component to the Interest Rate / Year									
56	Input Values for		Output Formula: Principal Component							
57	Interest rate / year	$2,648	$2,860	$3,089	$3,336	$3,603	$3,891	$4,202	$4,539	$4,902
58	7.00%	$3,176	$3,398	$3,636	$3,891	$4,163	$4,454	$4,766	$5,100	$5,457
59	8.00%	$2,648	$2,860	$3,089	$3,336	$3,603	$3,891	$4,202	$4,539	$4,902

Principal And Interest Payments Over Time

8% Interest Component

7% Interest Component

7% Principal Component

8% Principal Component

(y-axis: Principal And Interest Components, $0 to $25,000; x-axis: Time (Years), 0 to 30)

Excel 2003 Equivalent

To call up a Data Table in Excel 2003, click on **Data | Table**

From the graph, we see that the Interest Component is much lower at 7% than it is at 8%. Indeed you pay $3,000 less in interest ($21,000 vs. $24,000) in year 1. The difference in interest component gradually declines over time. The principal component stays nearly the same over time. The principal component is slightly more frontloaded at 7% than at 8%. That is, $528 *more* of your payment goes to principal in year 1 at 7% than at 8%. Then it switches and $2,080 *less* of your payment goes to principal in year 30.

Problems

1. To purchase a house, you take out a 30 year mortgage. The present value (loan amount) of the mortgage is $217,832. The mortgage charges an interest rate / year of 9.27%. What is the annual payment required by this mortgage? How much of each year's payment goes to paying interest and how much reducing the principal balance?

2. In purchasing a house, you need to obtain a mortgage with a present value (loan amount) of $175,000. You have a choice of: (A) a 30 year mortgage at an interest rate / year of 9.74% or (B) a 15 year mortgage at an interest rate / year of 9.46%. What is the annual payment required by the two alternative mortgages? How much of each year's payment goes to paying interest and how much reducing the principal balance by the two alternative mortgages? Which mortgage would you prefer?

3. Consider a 30 year mortgage for $442,264 as in the previous section. What would happen if the interest rate / year dropped from 9.21% to 7.95%. How much of each year's payment goes to paying interest vs. how much goes to reducing the principal under the two interest rates?

PART 2 VALUATION

Chapter 6 Bond Valuation

6.1 Annual Payments

Problem. On November 1, 2007, an 8 year Treasury Bond with a face value of $1,000.00, paying $45.00 in coupon payments per year had a discount rate per year (yield) of 4.26%. Consider a bond that paid a $45.00 coupon payment once per year. What is price of this annual payment bond?

Solution Strategy. We will calculate the bond price in three equivalent ways. First, we will calculate the bond price as the present value of the bond's cash flows. Second, we use a formula for the bond price. Third, we use Excel's PV function for a bond price.

FIGURE 6.1 Excel Model of Bond Pricing – Annual Payments.

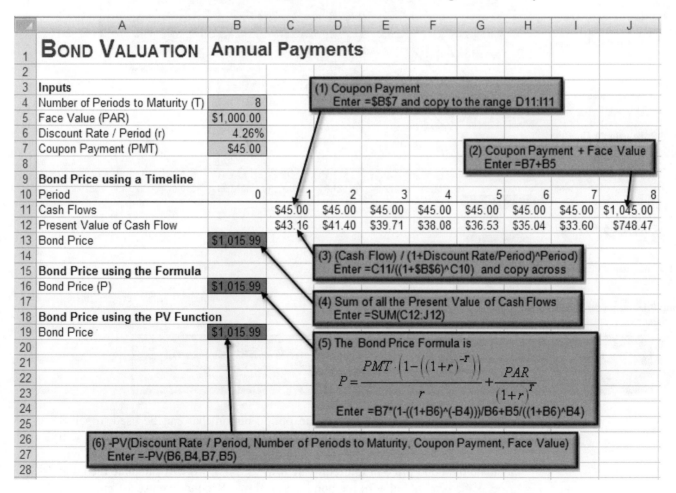

The resulting annual bond price is $1,015.99. Notice you get the same answer all three ways: using the cash flows, using the formula, or using the PV function!

6.2 EAR and APR

Problem. On November 1, 2007, a 4 year Treasury Bond with a face value of $1,000 and an annual coupon rate of 4.625% had a yield to maturity of 3.94%. This bond makes 2 (semi-annual) coupon payments per year and thus has 8 periods until maturity. What is price of this bond based on the Effective Annual Rate (EAR) convention? What is price of this bond based on the Annual Percentage Rate (APR) convention?

FIGURE 6.2 Excel Model of Bond Pricing – EAR and APR.

	A	B	C	D	E	F	G	H	I	J
1	**BOND VALUATION**	**EAR and APR**			**Annual Percentage Rate**					
2										
3	Inputs									
4	Rate Convention	○ EAR ● APR	2		(1) If Rate Convention = EAR,					
5	Annual Coupon Rate	4.625%			Then (1+Yield To Maturity)^(1 / (Number of Payments / Year)) - 1					
6	Yield to Maturity (Annualized)	3.94%			Else (Yield To Maturity) / Number of Payment / Year)					
7	Number of Payments / Year	2			Enter =IF(C4=1,((1+B6)^(1/B7))-1,B6/B7)					
8	Number of Periods to Maturity (T)	8								
9	Face Value (PAR)	$1,000.00			(2) Coupon Rate * Face Value / (Number of Payments / Year)					
10					Enter =B5*B9/B7					
11	Outputs									
12	Discount Rate / Period (r)	1.97%			(3) Period / (Number of Payments / Year)					
13	Coupon Payment (PMT)	$23.13			Enter =B16/$B$7 and copy across					
14										
15	**Bond Price using a Timeline**									
16	Period	0	1	2	3	4	5	6	7	8
17	Time (Years)	0.0	0.5	1.0	1.5	2.0	2.5	3.0	3.5	4.0
18	Cash Flows		$23.13	$23.13	$23.13	$23.13	$23.13	$23.13	$23.13	$1,023.13
19	Present Value of Cash Flow		$22.68	$22.24	$21.81	$21.39	$20.98	$20.57	$20.17	$875.28
20	Bond Price	$1,025.12								
21										
22	**Bond Price using the Formula**									
23	Bond Price	$1,025.12								
24										
25	**Bond Price using the PV Function**									
26	Bond Price	$1,025.12								
27										
28	**Bond Price using the PRICE Function (under APR)**									
29	Bond Price	$1,025.12								
30										
31		(4) If Rate Convention = EAR, Then Blank,								
32		Else =PRICE(DATE(2000,1,1),DATE(2000 + Number of Periods to Maturity / (Number of Payments / Year),1,1),								
33		Coupon Rate, Yield To Maturity, 100, (Number of Payments / Year)) * Number of Periods to Maturity / 100)								
34		Enter =IF(C4=1,"",PRICE(DATE(2000,1,1),DATE(2000+B8/B7,1,1),B5,B6,100,B7)*B9/100)								

Solution Strategy. We will create an option button that can be used to select either the EAR or APR rate convention. The choice of rate convention will determine the discount rate / period. For a given discount rate / period, we will calculate the bond price in four equivalent ways. First, we will calculate the bond price as the present value of the bond's cash flows. Second, we use a formula for the bond price. Third, we use Excel's PV function for a bond price. Fourth, we use Excel's Analysis ToolPak Add-In PRICE function, which only works under the APR convention.

Excel's Analysis ToolPak contains several advanced bond functions, including the PRICE function which uses the APR convention. To access any of these functions, you need to install the Analysis ToolPak. Otherwise you will get the error message #NAME?.

To install the Analysis ToolPak, click on the **Office** button, click on the Excel Options button at the bottom of the drop-down window, click on **Add-Ins**, highlight the **Analysis ToolPak** in the list of Inactive Applications, click on **Go**, check the **Analysis ToolPak**, and click on **OK**.

The bond price function is =PRICE(Settlement Date, Maturity Date, Annual Coupon Rate, Yield To Maturity, Redemption Value, Number of Payments). The Settlement Date is the date when you exchange money to purchase the bond. Specifying the exact day of settlement and maturity allows a very precise calculation. For our purpose, we simple want the difference between the two dates to equal the (8 Periods To Maturity) / (2 Payments / Year) = 4 Years To Maturity. This is easily accomplished by the use of the DATE function. The DATE Function has the format =DATE(Year, Month, Day). We will enter an arbitrary starting date of 1/1/2000 for the Settlement Date and then specify a formula for 1/1/2000 plus T / NOP for the Maturity Date. We also add an IF statement to test for the rate convention being used.

The resulting semi-annual bond price is $1,025.12 under APR and $1,026.54 under EAR. Notice you get the same answer all ways: using the cash flows, using the formula, using the PV function, or using the PRICE function under APR!

6.3 By Yield To Maturity

What is the relationship between bond price and yield to maturity? We can construct a graph to find out.

FIGURE 6.3 Excel Model of Bond Pricing - By Yield To Maturity.

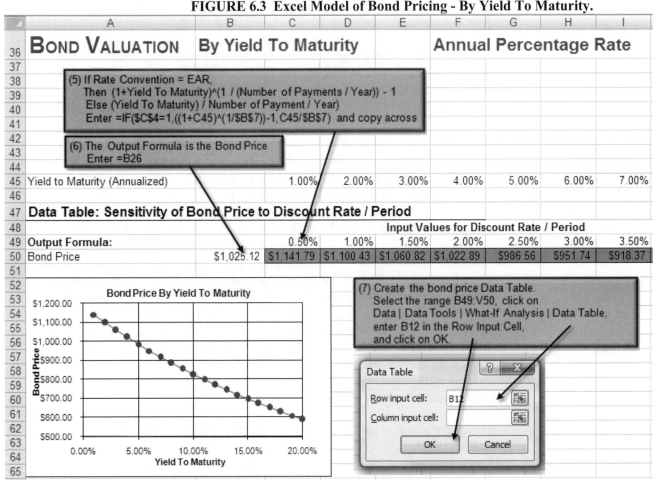

This graph shows the inverse relationship between bond price and yield to maturity. In other words, a higher discount rate (yield to maturity) lowers the present value of the bond's cash flows (price). The graph also shows that the relationship is curved (nonlinear) rather than being a straight line (linear).

6.4 Dynamic Chart

If you increased the coupon rate of a bond, what would happen to its price? If you increased the yield to maturity of a bond, what would happen to its price? You can answer these questions and more by creating a *Dynamic Chart* using "spin button." Spin buttons are up-arrow / down-arrow buttons that allow you to easily change the inputs to the model with the click of a mouse. Then Excel recalculates the model and instantly redraws the model outputs on the graph.

FIGURE 6.4 Excel Model of Bond Pricing – Dynamic Chart.

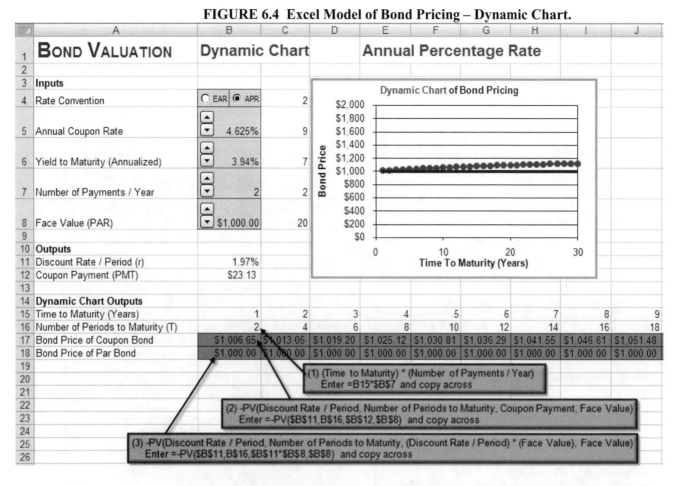

Your *Dynamic Chart* allows you to change the Bond Price inputs and instantly see the impact on a graph of the price of a coupon bond and par bond by time to maturity. This allows you to perform instant experiments on Bond Price. Below is a list of experiments that you might want to perform:

- What happens when the annual coupon rate is increased?
- What happens when the yield to maturity is increased?
- What happens when the number of payments / year is increased?
- What happens when the face value is increased?
- What is the relationship between the price of a par bond and time to maturity?
- What happens when the annual coupon rate is increased to the point that it equals the yield to maturity? What happens when it is increased further?

6.5 System of Five Bond Variables

There is a system of five bond variables: (1) Number of Periods to Maturity (T), (2) Face Value (PAR), (3) Discount Rate / Period (r), (4) Coupon Payments (PMT), and (5) Bond Price (P). Given any four of these variables, the fifth variable can be found by using Excel functions (and in some cases by formulas).

FIGURE 6.5 Excel Model of Bond Pricing - System of Five Bond Variables.

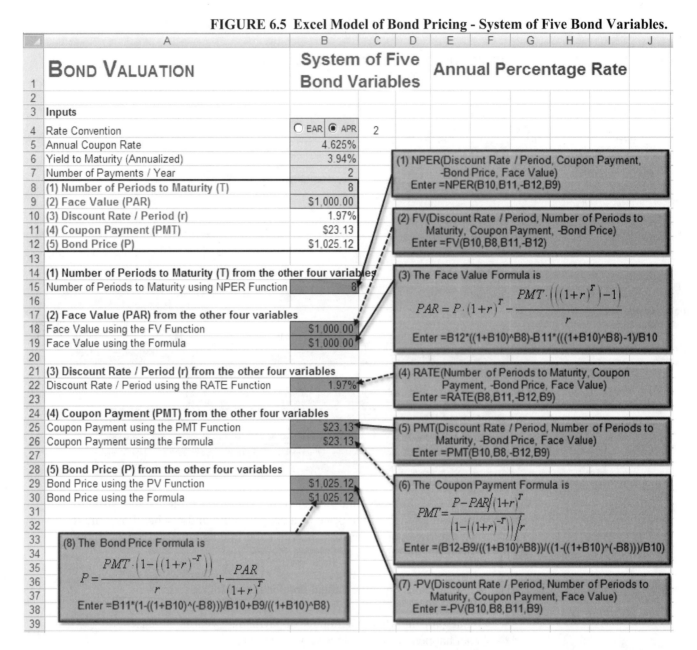

We see that the system of five bond variables is internally consistent. The five outputs in rows **15** through **30** (T=8, PAR=1000, r=1.97%, PMT=$23.13, P=$1,025.12) are identical to the five inputs in rows **8** through **12**. Thus, any of the five bond variables can be calculated from the other four in a fully consistent manner.

Problems

1. An annual bond has a face value of $1,000, makes an annual coupon payment of $12 per year, has a discount rate per year of 4.3%, and has 8 years to maturity. What is price of this bond?

2. A semi-annual bond has a face value of $1,000, an annual coupon rate of 4.60%, an yield to maturity of 8.1%, makes 2 (semi-annual) coupon payments per year, and 10 periods to maturity (or 5 years to maturity). Determine the price of this bond based on the Annual Percentage Rate (APR) convention and the price of this bond based on the Effective Annual Rate (EAR) convention.

3. Determine the relationship between bond price and yield to maturity by constructing a graph of the relationship.

4. Perform instant experiments on whether changing various inputs causes an increase or decrease in the Bond Price and by how much.

   (a.) What happens when the annual coupon rate is increased?
   (b.) What happens when the yield to maturity is increased?
   (c.) What happens when the number of payments / year is increased?
   (d.) What happens when the face value is increased?
   (e.) What is the relationship between the price of a par bond and time to maturity?

   (f.) What happens when the annual coupon rate is increased to the point that it equals the yield to maturity? What happens when it is increased further?

5. Given four of the bond variables, determine the fifth bond variable.

   (a.) Given Number of Periods to Maturity is 10, Face Value is $1,000, Discount Rate / Period is 3.2%, and Coupon Payment is $40, determine the Bond Price.
   (b.) Given Number of Periods to Maturity is 8, Face Value is $1,000, Discount Rate / Period is 4.5%, and the Bond Price is $880.00, determine the Coupon Payment.
   (c.) Given Number of Periods to Maturity is 6, Face Value is $1,000, Coupon Payment is $30, and the Bond Price is $865.00, determine Discount Rate / Period.
   (d.) Given Number of Periods to Maturity is 8, Discount Rate / Period is 3.8%, Coupon Payment is $45, and the Bond Price is $872.00, determine Face Value.
   (e.) Given Face Value is $1,000, Discount Rate / Period is 4.3%, Coupon Payment is $37, and the Bond Price is $887.00, determine the Number of Periods to Maturity.

Chapter 7 Estimating the Cost of Capital

7.1 Static CAPM Using Fama-MacBeth Method

Problem. Given monthly total return data on individual stocks, US portfolios, and country portfolios, estimate the Static CAPM under three market portfolio benchmarks (SPDR "Spider" Exchange Traded Fund, CRSP Value-Weighted Market Return, and Dow Jones World Stock Index) and using the standard Fama-MacBeth methodology. Then use the Static CAPM estimates to forecast each asset's expected return in the future (Jan 2007), or equivalently, each asset's cost of equity capital. Finally, determine how much variation of individual stocks, US portfolios, or country portfolios is explained by the Static CAPM.

Solution Strategy. First compute the monthly excess return of each asset. Then stage one of the Fama-MacBeth method is estimating the CAPM beta of an asset by doing a five-year, time-series regression of the asset's excess return on the excess return of a market portfolio benchmark. Repeat this time-series regression for many five-year windows and compute the average of the estimated CAPM betas. Then stage two of the Fama-Beth method is estimating the CAPM risk premium and intercept by doing a cross-sectional regression of the excess returns across assets in the following month on the CAPM beta from the immediately prior five-year window. Repeat this cross-sectional regression for many following months and compute the average of the estimated CAPM risk premium and intercept. Then use the estimated CAPM risk premium and intercept to forecast each asset's expected return, or equivalently, each asset's cost of equity capital. Finally, compute the R^2 ("explained variation") of both regressions.

FIGURE 7.1 Cost of Capital - Static CAPM Using Fama-MacBeth Method.

	A	B	C	D	E	F	G	H
1	COST OF CAPITAL Static CAPM Using Fama-MacBeth Method							
2								
3	Inputs							
4	Market Portfolio Benchmark	Market Portfolio Benchmark ○ SPDR ETF ● CRSP VWMR ○ DJ World Stock			2			
5	Asset Type	Asset Type ○ Stock ● US Port ○ Country Port			2			
6								
7		Stock	Stock	Stock	Stock	Stock	Stock	US Portfolio
8		Barrick	Hanson	IBM	Nokia	Telefonos	YPF	Small-Growth
130			(1) Monthly Return(Asset i, Month t) - Riskfree Rate(Month t) Enter =B10-$AC10 and copy to B133:V252					
131								
132	Monthly Excess Returns							
133	Dec 2006	-3.90%	-0.64%	1.66%	8.36%	8.23%	0.10%	-0.99%
134	Nov 2006	-2.79%	4.46%	5.27%	0.09%	8.59%	-1.37%	2.16%
135	Oct 2006	1.38%	3.37%	-0.53%	1.29%	-1.49%	3.08%	5.46%
136	Sep 2006	0.51%	-3.90%	12.28%	0.52%	2.73%	6.61%	0.68%
137	Aug 2006	-8.65%	13.94%	0.78%	-6.10%	6.34%	-4.25%	2.80%
138	Jul 2006	8.28%	3.32%	4.60%	4.80%	2.62%	1.60%	-6.16%
139	Jun 2006	3.66%	0.48%	0.38%	-2.42%	12.11%	9.58%	-1.05%

FIGURE 7.2 Excel Model of Estimating the Cost of Capital – Static CAPM Using Fama-MacBeth Method.

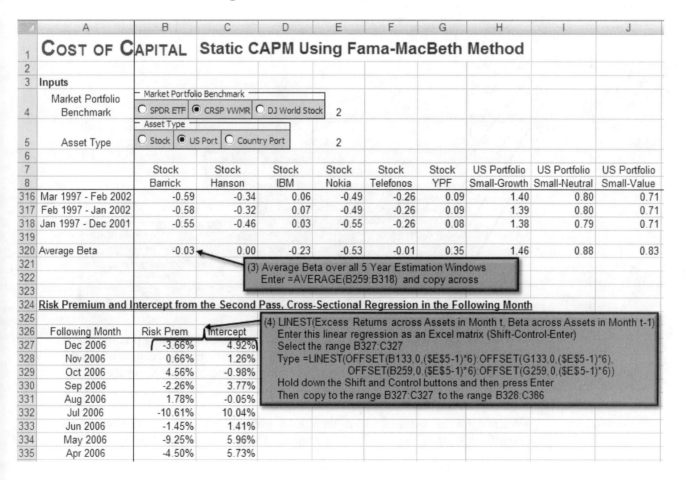

FIGURE 7.3 Excel Model of Estimating the Cost of Capital – Static CAPM Using Fama-MacBeth Method.

FIGURE 7.4 Excel Model of Estimating the Cost of Capital – Static CAPM Using Fama-MacBeth Method.

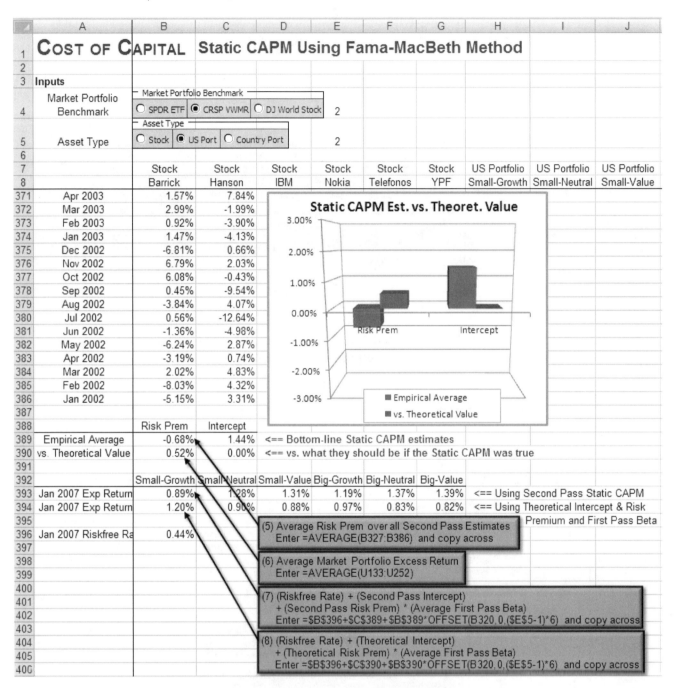

Row 389 contains the empirical average of the CAPM risk premium and intercept from the second-pass, cross-sectional regressions. Row 390 contains the theoretical value of the CAPM risk premium and intercept based on the CAPM beta from the first-pass, time-series regressions.

With a lot of extra work it would be possible to compute the statistical significance of the Static CAPM estimates. However, it is much simpler to just compare the empirical average and the theoretical value on a graph. It is clear at a glance that the empirical average and the theoretical value don't match very well.

It is interesting to make the same comparison for different market portfolio benchmarks by clicking on the option buttons in row 4 and for different asset types by clicking on the option buttons in row 5. Often the empirical average CAPM risk premium is negative, which doesn't make any economic sense. Often the empirical average of the CAPM intercept is far away from zero, which doesn't make any economic sense.

Row 393 contains the Static CAPM forecast of each asset's expected return in the future (Jan 2007), or equivalently, of each asset's cost of equity capital. This is a key output of this spreadsheet. However, given lack of economically sensible estimates for the Static CAPM, one should be very cautious about using the forecasts of each asset's expected return / cost of equity capital.

FIGURE 7.5 Excel Model of Estimating the Cost of Capital – Static CAPM Using Fama-MacBeth Method.

	A	B	C	D	E	F	G	H	I	J
1	COST OF CAPITAL		Static CAPM Using Fama-MacBeth Method							
2										
3	Inputs									
4	Market Portfolio Benchmark	Market Portfolio Benchmark: SPDR ETF / ● CRSP VWMR / DJ World Stock			2					
5	Asset Type	Asset Type: Stock / ● US Port / Country Port			2					
6										
7		Stock	Stock	Stock	Stock	Stock	Stock	US Portfolio	US Portfolio	US Portfolio
8		Barrick	Hanson	IBM	Nokia	Telefonos	YPF	Small-Growth	Small-Neutral	Small-Value
408										
409		(9) LINEST(Asset Excess Returns over 5 Years, Market Port Benchmark Excess Returns over 5 Yrs)								
410		INDEX(LINEST(...), 3, 1) selects the R² of the regression above								
411		Enter =INDEX(LINEST(B134:B193,OFFSET($T134,0,($E$4-1)):OFFSET($T193,0,$E$4-1),,TRUE),3,1)								
412		and copy to B417:S476								
413	R² (Explained Variation as a Percentage of Total Variation) from the First Pass, Time-Series Regression									
414										
415	5 Yr Estimation Per:									
416	Beg Mon - End Mon	Barrick	Hanson	IBM	Nokia	Telefonos	YPF	Small-Growth	Small-Neutral	Small-Value
417	Dec 2001 - Nov 2006	1.5%	4.9%	4.9%	0.1%	0.1%	0.5%	81.7%	74.9%	65.5%
418	Nov 2001 - Oct 2006	1.9%	4.2%	4.0%	0.0%	0.2%	1.7%	82.0%	75.2%	66.7%
419	Oct 2001 - Sep 2006	1.8%	3.8%	3.7%	0.0%	0.2%	1.8%	80.3%	75.1%	66.6%
420	Sep 2001 - Aug 2006	3.3%	4.6%	7.5%	1.4%	0.0%	1.9%	82.5%	78.0%	70.5%
421	Aug 2001 - Jul 2006	2.8%	6.1%	5.7%	1.1%	0.3%	3.5%	82.8%	77.3%	69.5%
422	Jul 2001 - Jun 2006	2.6%	5.4%	5.3%	0.5%	0.2%	3.8%	82.7%	77.6%	69.7%
423	Jun 2001 - May 2006	2.8%	5.7%	4.8%	0.5%	0.4%	4.1%	79.7%	75.2%	69.2%
424	May 2001 - Apr 2006	2.4%	5.5%	5.2%	0.7%	0.6%	3.6%	79.3%	74.6%	68.1%
425	Apr 2001 - Mar 2006	2.3%	6.4%	5.4%	1.4%	0.5%	3.8%	80.0%	73.3%	66.8%

FIGURE 7.6 Excel Model of Estimating the Cost of Capital – Static CAPM Using Fama-MacBeth Method.

	A	B	C	D	E	F	G	H	I	J
1	COST OF CAPITAL		Static CAPM Using Fama-MacBeth Method							
2										
3	**Inputs**									
4	Market Portfolio Benchmark	⊙ SPDR ETF ⊙ CRSP VWMR ⊙ DJ World Stock			2					
5	Asset Type	⊙ Stock ⊙ US Port ⊙ Country Port			2					
6										
7		Stock	Stock	Stock	Stock	Stock	Stock	US Portfolio	US Portfolio	US Portfolio
8		Barrick	Hanson	IBM	Nokia	Telefonos	YPF	Small-Growth	Small-Neutral	Small-Value
474	Mar 1997 - Feb 2002	7.5%	3.4%	0.1%	2.6%	1.5%	0.2%	60.4%	55.9%	52.2%
475	Feb 1997 - Jan 2002	7.0%	3.1%	0.1%	2.7%	1.5%	0.3%	60.1%	55.8%	52.1%
476	Jan 1997 - Dec 2001	6.5%	4.1%	0.0%	3.4%	1.5%	0.2%	59.9%	55.8%	52.6%
477										
478	Average R^2	2.8%	1.7%	2.0%	3.4%	0.4%	2.5%	69.6%	62.0%	56.1%

(10) Average R^2 over all 5 Year Estimation Windows
Enter =AVERAGE(B417:B476) and copy across

(11) LINEST(Excess Returns across Assets in Month t, Beta across Assets in Month t)
INDEX(LINEST(...), 3, 1) selects the R^2 of the regression above
Enter =INDEX(LINEST(OFFSET(B133,0,($E$5-1)*6):OFFSET(G133,0,($E$5-1)*6),
OFFSET(B259,0,($E$5-1)*6):OFFSET(G259,0,($E$5-1)*6),,TRUE),3,1)
and copy down

	A	B
489	R^2 (Explained Variation as a Percentage of Total Variation) from the Second Pass, Cross-sectional Regression in the Following Mo	
490		
491	Following Month	R^2
492	Dec 2006	36.1%
493	Nov 2006	4.3%
494	Oct 2006	64.9%
495	Sep 2006	46.0%
496	Aug 2006	14.0%
497	Jul 2006	73.8%
498	Jun 2006	14.0%

The Average R^2 of the first-pass, time-series regression tells us how much of the fluctuation in an asset's excess return can be explained by market portfolio's excess return. An R^2 of 0% means the two variables are unrelated vs. an R^2 of 100% means the two variables are move together perfectly. With single-digit R^2s, the individual stocks are poorly explained. By contrast, the US portfolios are pretty well-explained by US benchmarks and country portfolios are pretty well-explained by a world benchmark.

FIGURE 7.7 Excel Model of Estimating the Cost of Capital – Static CAPM Using Fama-MacBeth Method.

	A	B	C	D	E	F	G	H	I
1	COST OF CAPITAL		Static CAPM Using Fama-MacBeth Method						
2									
3	**Inputs**								
4	Market Portfolio Benchmark	Market Portfolio Benchmark ○ SPDR ETF ◉ CRSP VWMR ○ DJ World Stock			2				
5	Asset Type	Asset Type ○ Stock ◉ US Port ○ Country Port			2				
6									
7		Stock	Stock	Stock	Stock	Stock	Stock	US Portfolio	US Portfolio
8		Barrick	Hanson	IBM	Nokia	Telefonos	YPF	Small-Growth	Small-Neutral
547	May 2002	62.8%							
548	Apr 2002	4.9%							
549	Mar 2002	6.2%							
550	Feb 2002	69.5%							
551	Jan 2002	34.3%							
552									
553	Average R^2	30.8%							
554									
555		(12) Average R^2 over all Following Months in Second Pass Regressions							
556		Enter =AVERAGE(B492:B551)							
557									

The Average R^2 of the second-pass, cross-sectional regression tells us how much of the fluctuation in the excess returns across assets in the following month can be explained by the CAPM beta from the immediately prior five-year window. With an Average R^2 of around 30%, the individual stocks and US portfolios are modestly explained by their CAPM betas. With an Average R^2 of below 20%, the country portfolio are very modestly explained by their CAPM betas.

7.2 APT or Intertemporal CAPM Using Fama-McBeth Method

Problem. Given monthly total return data on individual stocks, US portfolios, and country portfolios, estimate the APT or Intertemporal CAPM (ICAPM) under two sets of factors (Fama-French 3 factors and 3 macro factors) and using the standard Fama-MacBeth methodology. Then use the APT or ICAPM estimates from Jan 1997 – Dec 2006 data to forecast each asset's expected return in the future (Jan 2007), or equivalently, each asset's cost of equity capital. Finally, determine how much variation of individual stocks, US portfolios, or country portfolios is explained by the APT or ICAPM.

Solution Strategy. First carry over the monthly excess return of each asset from the other sheet. Then stage one of the Fama-MacBeth method is estimating the APT or ICAPM factor betas of an asset by doing a five-year, time-series regression of the asset's excess return on sets of APT or ICAPM factors. Repeat this time-series regression for many five-year windows and compute the average of the estimated APT or ICAPM factor betas. Then stage two of the Fama-Beth method is estimating the APT or ICAPM factor risk premia and intercept by doing a cross-sectional regression of the excess returns across assets in the following month on the APT or ICAPM factor betas from the immediately prior five-year window. Repeat this cross-sectional regression for many following months and compute the average of the estimated APT or ICAPM factor risk premia and intercept. Then use the estimated APT or ICAPM factor risk premia and intercept to forecast each asset's expected return in the future (Jan 2007), or equivalently, each asset's cost of equity capital. Finally, compute the R^2 ("explained variation") of both regressions.

FIGURE 7.8 Excel Model of Estimating the Cost of Capital – APT or Intertemporal CAPM Using Fama-MacBeth Method.

	A	B	C	D	E	F	G	H	I
1	COST OF CAPITAL APT or Intertemporal CAPM Using Fama-MacBeth Method								
2									
3	Inputs								
4	APT or ICAPM Factors	APT or ICAPM Factors ⦿ Fama-French 3 Factors ○ 3 Macro Factors			1				
5	Asset Type	Asset Type ⦿ Stock ○ US Port ○ Country Port			1	(1) Monthly Return from Sheet 9.1 Enter ='9.1'!B10 and copy to D10:AE129			
6									
7				Stock	Stock	Stock	Stock	Stock	Stock
8				Barrick	Hanson	IBM	Nokia	Telefonos	YPF
9	**Monthly Returns**								
10	Dec 2006			-3.50%	-0.24%	2.06%	8.76%	8.63%	0.50%
11	Nov 2006			-2.37%	4.88%	5.69%	0.51%	9.01%	-0.95%
12	Oct 2006			1.79%	3.78%	-0.12%	1.70%	-1.08%	3.49%
13	Sep 2006			0.92%	-3.49%	12.69%	0.93%	3.14%	7.02%
14	Aug 2006			-8.23%	14.36%	1.20%	-5.68%	6.76%	-3.83%
15	Jul 2006			8.68%	3.72%	5.00%	5.20%	3.02%	2.00%
16	Jun 2006			4.06%	0.88%	0.78%	-2.02%	12.51%	9.98%

FIGURE 7.9 Excel Model of Estimating the Cost of Capital – APT or Intertemporal CAPM Using Fama-MacBeth Method.

	A	B	C	D	E	F	G	H	I
1	**COST OF CAPITAL APT or Intertemporal CAPM Using Fama-MacBeth Method**								
2									
3	Inputs								
4	APT or ICAPM Factors	APT or ICAPM Factors ⦿ Fama-French 3 Factors ◯ 3 Macro Factors			1				
5	Asset Type	Asset Type ⦿ Stock ◯ US Port ◯ Country Port			1				
6									
7				Stock	Stock	Stock	Stock	Stock	Stock
8				Barrick	Hanson	IBM	Nokia	Telefonos	YPF

130	(2) LINEST(Asset Returns over 5 Years, 3 Factor Innovations over 5 Yrs)
131	Enter this linear regression as an Excel matrix (Shift-Control-Enter)
132	Select D143:D145
133	Type =TRANSPOSE(LINEST(OFFSET(D$11,$B143,0):OFFSET(D$70,$B143,0),
134	OFFSET($Y$11,$B143,($E$4-1)*3):OFFSET($AA$70,$B143,($E$4-1)*3)))
135	Hold down the Shift and Control buttons and then press Enter
136	Then copy to the range D143:D145 to the range E143:U145; Then copy the range D143:U145 to the range D146:U148;
137	Then copy the doubled range D143:U148 to the range D149:U154; Keep doubling until row 322 is reached.

	A	B	C	D	E	F	G	H
138								
139	**Three Factor Betas from the First Pass, Time-Series Regression**							
140								
141	5 Yr Estimation Per:	Row						
142	Beg Mon - End Mon	Offset	Factors	Barrick	Hanson	IBM	Nokia	Telefonos	YPF
143	Dec 2001 - Nov 2006	0	FF HML	-0.10	-0.67	-0.95	-1.12	-0.64	-1.84
144			FF SMB	0.15	0.16	0.11	-1.31	-0.35	-0.95
145			FF Mkt-RF	0.24	0.27	-0.67	0.05	0.03	0.17
146	Nov 2001 - Oct 2006	1	FF HML	-0.09	-0.69	-0.90	-1.09	-0.62	-1.74
147			FF SMB	0.14	0.18	0.07	-1.33	-0.37	-1.04
148			FF Mkt-RF	0.27	0.23	-0.59	0.11	0.06	0.38
149	Oct 2001 - Sep 2006	2	FF HML	0.06	-0.41	-0.93	-1.38	-0.48	-1.69
150			FF SMB	0.06	0.04	0.08	-1.19	-0.44	-1.07
151			FF Mkt-RF	0.30	0.28	-0.59	0.05	0.09	0.39
152	Sep 2001 - Aug 2006	3	FF HML	0.08	-0.43	-0.91	-1.45	-0.49	-1.68
153			FF SMB	0.14	0.01	0.01	-1.45	-0.46	-1.02
154			FF Mkt-RF	0.37	0.29	-0.73	-0.14	0.06	0.43
155	Aug 2001 - Jul 2006	4	FF HML	0.05	-0.40	-0.98	-1.50	-0.51	-1.84
156			FF SMB	0.20	-0.04	-0.08	-1.43	-0.53	-1.11
157			FF Mkt-RF	0.31	0.35	-0.64	-0.16	0.14	0.53

FIGURE 7.10 Excel Model of Estimating the Cost of Capital – APT or Intertemporal CAPM Using Fama-MacBeth Method.

	A	B	C	D	E	F	G	H	I
1	COST OF CAPITAL APT or Intertemporal CAPM Using Fama-MacBeth Method								
2									
3	**Inputs**								
4	APT or ICAPM Factors	APT or ICAPM Factors ⦿ Fama-French 3 Factors ○ 3 Macro Factors			1				
5	Asset Type	Asset Type ⦿ Stock ○ US Port ○ Country Port			1				
6									
7				Stock	Stock	Stock	Stock	Stock	Stock
8				Barrick	Hanson	IBM	Nokia	Telefonos	YPF
314	Mar 1997 - Feb 2002	57	FF HML	-0.19	-0.23	0.02	-1.14	-0.48	-0.64
315			FF SMB	-0.47	-0.37	0.09	-0.37	0.04	-0.46
316			FF Mkt-RF	-0.60	-0.40	0.05	-1.09	-0.56	-0.20
317	Feb 1997 - Jan 2002	58	FF HML	-0.27	-0.26	-0.02	-1.14	-0.50	-0.65
318			FF SMB	-0.48	-0.37	0.08	-0.37	0.04	-0.46
319			FF Mkt-RF	-0.63	-0.40	0.04	-1.10	-0.56	-0.20
320	Jan 1997 - Dec 2001	59	FF HML	-0.30	-0.14	0.05	-1.04	-0.49	-0.64
321			FF SMB	-0.51	-0.23	0.14	-0.29	0.04	-0.45
322			FF Mkt-RF	-0.63	-0.50	0.02	-1.12	-0.56	-0.21
323									
324		Average Factor Betas		Barrick	Hanson	IBM	Nokia	Telefonos	YPF
325			FF HML	0.17	-0.05	-0.46	-1.23	-0.31	-1.19
326			FF SMB	-0.07	-0.23	-0.04	-0.94	-0.16	-0.95
327			FF Mkt-RF	0.06	0.04	-0.41	-0.87	-0.12	0.07
328									
329									
330			(3) LINEST(Returns across Assets in Month t, Factor Betas across Assets in Month t)						
331			Enter this linear regression as an Excel matrix (Shift-Control-Enter)						
332			Select the range D340:G340						
333			Type =LINEST(OFFSET(D10,0,($E$5-1)*6):OFFSET(I10,0,($E$5-1)*6),						
334			OFFSET($D$143,B340,($E$5-1)*6):OFFSET($I$145,B340,($E$5-1)*6))						
335			Hold down the Shift and Control buttons and then press Enter						
336			Then copy to the range D340:G340 to the range D341:G399						
337	**Factor Risk Premia and Intercept from the Second Pass, Cross-Sectional Regression in the Following Month**								
338		Row							
339	Following Month	Offset		FF Mkt-RF	FF SMB	FF HML	Intercept		
340	Dec 2006	0		-6.62%	-8.45%	4.84%	4.02%		
341	Nov 2006	3		-5.84%	1.49%	-0.50%	3.39%		
342	Oct 2006	6		5.94%	3.89%	-3.74%	-0.29%		
343	Sep 2006	9		-5.56%	6.75%	-8.17%	0.26%		
344	Aug 2006	12		1.43%	3.74%	0.43%	2.87%		
345	Jul 2006	15		-1.00%	1.79%	0.38%	5.82%		
346	Jun 2006	18		4.59%	-7.84%	4.70%	4.24%		

FIGURE 7.11 Excel Model of Estimating the Cost of Capital – APT or Intertemporal CAPM Using Fama-MacBeth Method.

	A	B	C	D	E	F	G	H	I	J
1	COST OF CAPITAL APT or Intertemporal CAPM Using Fama-MacBeth Method									
2										
3	Inputs									
4	APT or ICAPM Factors	APT or ICAPM Factors: ◉ Fama-French 3 Factors ○ 3 Macro Factors		1						
5	Asset Type	Asset Type: ◉ Stock ○ US Port ○ Country Port		1						
6										
7				Stock	Stock	Stock	Stock	Stock	Stock	US Portfolio
8				Barrick	Hanson	IBM	Nokia	Telefonos	YPF	Small-Growth
397	Mar 2002	171		-27.27%	-18.35%	36.97%	-10.99%			
398	Feb 2002	174		2.53%	-2.98%	4.97%	8.79%			
399	Jan 2002	177		-4.61%	-16.37%	13.76%	-2.55%			
400										
401				FF Mkt-RF	FF SMB	FF HML				
402	Factor Premia			Premium	Premium	Premium	Intercept			
403	Average			1.95%	-2.89%	0.56%	1.21%	<= Bottom-line APT or Intertemporal		
404								CAPM estimates		
405	Expected Return using APT or ICAPM Est.			Barrick	Hanson	IBM	Nokia	Telefonos	YPF	
406	Jan 2007	Fama-French 3 Factors		2.07%	2.37%	0.72%	1.99%	1.71%	3.88%	
407										
408		Jan 2007 Riskfree Rate		0.44%						
409						(4) Average Factor Risk Prem over all Second Pass Estimates Enter =AVERAGE(D340:D399) and copy across				
410										
411					(5) (Riskfree Rate) + (Second Pass Intercept)					
412					+ (Second Pass Factor 1 Risk Prem) * (First Pass Factor 1 Beta)					
413					+ (Second Pass Factor 2 Risk Prem) * (First Pass Factor 2 Beta)					
414					+ (Second Pass Factor 3 Risk Prem) * (First Pass Factor 3 Beta)					
415				Enter =$D$408+$G$403+$D$403*OFFSET(D327,0,($E$5-1)*6)						
416				+$E$403*OFFSET(D326,0,($E$5-1))						
417				+$F$403*OFFSET(D325,0,($E$5-1)*6) and copy across						
418										

Row 403 contains the empirical average of the APT or ICAPM factor risk premia and intercept from the second-pass, cross-sectional regressions. Given the wide flexibility in specifying APT or ICAPM factors in terms of either long positions or short positions, it is legitimately possible that risk premia could be either positive or negative.

Row 406 contains the APT or ICAPM forecast of each asset's expected return in the future (Jan 2007), or equivalently, of each asset's cost of equity capital. This is a key output of this spreadsheet.

FIGURE 7.12 Excel Model of Estimating the Cost of Capital – APT or Intertemporal CAPM Using Fama-MacBeth Method.

	A	B	C	D	E	F	G	H	I
1	COST OF CAPITAL APT or Intertemporal CAPM Using Fama-MacBeth Method								
2									
3	Inputs								
4	APT or ICAPM Factors	APT or ICAPM Factors ⦿ Fama-French 3 Factors ○ 3 Macro Factors			1				
5	Asset Type	Asset Type ⦿ Stock ○ US Port ○ Country Port			1				
6									
7				Stock	Stock	Stock	Stock	Stock	Stock
8				Barrick	Hanson	IBM	Nokia	Telefonos	YPF
419									
420	(6) LINEST(Asset Returns over 5 Years, Three Factor Innovations over 5 Yrs)								
421	INDEX(LINEST(...), 3, 1) selects the R^2 of the regression above								
422	Enter =INDEX(LINEST(OFFSET(D$11,$B429,0):OFFSET(D$70,$B429,0),								
423	OFFSET($Y$11,$B429,($E$4-1)*3):OFFSET($AA$70,$B429,($E$4-1)*3),,TRUE),3,1)								
424	and copy to D429:U488								
425	R^2 (Explained Variation as a Percentage of Total Variation) from the First Pass, Time-Series Regression								
426									
427	5 Yr Estimation Per:	Row							
428	Beg Mon - End Mon	Offset		Barrick	Hanson	IBM	Nokia	Telefonos	YPF
429	Dec 2001 - Nov 2006	0		1.7%	8.7%	9.9%	15.8%	7.6%	17.2%
430	Nov 2001 - Oct 2006	1		2.1%	8.4%	8.6%	15.9%	7.8%	17.4%
431	Oct 2001 - Sep 2006	2		1.8%	5.6%	9.7%	16.2%	7.1%	17.7%
432	Sep 2001 - Aug 2006	3		3.5%	6.6%	12.9%	20.3%	7.5%	17.4%
433	Aug 2001 - Jul 2006	4		3.1%	7.6%	11.9%	21.0%	9.3%	21.4%
434	Jul 2001 - Jun 2006	5		3.1%	6.2%	12.9%	19.9%	9.1%	22.3%
435	Jun 2001 - May 2006	6		3.1%	6.5%	11.1%	19.9%	9.7%	22.7%
436	May 2001 - Apr 2006	7		2.5%	6.2%	11.0%	22.3%	9.2%	24.3%
437	Apr 2001 - Mar 2006	8		2.4%	7.1%	10.8%	18.4%	8.9%	22.6%
438	Mar 2001 - Feb 2006	9		1.5%	2.7%	10.8%	13.1%	5.9%	22.0%

FIGURE 7.13 Excel Model of Estimating the Cost of Capital – APT or Intertemporal CAPM Using Fama-MacBeth Method.

	A	B	C	D	E	F	G	H	I	J
1	COST OF CAPITAL APT or Intertemporal CAPM Using Fama-MacBeth Method									
2										
3	Inputs									
4	APT or ICAPM Factors		APT or ICAPM Factors ⦿ Fama-French 3 Factors ○ 3 Macro Factors		1					
5	Asset Type		Asset Type ⦿ Stock ○ US Port ○ Country Port		1					
6										
7				Stock	Stock	Stock	Stock	Stock	Stock	US Portfolio
8				Barrick	Hanson	IBM	Nokia	Telefonos	YPF	Small-Growth
486	Mar 1997 - Feb 2002	57		11.0%	6.0%	0.3%	7.6%	4.7%	5.3%	97.8%
487	Feb 1997 - Jan 2002	58		10.2%	5.8%	0.4%	7.7%	4.9%	5.5%	97.9%
488	Jan 1997 - Dec 2001	59		10.1%	4.8%	0.4%	7.8%	4.8%	5.1%	98.2%
489										
490	Average R^2			5.2%	4.1%	4.5%	13.4%	4.0%	17.1%	97.4%
491										
492				(7) Average R^2 over all 5 Year Estimation Windows						
493				Enter =AVERAGE(D429:D488) and copy across						
494										
495				(8) LINEST(Returns across Assets in Month t, Factor Betas across Assets in Month t)						
496				INDEX(LINEST(...), 3, 1) selects the R^2 of the regression above						
497				Enter =INDEX(LINEST(OFFSET(D10,0,($E$5-1)*6):OFFSET(I10,0,($E$5-1)*6),						
498				OFFSET($D$143,B340,($E$5-1)*6):OFFSET($I$145,B340,($E$5-1)*6),,TRUE),3,1)						
499				and copy down						
500										
501	R^2 (Explained Variation as a Percentage of Total Variation) from the Second Pass, Cross-sectional Regression in the Following Month									
502										
503	Following Month			R^2						
504	Dec 2006			60.5%						
505	Nov 2006			29.7%						
506	Oct 2006			76.1%						
507	Sep 2006			65.1%						
508	Aug 2006			10.4%						
509	Jul 2006			36.2%						
510	Jun 2006			32.8%						
511	May 2006			40.0%						

The Average R^2 of the first-pass, time-series regression tells us how much of the fluctuation in an asset's excess return can be explained by the APT or ICAPM factors. An R^2 of 0% means the two variables are unrelated vs. an R^2 of 100% means the two variables are move together perfectly. With single-digit R^2s, the individual stocks are poorly explained. With an R^2 over 90%, the US portfolios are extremely well-explained by US-based APT or ICAPM factors. With an R^2 around 50%, country portfolios are somewhat-explained by US-based APT or ICAPM factors.

FIGURE 7.14 Excel Model of Estimating the Cost of Capital – APT or Intertemporal CAPM Using Fama-MacBeth Method.

	A	B	C	D	E	F	G	H	I
1	COST OF CAPITAL APT or Intertemporal CAPM Using Fama-MacBeth Method								
2									
3	Inputs								
4	APT or ICAPM Factors	⊙ Fama-French 3 Factors ○ 3 Macro Factors		1					
5	Asset Type	⊙ Stock ○ US Port ○ Country Port		1					
6									
7				Stock	Stock	Stock	Stock	Stock	Stock
8				Barrick	Hanson	IBM	Nokia	Telefonos	YPF
559	May 2002			94.3%					
560	Apr 2002			93.0%					
561	Mar 2002			79.5%					
562	Feb 2002			29.4%					
563	Jan 2002			54.9%					
564									
565	Average R²			63.4%					
566									
567									
568				(9) Average R² over all Following Months in Second Pass Regressions Enter =AVERAGE(D504:D563)					
569									

The Average R^2 of the second-pass, cross-sectional regression tells us how much of the fluctuation in the excess returns across assets in the following month can be explained by the APT or ICAPM factor betas from the immediately prior five-year window. With an Average R^2 of 50% - 70%, the individual stocks, US portfolios, and country portfolios are pretty well-explained by their APT or ICAPM factors.[2]

Problems

1. Download ten years of monthly total return data for individual stocks, US portfolios, and country portfolios. Then use that data to estimate the Static CAPM under three market portfolio benchmarks (SPDR "Spider" Exchange Traded Fund, CRSP Value-Weighted Market Return, and Dow Jones World Stock Index) and using the standard Fama-MacBeth methodology. Then use the Static CAPM estimates to forecast each asset's expected return in the next future month, or equivalently, each asset's cost of equity capital.

---

[2] Lewellen, Nagel and Shaken (2007) suggest that apparently high cross-sectional R^2 provide quite weak support for an asset pricing model. They offer a number of suggestions for improving empirical asset pricing tests, include expanding the set of assets tested to include industry portfolios and using Generalized Least Squares (GLS) R^2, rather than regular regression (OLS) R^2. They test seven popular asset pricing models, including the Static CAPM and the Fama-French 3 Factor model. They find that for an expanded set of assets which includes industry portfolios, the GLS R^2 is less than 10% for all seven asset pricing models. See Lewellen, J., S. Nagel, and J. Shaken, 2007, A Skeptical Appraisal of Asset-Pricing Tests, Emory working paper.

Finally, determine how much variation of individual stocks, US portfolios, or country portfolios is explained by the Static CAPM.

2. Download ten years of monthly total return data for individual stocks, US portfolios, and country portfolios. Then use that data to estimate the APT or Intertemporal CAPM (ICAPM) under two sets of factors (Fama-French 3 factors and 3 macro factors) and using the standard Fama-MacBeth methodology. Then use the APT or ICAPM estimates to forecast each asset's expected return in the next future month, or equivalently, each asset's cost of equity capital. Finally, determine how much variation of individual stocks, US portfolios, or country portfolios is explained by the APT or ICAPM.

Chapter 8 Stock Valuation

8.1 Dividend Discount Model

Problem. Currently a stock pays a dividend per share of $6.64. A security analyst projects the future dividend growth rate over the next five years to be 12.0%, 11.0%, 10.0%, 9.0%, 8.0% and then 7.0% each year thereafter to infinity. The levered cost of equity capital for the firm is 12.0% per year. What is the stock's value / share?

Solution Strategy. Construct a two-stage discounted dividend model. In stage one, explicitly forecast the firm's dividend over a five-year horizon. In stage two, forecast the firm's dividend from year six to infinity and calculate its continuation value as the present value of this infinitely growing annuity. Then, discount the future dividends and the date 5 continuation value back to the present to get the stock's value.

FIGURE 8.1 Excel Model for Stock Valuation – Dividend Discount Model.

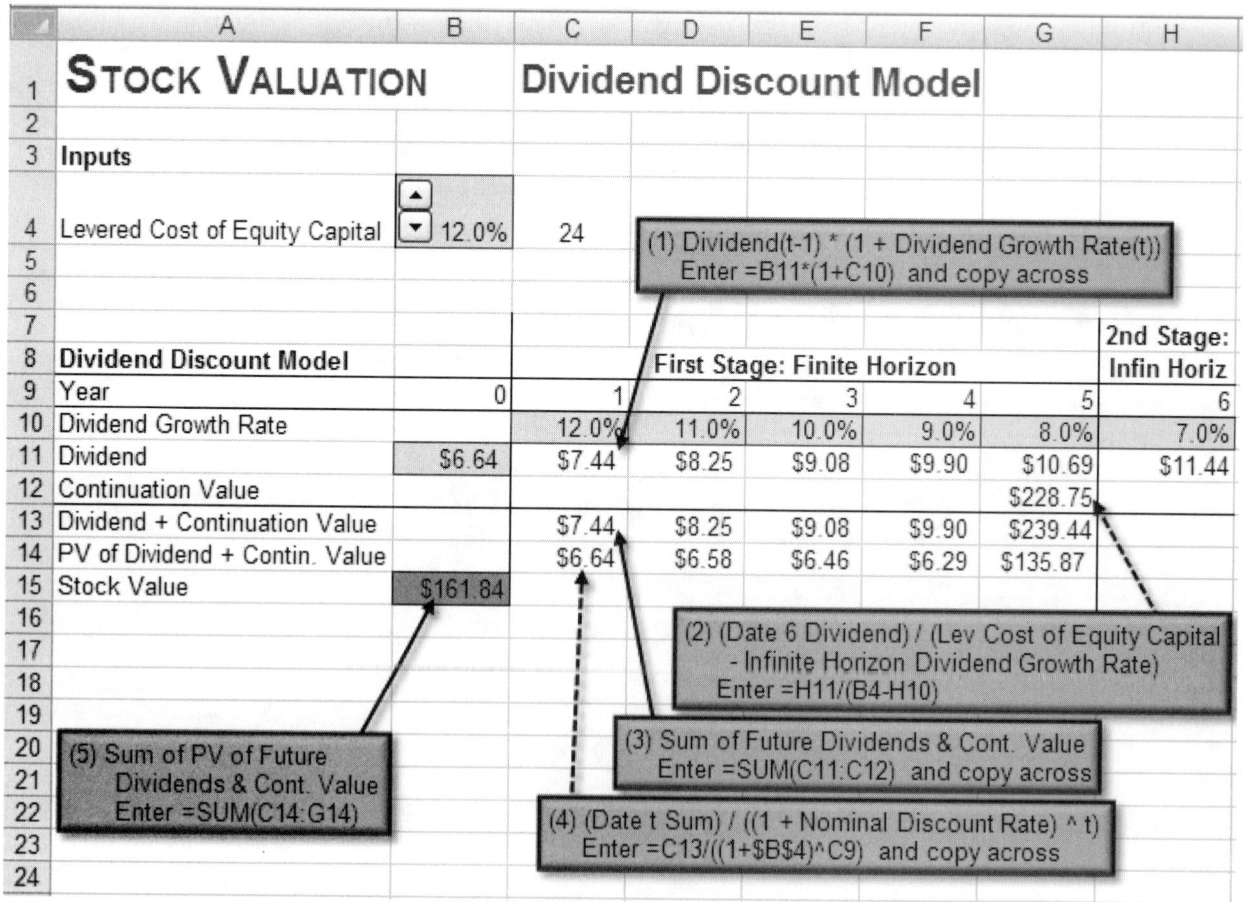

	A	B	C	D	E	F	G	H
1	STOCK VALUATION		Dividend Discount Model					
2								
3	Inputs							
4	Levered Cost of Equity Capital	12.0%	24					
5								
6								
7								2nd Stage:
8	Dividend Discount Model			First Stage: Finite Horizon				Infin Horiz
9	Year	0	1	2	3	4	5	6
10	Dividend Growth Rate		12.0%	11.0%	10.0%	9.0%	8.0%	7.0%
11	Dividend	$6.64	$7.44	$8.25	$9.08	$9.90	$10.69	$11.44
12	Continuation Value						$228.75	
13	Dividend + Continuation Value		$7.44	$8.25	$9.08	$9.90	$239.44	
14	PV of Dividend + Contin. Value		$6.64	$6.58	$6.46	$6.29	$135.87	
15	Stock Value	$161.84						

The stock value is estimated to be $161.84.

Problems

1. Currently a stock pays a dividend per share of $43.37. A security analyst projects the future dividend growth rate over the next five years to be 21.0%, 18.0%, 15.0%, 13.5%, 11.5% and then 11.0% each year thereafter to infinity. The levered cost of equity capital for the firm is 13.4% per year. What is the stock's value / share?

Chapter 9 Firm and Project Valuation

9.1 Cash Flows for Five Equivalent Methods

Problem. The expected future cash flows for a firm have been forecasted in two stages correspond to two time periods. Stage one is a finite horizon from years 1 to 5. Stage two is the remaining infinite horizon from year 6 to infinity. Given these forecasted cash flows, compute the current value of the firm and the value added by the firm using five equivalent methods: (1) Adjusted Present Value, (2) Free Cash Flow to Equity, (3) Free Cash Flow to the Firm, (4) Dividend Discount Model, and (5) Residual Income. Given expected future cash flows for a project, compute the present value of future cash flows and the NPV of the project using the same five equivalent methods.

Solution Strategy. In this section, compute the cash flows streams that will be used by the five valuation methods: (1) Free Cash Flow to Equity, (2) Dividends, (3) Tax Shield Benefit, (4) Free Cash Flow to the Firm, and (5) Economic Profit. In subsequent sections, compute the current value of the firm and the value added by the firm using each of the five equivalent methods in turn. In the last section, eliminate stage two cash flows and recompute the value of the firm and the value added by the firm using the same five methods. Then, switch to evaluating a project and compute the value of future cash flows and the NPV of the project using the same five methods. Finally, restore stage two cash flows and compute the value of future cash flows and the NPV of the project using the same five methods.

FIGURE 9.1 Firm and Project Valuation – Cash Flows for 5 Equiv Methods.

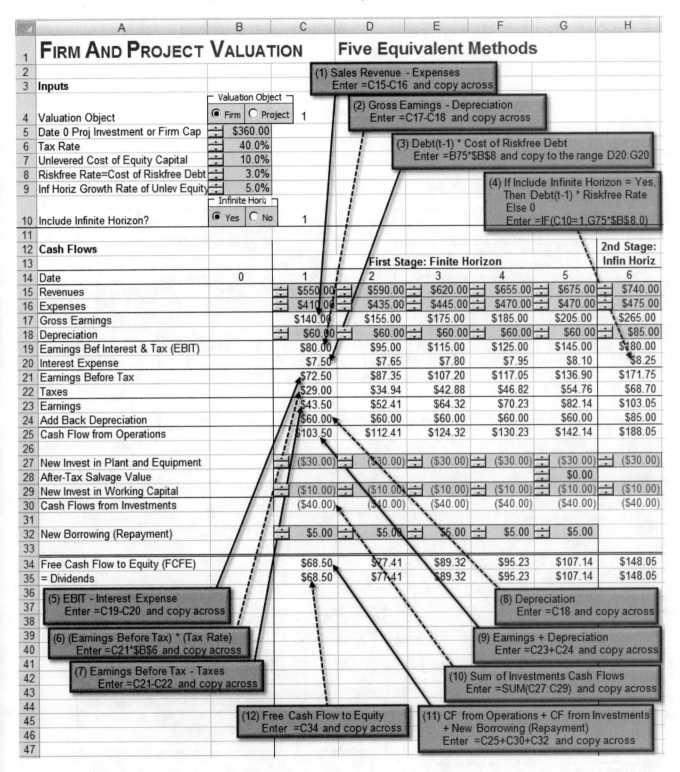

FIGURE 9.2 Firm and Project Valuation – Cash Flows for 5 Equiv Methods.

	A	B	C	D	E	F	G	H
1	**FIRM AND PROJECT VALUATION**			**Five Equivalent Methods**				
2								
3	**Inputs**							
4	Valuation Object	Valuation Object ◉ Firm ○ Project	1					
5	Date 0 Proj Investment or Firm Cap	$360.00						
6	Tax Rate	40.0%						
7	Unlevered Cost of Equity Capital	10.0%						
8	Riskfree Rate=Cost of Riskfree De	3.0%						
9	Inf Horiz Growth Rate of Unlev Equi	5.0%						
10	Include Infinite Horizon?	Infinite Horiz ◉ Yes ○ No	1					
48								
49–59								

(13) Interest Expense Enter =C20 and copy across

(17) FCFE + CFD + Tax Shield Benefit Enter =C34+C62-C64 and copy across

(14) - New Borrowing (Repayment) Enter =-C32 and copy across

(18) Earnings Enter =C23 and copy across

(15) Interest + Less New Borrow (Repay) Enter =C60+C61 and copy across

(19) (1 - Tax Rate) * Interest Expense Enter =(1-$B$6)*C20 and copy across

(16) Debt(t-1) * Cost of Riskfree Debt * Tax Rate Enter =B75*$B$8*$B$6 and copy across

(20) Earnings + After-tax Interest Expense Enter =C68+C69 and copy across

	A	B	C	D	E	F	G	H
60	Interest		$7.50	$7.65	$7.80	$7.95	$8.10	$8.25
61	Less New Borrowing (Repayment)		($5.00)	($5.00)	($5.00)	($5.00)	($5.00)	$0.00
62	Cash Flow to Debtholders (CFD)		$2.50	$2.65	$2.80	$2.95	$3.10	$8.25
63								
64	Tax Shield Benefit		$3.00	$3.06	$3.12	$3.18	$3.24	$3.30
65	Free Cash Flow to the Firm (FCFF)		$68.00	$77.00	$89.00	$95.00	$107.00	$153.00
66								
67	**Alternative Way to get FCFF**							
68	Earnings		$43.50	$52.41	$64.32	$70.23	$82.14	$103.05
69	After-tax Interest Expense		$4.50	$4.59	$4.68	$4.77	$4.86	$4.95
70	Net Oper. Profit After Tax (NOPAT)		$48.00	$57.00	$69.00	$75.00	$87.00	$108.00
71	Depreciation		$60.00	$60.00	$60.00	$60.00	$60.00	$85.00
72	Cash Flows from Investments		($40.00)	($40.00)	($40.00)	($40.00)	($40.00)	($40.00)
73	Free Cash Flow to the Firm (FCFF)		$68.00	$77.00	$89.00	$95.00	$107.00	$153.00
74								
75	Debt (D)	$250.00	$255.00	$260.00	$265.00	$270.00	$275.00	
76	Book Value of Equity	$110.00	$85.00	$60.00	$35.00	$10.00	($15.00)	
77								
78	**Economic Profit**							
79	Net Oper. Profit After Tax (NOPAT)		$48.00	$57.00	$69.00	$75.00	$87.00	$108.00
80	Capital Charge		$10.50	$8.13	$5.76	$3.36	$0.96	($1.47)
81	Economic Profit		$37.50	$48.87	$63.24	$71.64	$86.04	$109.47

(21) Date 0 Firm Capital - Debt Enter =B5-B74

(26) BV Equity(t-1) - Deprec - New Invest in Plant & Equip - New Invest in Working Cap - New Borrowing (Repayment) Enter =B70-C10-C27-C29-C32 and copy across

(22) Depreciation Enter =C18 and copy across

(23) Cash Flows From Investments Enter =C30 and copy across

(27) NOPAT Enter =C70 and copy across

(24) NOPAT + Depreciation + Cash Flow from Invest Enter =C70+C71+C72 and copy across

(28) Cost of Firm Capital * Book Value of Equity(t-1) Enter =C187*B76 and copy to D80:G80

(29) If Include Inf Horiz = Yes, Then Cost of Firm Capital * Book Value of Equity(t-1) Else 0 Enter =IF(C10=1,H187*G76,0)

(25) Debt(t-1) + New Borrowing (Repayment) Enter =B75+C32 and copy across

(30) NOPAT - Capital Charge Enter =C79-C80 and copy across

9.2 Adjusted Present Value

Problem. Given the cash flow streams, compute the current value of the firm and the value added by the firm using Adjusted Present Value.

Soluton Strategy. Take the Free Cash Flow to the Firm and discount at the Unlevered Cost of Equity Capital to obtain the Value of the Unlevered Firm. Take the Tax Shield Benefit and discount at the Cost of Riskfree Debt to obtain the Value of the Tax Shield. Sum the Value of the Unlevered Firm and the Value of the Tax Shield to get the Value of the Firm. Subtract Date 0 Capital to get the Value Added by the Firm.

FIGURE 9.3 Firm and Project Valuation – Adjusted Present Value.

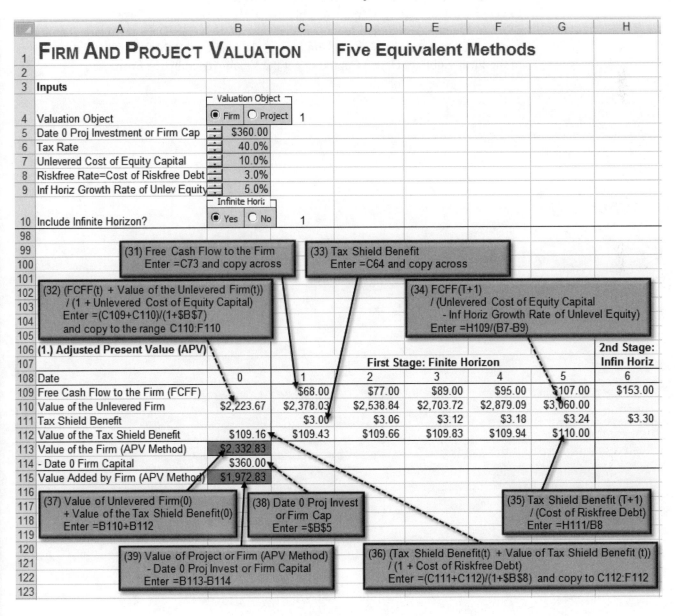

The value of the firm is $2,332.83. This is the amount of money you would be willing to pay if you were going to buy the firm on Date 0, since the Date 0 Firm Capital is already sunk into the firm. Considering that the firm is currently using $360.00 in capital, the (Net Present) Value Added by the Firm is $1,972.83.

9.3 Free Cash Flow To Equity

Problem. Given the cash flow streams, compute the current value of the firm and the value added by the firm using Free Cash Flow to Equity.

Soluton Strategy. Take the Free Cash Flow to Equity and discount at the Levered Cost of Equity Capital to obtain the Value of Equity. Take the Cash Flow to Debtholders and discount at the Cost of Riskfree Debt to obtain the Value of Debt. Sum the Value of Equity and the Value of Debt to get the Value of the Firm. Subtract Date 0 Capital to get the Value Added by the Firm.

FIGURE 9.4 Firm and Project Valuation – Free Cash Flow To Equity.

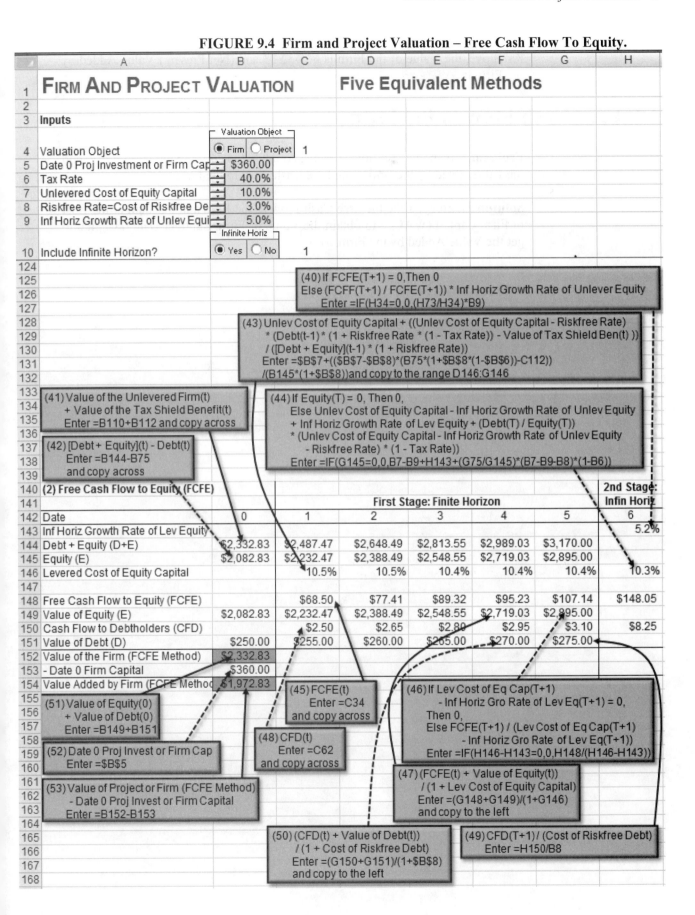

As above, the Value of the Firm is $2,332.83 and (Net Present) Value Added by the Firm is $1,972.83.

9.4 Free Cash Flow to the Firm

Problem. Given the cash flow streams, compute the current value of the firm and the value added by the firm using Free Cash Flow to the Firm.

Soluton Strategy. Take the Free Cash Flow to the Firm and discount at the Cost of Firm Capital (WACC) to obtain the Value of Firm. Subtract Date 0 Capital to get the Value Added by the Firm.

FIGURE 9.5 Firm and Project Valuation – Free Cash Flow To The Firm.

	A	B	C	D	E	F	G	H
1	**FIRM AND PROJECT VALUATION**			**Five Equivalent Methods**				
2								
3	Inputs							
4	Valuation Object	⊙ Firm ○ Project	1					
5	Date 0 Proj Investment or Firm Cap	$360.00						
6	Tax Rate	40.0%						
7	Unlevered Cost of Equity Capital	10.0%						
8	Riskfree Rate=Cost of Riskfree Debt	3.0%						
9	Inf Horiz Growth Rate of Unlev Equity	5.0%						
10	Include Infinite Horizon?	⊙ Yes ○ No	1					

(55) Equity(t) / [Debt + Equity](t)
Enter B145/B144 and copy to C185:F185

(56) If [Debt + Equity](T) = 0, Then 0,
Else Equity(T) / [Debt + Equity](T)
Enter =IF(G144=0,0,G145/G144)

(54) Inf Horiz Growth Rate
of Unlev Equity
Enter =B9

(57) Debt(t) / [Debt + Equity](t)
Enter =B75/B144 and copy to C186:F186

(58) If [Debt + Equity](T) = 0, Then 0,
Else Equity(T) / [Debt + Equity](T)
Enter =IF(G144=0,0,G75/G144)

(59) (Lev Cost of Equity Cap) * (Equity Weight)
+ (1 - Tax Rate) * (Cost of Riskfree Debt)
* (Debt Weight)
Enter =C146*B185+(1-$B$6)*$B$8*B186
and copy to the range D187:G187

(60) Inf Horiz Growth Rate of the Firm + (Equity Weight)
* (Lev Cost of Equity Cap - Inf Horizon Gro Rate of Lev Equity)
+ (Debt Weight) * (1 - Tax Rate) * (Cost of Riskfree Debt)
Enter =H184+G185*(H146-H143)+G186*(1-$B$6)*$B$8

	A	B	C	D	E	F	G	H
181	(3) Free Cash Flow to the Firm (FCFF)							2nd Stage
182				First Stage: Finite Horizon				Infin Horiz
183	Date	0	1	2	3	4	5	6
184	Inf Horiz Growth Rate of the Firm							5.0%
185	Equity Weight (E / (D+E))	89.3%	89.7%	90.2%	90.6%	91.0%	91.3%	
186	Debt Weight (D / (D+E))	10.7%	10.3%	9.8%	9.4%	9.0%	8.7%	
187	Cost of Firm Capital (WACC)		9.54%	9.57%	9.59%	9.61%	9.63%	9.8%
188								
189	Free Cash Flow to the Firm (FCFF)		$68.00	$77.00	$89.00	$95.00	$107.00	$153.00
190	Value of the Firm (FCFF Method)	$2,332.83	$2,487.47	$2,648.49	$2,813.55	$2,989.03	$3,170.00	
191	- Date 0 Firm Capital	$360.00						
192	Value Added by Firm (FCFF Method)	$1,972.83						

(64) Date 0 Proj Invest or Firm Cap
Enter =$B$5

(61) FCFF(t)
Enter =C73
and copy across

(62) If Cost of Firm Cap(T+1)
- Inf Horiz Gro Rate of the Firm(T+1) = 0,
Then 0,
Else FCFF(T+1) / (Cost of Firm Cap(T+
- Inf Horiz Gro Rate of the Firm(T+1))
Enter =IF(H187-H184=0,0,H189/(H187-H184))

(65) Value of Project or Firm (FCFF Method)
- Date 0 Proj Invest or Firm Capital
Enter =B190-B191

(63) (FCFF(t) + Value of the Firm (t))
/ (1 + Cost of Firm Capital(t))
Enter =(G189+G190)/(1+G187)
and copy to the left

As above, the Value of the Firm is $2,332.83 and (Net Present) Value Added by the Firm is $1,972.83.

9.5 Dividend Discount Model

Problem. Given the cash flow streams, compute the current value of the firm and the value added by the firm using a Dividend Discount Model.

Soluton Strategy. Take the Dividends and discount at the Levered Cost of Equity Capital to obtain the Value of Equity. Take the Cash Flow to Debtholders and discount at the Cost of Riskfree Debt to obtain the Value of Debt. Sum the Value of Equity and the Value of Debt to get the Value of the Firm. Subtract Date 0 Capital to get the Value Added by the Firm.

FIGURE 9.6 Firm and Project Valuation – Dividend Discount Model.

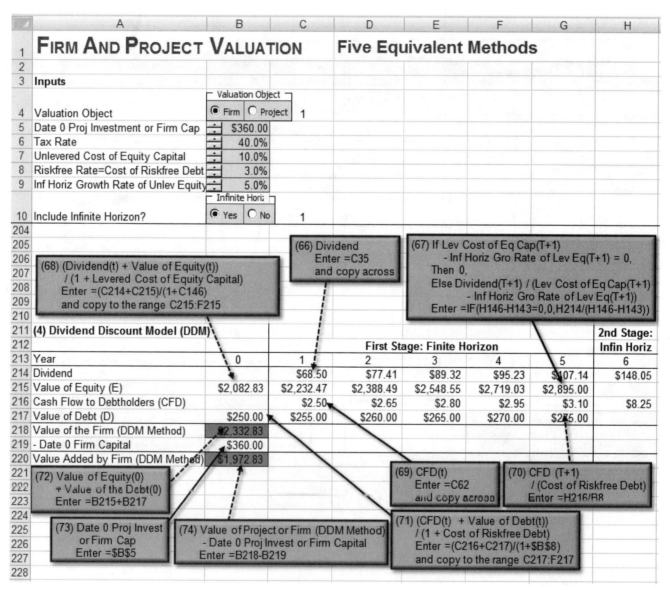

As above, the Value of the Firm is $2,332.83 and (Net Present) Value Added by the Firm is $1,972.83.

9.6 Residual Income

Problem. Given the cash flow streams, compute the current value of the firm and the value added by the firm using Residual Income.

Soluton Strategy. Take the Economic Profit and discount at the Cost of Firm Capital (WACC) to obtain the Value of Economic Profit. Add the Date 0 Book Value of the Firm to get the Value of the Firm. Subtract Date 0 Capital to get the Value Added by the Firm.

FIGURE 9.7 Firm and Project Valuation – Residual Income.

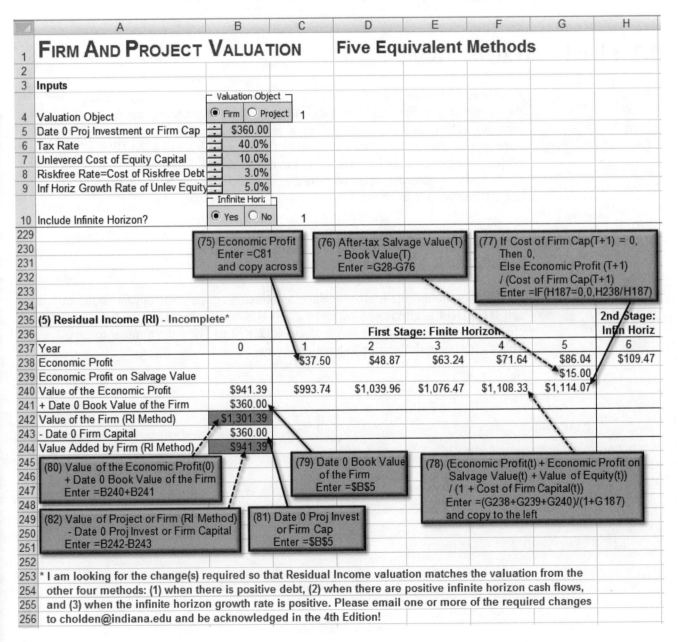

Unfortunately the Residual Income valuation is incomplete. In principle, it should match the results of the other four valuation methods. However, the current spreadsheet does not match. It currently gives the Value of the Firm is $1,301.39 and (Net Present) Value Added by the firm's capital is $941.39. As will be demonstrated shortly, the current spreadsheet does produce a Residual Income valuation that matches the other four valuation methods in the special case of no infinite horizon and no debt in any period.

I'm not sure how to fix this and would be grateful for your help. Please email one or more of the required changes to make the Residual Income valuation match the valuation from the other four methods under more general conditions. I will be delighted to acknowledge your contribution in the 4th Edition of this book!

9.7 Five Equivalent Methods

Problem. Eliminate the (stage two) infinite horizon cash flows and recompute the value of the firm and the value added by the firm using the same five methods. Then, switch to evaluating a project while maintaining no infinite horizon cash flows. Compute the value of future cash flows and the NPV of the project using the same five methods. Finally, restore the infinite horizon cash flows and compute the value of future cash flows and the NPV of the project using the same five methods.

Start by considering the special case of no infinite horizon and no debt in any period. Essentially, we are assuming that that firm lasts for 5 years and then is liquidated for an After-Tax Salvage Value of $300.

Eliminating the infinite horizon is done by clicking on the "**No**" option button in cell **B10**. Debt is eliminated by editing cell **B75** to be =0+(K75-50)*10 and by clicking on the spin buttons in the range **C32:F32** to bring them down to zero. This yields the cash flows and valuations below.

FIGURE 9.8 Five Equivalent Methods – Firm and No Infinite Horizon.

	A	B	C	D	E	F	G	H
1	**FIRM AND PROJECT VALUATION**				**Five Equivalent Methods**			
2								
3	Inputs							
4	Valuation Object	⊙ Firm ○ Project		1				
5	Date 0 Proj Investment or Firm Cap	$360.00						
6	Tax Rate	40.0%						
7	Unlevered Cost of Equity Capital	10.0%						
8	Riskfree Rate=Cost of Riskfree Debt	3.0%						
9	Inf Horiz Growth Rate of Unlev Equity	5.0%						
10	Include Infinite Horizon?	○ Yes ⊙ No		2				
11								
12	**Cash Flows**							**2nd Stage: Infin Horiz**
13				First Stage: Finite Horizon				
14	Date	0	1	2	3	4	5	6
15	Revenues		$550.00	$590.00	$620.00	$655.00	$675.00	$0.00
16	Expenses		$410.00	$435.00	$445.00	$470.00	$470.00	$0.00
17	Gross Earnings		$140.00	$155.00	$175.00	$185.00	$205.00	$0.00
18	Depreciation		$60.00	$60.00	$60.00	$60.00	$60.00	$0.00
19	Earnings Bef Interest & Tax (EBIT)		$80.00	$95.00	$115.00	$125.00	$145.00	$0.00
20	Interest Expense		$0.00	$0.00	$0.00	$0.00	$0.00	$0.00
21	Earnings Before Tax		$80.00	$95.00	$115.00	$125.00	$145.00	$0.00
22	Taxes		$32.00	$38.00	$46.00	$50.00	$58.00	$0.00
23	Earnings		$48.00	$57.00	$69.00	$75.00	$87.00	$0.00
24	Add Back Depreciation		$60.00	$60.00	$60.00	$60.00	$60.00	$0.00
25	Cash Flow from Operations		$108.00	$117.00	$129.00	$135.00	$147.00	$0.00
26								
27	New Invest in Plant and Equipment		($30.00)	($30.00)	($30.00)	($30.00)	($30.00)	$0.00
28	After-Tax Salvage Value						$300.00	
29	New Invest in Working Capital		($10.00)	($10.00)	($10.00)	($10.00)	($10.00)	$0.00
30	Cash Flows from Investments		($40.00)	($40.00)	($40.00)	($40.00)	$260.00	$0.00
31								
32	New Borrowing (Repayment)		$0.00	$0.00	$0.00	$0.00	$0.00	
33								
34	Free Cash Flow to Equity (FCFE)		$68.00	$77.00	$89.00	$95.00	$407.00	$0.00
35	= Dividends		$68.00	$77.00	$89.00	$95.00	$407.00	$0.00
36								
60	Interest		$0.00	$0.00	$0.00	$0.00	$0.00	$0.00
61	Less New Borrowing (Repayment)		$0.00	$0.00	$0.00	$0.00	$0.00	$0.00
62	Cash Flow to Debtholders (CFD)		$0.00	$0.00	$0.00	$0.00	$0.00	$0.00
63								
64	Tax Shield Benefit		$0.00	$0.00	$0.00	$0.00	$0.00	$0.00
65	Free Cash Flow to the Firm (FCFF)		$68.00	$77.00	$89.00	$95.00	$407.00	$0.00
66								
67	**Alternative Way to get FCFF**							
68	Earnings		$48.00	$57.00	$69.00	$75.00	$87.00	$0.00
69	After-tax Interest Expense		$0.00	$0.00	$0.00	$0.00	$0.00	$0.00
70	Net Oper. Profit After Tax (NOPAT)		$48.00	$57.00	$69.00	$75.00	$87.00	$0.00
71	Depreciation		$60.00	$60.00	$60.00	$60.00	$60.00	$0.00
72	Cash Flows from Investments		($40.00)	($40.00)	($40.00)	($40.00)	$260.00	$0.00
73	Free Cash Flow to the Firm (FCFF)		$68.00	$77.00	$89.00	$95.00	$407.00	$0.00
74								
75	Debt (D)	$0.00	$0.00	$0.00	$0.00	$0.00	$0.00	
76	Book Value of Equity	$360.00	$340.00	$320.00	$300.00	$280.00	$260.00	
77								
78	**Economic Profit**							
79	Net Oper. Profit After Tax (NOPAT)		$48.00	$57.00	$69.00	$75.00	$87.00	$0.00
80	Capital Charge		$36.00	$34.00	$32.00	$30.00	$28.00	$0.00
81	Economic Profit		$12.00	$23.00	$37.00	$45.00	$59.00	$0.00

FIGURE 9.9 Five Equivalent Methods – Firm and No Infinite Horizon.

	A	B	C	D	E	F	G	H
106	**(1.) Adjusted Present Value (APV)**							2nd Stage:
107				First Stage: Finite Horizon				Infin Horiz
108	Date	0	1	2	3	4	5	6
109	Free Cash Flow to the Firm (FCFF)		$68.00	$77.00	$89.00	$95.00	$407.00	$0.00
110	Value of the Unlevered Firm	$509.92	$492.92	$465.21	$422.73	$370.00	$0.00	
111	Tax Shield Benefit		$0.00	$0.00	$0.00	$0.00	$0.00	$0.00
112	Value of the Tax Shield Benefit	$0.00	$0.00	$0.00	$0.00	$0.00	$0.00	
113	Value of the Firm (APV Method)	$509.92						
114	- Date 0 Firm Capital	$360.00						
115	Value Added by Firm (APV Method)	$149.92						
116								
140	**(2) Free Cash Flow to Equity (FCFE)**							2nd Stage:
141				First Stage: Finite Horizon				Infin Horiz
142	Date	0	1	2	3	4	5	6
143	Inf Horiz Growth Rate of Lev Equity							0.0%
144	Debt + Equity (D+E)	$509.92	$492.92	$465.21	$422.73	$370.00	$0.00	
145	Equity (E)	$509.92	$492.92	$465.21	$422.73	$370.00	$0.00	
146	Levered Cost of Equity Capital		10.0%	10.0%	10.0%	10.0%	10.0%	0.0%
147								
148	Free Cash Flow to Equity (FCFE)		$68.00	$77.00	$89.00	$95.00	$407.00	$0.00
149	Value of Equity (E)	$509.92	$492.92	$465.21	$422.73	$370.00	$0.00	
150	Cash Flow to Debtholders (CFD)		$0.00	$0.00	$0.00	$0.00	$0.00	$0.00
151	Value of Debt (D)	$0.00	$0.00	$0.00	$0.00	$0.00	$0.00	
152	Value of the Firm (FCFE Method)	$509.92						
153	- Date 0 Firm Capital	$360.00						
154	Value Added by Firm (FCFE Method)	$149.92						
155								
181	**(3) Free Cash Flow to the Firm (FCFF)**							2nd Stage:
182				First Stage: Finite Horizon				Infin Horiz
183	Date	0	1	2	3	4	5	6
184	Inf Horiz Growth Rate of the Firm							5.0%
185	Equity Weight (E / (D+E))	100.0%	100.0%	100.0%	100.0%	100.0%	0.0%	
186	Debt Weight (D / (D+E))	0.0%	0.0%	0.0%	0.0%	0.0%	0.0%	
187	Cost of Firm Capital (WACC)		10.00%	10.00%	10.00%	10.00%	10.00%	5.0%
188								
189	Free Cash Flow to the Firm (FCFF)		$68.00	$77.00	$89.00	$95.00	$407.00	$0.00
190	Value of the Firm (FCFF Method)	$509.92	$492.92	$465.21	$422.73	$370.00	$0.00	
191	- Date 0 Firm Capital	$360.00						
192	Value Added by Firm (FCFF Method)	$149.92						
193								
211	**(4) Dividend Discount Model (DDM)**							2nd Stage:
212				First Stage: Finite Horizon				Infin Horiz
213	Year	0	1	2	3	4	5	6
214	Dividend		$68.00	$77.00	$89.00	$95.00	$407.00	$0.00
215	Value of Equity (E)	$509.92	$492.92	$465.21	$422.73	$370.00	$0.00	
216	Cash Flow to Debtholders (CFD)		$0.00	$0.00	$0.00	$0.00	$0.00	$0.00
217	Value of Debt (D)	$0.00	$0.00	$0.00	$0.00	$0.00	$0.00	
218	Value of the Firm (DDM Method)	$509.92						
219	- Date 0 Firm Capital	$360.00						
220	Value Added by Firm (DDM Method)	$149.92						
221								
235	**(5) Residual Income (RI) - Incomplete***							2nd Stage:
236				First Stage: Finite Horizon				Infin Horiz
237	Year	0	1	2	3	4	5	6
238	Economic Profit		$12.00	$23.00	$37.00	$45.00	$59.00	$0.00
239	Economic Profit on Salvage Value						$40.00	
240	Value of the Economic Profit	$149.92	$152.92	$145.21	$122.73	$90.00	$0.00	
241	+ Date 0 Book Value of the Firm	$360.00						
242	Value of the Firm (RI Method)	$509.92						
243	- Date 0 Firm Capital	$360.00						
244	Value Added by Firm (RI Method)	$149.92						

Now all five valuation methods match. The Value of the Firm is $509.92 and (Net Present) Value Added by the Firm is $149.92. It makes sense that these valuations are much lower than before because we have eliminated the (second stage) infinite horizon cash flows from period 6 to infinity.

Now switch to considering a project. The main difference between a firm and a project is how the date 0 cash flow is treated. With a firm, the date 0 capital is already invested in the firm, so the Value of the Firm is the present value of all future cash flows excluding the date 0 capital. With a project, the date 0 capital has not been invested yet and we are trying to decide whether to proceed with the project or not. So the Net Present Value of the project is the present value of all future cash flows minus the cost of the Date 0 Project Investment.

Switching to the project is done by clicking on the "**Project**" option button in cell **B4**. Click on the spin buttons in the range **C32:F32** to reset the New Borrowing each year to zero. There is no infinite horizon, so it is assumed that the project lasts for 5 years and then is liquidated for an After-Tax Salvage Value. To highlight the contrast between a project and a firm, we have assumed that the project involved a single investment on date 0 and no further investments in plant and equipment or working capital on future dates. However, this assumption could be relaxed and the spreadsheet would handle it just fine.

FIGURE 9.10 Five Equivalent Methods – Project and No Infinite Horizon.

	A	B	C	D	E	F	G	H
1	**FIRM AND PROJECT VALUATION**			**Five Equivalent Methods**				
2								
3	**Inputs**							
4	Valuation Object	⊙ Firm ● Project	2					
5	Date 0 Proj Investment or Firm Cap	$360.00						
6	Tax Rate	40.0%						
7	Unlevered Cost of Equity Capital	10.0%						
8	Riskfree Rate=Cost of Riskfree Debt	3.0%						
9	Inf Horiz Growth Rate of Unlev Equity	5.0%						
10	Include Infinite Horizon?	⊙ Yes ● No	2					
11								
12	**Cash Flows**							2nd Stage:
13					First Stage: Finite Horizon			Infin Horiz
14	Date	0	1	2	3	4	5	6
15	Revenues		$550.00	$590.00	$620.00	$655.00	$675.00	$0.00
16	Expenses		$410.00	$435.00	$445.00	$470.00	$470.00	$0.00
17	Gross Earnings		$140.00	$155.00	$175.00	$185.00	$205.00	$0.00
18	Depreciation		$60.00	$60.00	$60.00	$60.00	$60.00	$0.00
19	Earnings Bef Interest & Tax (EBIT)		$80.00	$95.00	$115.00	$125.00	$145.00	$0.00
20	Interest Expense		$0.00	$0.00	$0.00	$0.00	$0.00	$0.00
21	Earnings Before Tax		$80.00	$95.00	$115.00	$125.00	$145.00	$0.00
22	Taxes		$32.00	$38.00	$46.00	$50.00	$58.00	$0.00
23	Earnings		$48.00	$57.00	$69.00	$75.00	$87.00	$0.00
24	Add Back Depreciation		$60.00	$60.00	$60.00	$60.00	$60.00	$0.00
25	Cash Flow from Operations		$108.00	$117.00	$129.00	$135.00	$147.00	$0.00
26								
27	New Invest in Plant and Equipment		$0.00	$0.00	$0.00	$0.00	$0.00	$0.00
28	After-Tax Salvage Value						$300.00	
29	New Invest in Working Capital		$0.00	$0.00	$0.00	$0.00	$0.00	$0.00
30	Cash Flows from Investments		$0.00	$0.00	$0.00	$0.00	$300.00	$0.00
31								
32	New Borrowing (Repayment)		$0.00	$0.00	$0.00	$0.00	$0.00	
33								
34	Free Cash Flow to Equity (FCFE)		$108.00	$117.00	$129.00	$135.00	$447.00	$0.00
35	= Dividends		$108.00	$117.00	$129.00	$135.00	$447.00	$0.00
36								
60	Interest		$0.00	$0.00	$0.00	$0.00	$0.00	$0.00
61	Less New Borrowing (Repayment)		$0.00	$0.00	$0.00	$0.00	$0.00	$0.00
62	Cash Flow to Debtholders (CFD)		$0.00	$0.00	$0.00	$0.00	$0.00	$0.00
63								
64	Tax Shield Benefit		$0.00	$0.00	$0.00	$0.00	$0.00	$0.00
65	Free Cash Flow to the Firm (FCFF)		$108.00	$117.00	$129.00	$135.00	$447.00	$0.00
66								
67	**Alternative Way to get FCFF**							
68	Earnings		$48.00	$57.00	$69.00	$75.00	$87.00	$0.00
69	After-tax Interest Expense		$0.00	$0.00	$0.00	$0.00	$0.00	$0.00
70	Net Oper. Profit After Tax (NOPAT)		$48.00	$57.00	$69.00	$75.00	$87.00	$0.00
71	Depreciation		$60.00	$60.00	$60.00	$60.00	$60.00	$0.00
72	Cash Flows from Investments		$0.00	$0.00	$0.00	$0.00	$300.00	$0.00
73	Free Cash Flow to the Firm (FCFF)		$108.00	$117.00	$129.00	$135.00	$447.00	$0.00
74								
75	Debt (D)	$0.00	$0.00	$0.00	$0.00	$0.00	$0.00	
76	Book Value of Equity	$360.00	$300.00	$240.00	$180.00	$120.00	$60.00	

FIGURE 9.11 Five Equivalent Methods – Project and No Infinite Horizon.

	A	B	C	D	E	F	G	H
106	**(1.) Adjusted Present Value (APV)**							**2nd Stage:**
107			First Stage: Finite Horizon					Infin Horiz
108	Date	0	1	2	3	4	5	6
109	Free Cash Flow to the Firm (FCFF)		$108.00	$117.00	$129.00	$135.00	$447.00	$0.00
110	Value of the Unlevered Firm	$661.55	$619.71	$564.68	$492.15	$406.36	$0.00	
111	Tax Shield Benefit		$0.00	$0.00	$0.00	$0.00	$0.00	$0.00
112	Value of the Tax Shield Benefit	$0.00	$0.00	$0.00	$0.00	$0.00	$0.00	
113	Value of Fut Cash Flows (APV Met)	$661.55						
114	- Date 0 Project Investment	$360.00						
115	NPV of Project (APV Method)	$301.55						
116								
140	**(2) Free Cash Flow to Equity (FCFE)**							**2nd Stage:**
141			First Stage: Finite Horizon					Infin Horiz
142	Date	0	1	2	3	4	5	6
143	Inf Horiz Growth Rate of Lev Equity							0.0%
144	Debt + Equity (D+E)	$661.55	$619.71	$564.68	$492.15	$406.36	$0.00	
145	Equity (E)	$661.55	$619.71	$564.68	$492.15	$406.36	$0.00	
146	Levered Cost of Equity Capital		10.0%	10.0%	10.0%	10.0%	10.0%	0.0%
147								
148	Free Cash Flow to Equity (FCFE)		$108.00	$117.00	$129.00	$135.00	$447.00	$0.00
149	Value of Equity (E)	$661.55	$619.71	$564.68	$492.15	$406.36	$0.00	
150	Cash Flow to Debtholders (CFD)		$0.00	$0.00	$0.00	$0.00	$0.00	$0.00
151	Value of Debt (D)	$0.00	$0.00	$0.00	$0.00	$0.00	$0.00	
152	Value of Fut Cash Flows (FCFE Met)	$661.55						
153	- Date 0 Project Investment	$360.00						
154	NPV of Project (FCFE Method)	$301.55						
155								
181	**(3) Free Cash Flow to the Firm (FCFF)**							**2nd Stage:**
182			First Stage: Finite Horizon					Infin Horiz
183	Date	0	1	2	3	4	5	6
184	Inf Horiz Growth Rate of the Firm							5.0%
185	Equity Weight (E / (D+E))	100.0%	100.0%	100.0%	100.0%	100.0%	0.0%	
186	Debt Weight (D / (D+E))	0.0%	0.0%	0.0%	0.0%	0.0%	0.0%	
187	Cost of Firm Capital (WACC)		10.00%	10.00%	10.00%	10.00%	10.00%	5.0%
188								
189	Free Cash Flow to the Firm (FCFF)		$108.00	$117.00	$129.00	$135.00	$447.00	$0.00
190	Value of Fut Cash Flows (FCFF Met)	$661.55	$619.71	$564.68	$492.15	$406.36	$0.00	
191	- Date 0 Project Investment	$360.00						
192	NPV of Project (FCFF Method)	$301.55						
193								
211	**(4) Dividend Discount Model (DDM)**							**2nd Stage:**
212			First Stage: Finite Horizon					Infin Horiz
213	Year	0	1	2	3	4	5	6
214	Dividend		$108.00	$117.00	$129.00	$135.00	$447.00	$0.00
215	Value of Equity (E)	$661.55	$619.71	$564.68	$492.15	$406.36	$0.00	
216	Cash Flow to Debtholders (CFD)		$0.00	$0.00	$0.00	$0.00	$0.00	$0.00
217	Value of Debt (D)	$0.00	$0.00	$0.00	$0.00	$0.00	$0.00	
218	Value of Fut Cash Flows (DDM Met)	$661.55						
219	- Date 0 Project Investment	$360.00						
220	NPV of Project (DDM Method)	$301.55						
221								
235	**(5) Residual Income (RI)** - Incomplete*							**2nd Stage:**
236			First Stage: Finite Horizon					Infin Horiz
237	Year	0	1	2	3	4	5	6
238	Economic Profit		$12.00	$27.00	$45.00	$57.00	$75.00	$0.00
239	Economic Profit on Salvage Value						$240.00	
240	Value of the Economic Profit	$301.55	$319.71	$324.68	$312.15	$286.36	$0.00	
241	+ Date 0 Book Value of the Firm	$360.00						
242	Value of Fut Cash Flows (RI Method)	$661.55						
243	- Date 0 Project Investment	$360.00						
244	NPV of Project (RI Method)	$301.55						

All five valuation methods produce the same results. The Value of Future Cash Flows is $661.55. After subtracting the cost of the Date 0 Project Investment, the Net Present Value of the Project is $301.55, so the project should be accepted.

Finally, restore the stage two cash flows by clicking on the "**Yes**" option button in cell **B10**.

FIGURE 9.12 Five Equivalent Methods – Project and Yes Infinite Horizon.

	A	B	C	D	E	F	G	H
1	**FIRM AND PROJECT VALUATION**				**Five Equivalent Methods**			
2								
3	**Inputs**							
4	Valuation Object	○ Firm ● Project	2					
5	Date 0 Proj Investment or Firm Cap	$360.00						
6	Tax Rate	40.0%						
7	Unlevered Cost of Equity Capital	10.0%						
8	Riskfree Rate=Cost of Riskfree Debt	3.0%						
9	Inf Horiz Growth Rate of Unlev Equity	5.0%						
10	Include Infinite Horizon?	● Yes ○ No	1					
11								
12	**Cash Flows**							**2nd Stage:**
13					**First Stage: Finite Horizon**			**Infin Horiz**
14	Date	0	1	2	3	4	5	6
15	Revenues		$550.00	$590.00	$620.00	$655.00	$675.00	$740.00
16	Expenses		$410.00	$435.00	$445.00	$470.00	$470.00	$475.00
17	Gross Earnings		$140.00	$155.00	$175.00	$185.00	$205.00	$265.00
18	Depreciation		$60.00	$60.00	$60.00	$60.00	$60.00	$85.00
19	Earnings Bef Interest & Tax (EBIT)		$80.00	$95.00	$115.00	$125.00	$145.00	$180.00
20	Interest Expense		$0.00	$0.00	$0.00	$0.00	$0.00	$0.00
21	Earnings Before Tax		$80.00	$95.00	$115.00	$125.00	$145.00	$180.00
22	Taxes		$32.00	$38.00	$46.00	$50.00	$58.00	$72.00
23	Earnings		$48.00	$57.00	$69.00	$75.00	$87.00	$108.00
24	Add Back Depreciation		$60.00	$60.00	$60.00	$60.00	$60.00	$85.00
25	Cash Flow from Operations		$108.00	$117.00	$129.00	$135.00	$147.00	$193.00
26								
27	New Invest in Plant and Equipment		$0.00	$0.00	$0.00	$0.00	$0.00	$0.00
28	After-Tax Salvage Value						$0.00	
29	New Invest in Working Capital		$0.00	$0.00	$0.00	$0.00	$0.00	$0.00
30	Cash Flows from Investments		$0.00	$0.00	$0.00	$0.00	$0.00	$0.00
31								
32	New Borrowing (Repayment)		$0.00	$0.00	$0.00	$0.00	$0.00	
33								
34	Free Cash Flow to Equity (FCFE)		$108.00	$117.00	$129.00	$135.00	$147.00	$193.00
35	= Dividends		$108.00	$117.00	$129.00	$135.00	$147.00	$193.00
36								
60	Interest		$0.00	$0.00	$0.00	$0.00	$0.00	$0.00
61	Less New Borrowing (Repayment)		$0.00	$0.00	$0.00	$0.00	$0.00	$0.00
62	Cash Flow to Debtholders (CFD)		$0.00	$0.00	$0.00	$0.00	$0.00	$0.00
63								
64	Tax Shield Benefit		$0.00	$0.00	$0.00	$0.00	$0.00	$0.00
65	Free Cash Flow to the Firm (FCFF)		$108.00	$117.00	$129.00	$135.00	$147.00	$193.00
66								
67	**Alternative Way to get FCFF**							
68	Earnings		$48.00	$57.00	$69.00	$75.00	$87.00	$108.00
69	After-tax Interest Expense		$0.00	$0.00	$0.00	$0.00	$0.00	$0.00
70	Net Oper. Profit After Tax (NOPAT)		$48.00	$57.00	$69.00	$75.00	$87.00	$108.00
71	Depreciation		$60.00	$60.00	$60.00	$60.00	$60.00	$85.00
72	Cash Flows from Investments		$0.00	$0.00	$0.00	$0.00	$0.00	$0.00
73	Free Cash Flow to the Firm (FCFF)		$108.00	$117.00	$129.00	$135.00	$147.00	$193.00
74								
75	Debt (D)	$0.00	$0.00	$0.00	$0.00	$0.00	$0.00	
76	Book Value of Equity	$360.00	$300.00	$240.00	$180.00	$120.00	$60.00	
77								
78	**Economic Profit**							
79	Net Oper. Profit After Tax (NOPAT)		$48.00	$57.00	$69.00	$75.00	$87.00	$108.00
80	Capital Charge		$36.00	$30.00	$24.00	$18.00	$12.00	$6.00
81	Economic Profit		$12.00	$27.00	$45.00	$57.00	$75.00	$102.00

FIGURE 9.13 Five Equivalent Methods – Project and Yes Infinite Horizon.

	A	B	C	D	E	F	G	H
106	(1.) Adjusted Present Value (APV)							2nd Stage:
107				First Stage: Finite Horizon				Infin Horiz
108	Date	0	1	2	3	4	5	6
109	Free Cash Flow to the Firm (FCFF)		$108.00	$117.00	$129.00	$135.00	$147.00	$193.00
110	Value of the Unlevered Firm	$2,872.03	$3,051.24	$3,239.36	$3,434.30	$3,642.73	$3,860.00	
111	Tax Shield Benefit		$0.00	$0.00	$0.00	$0.00	$0.00	$0.00
112	Value of the Tax Shield Benefit	$0.00	$0.00	$0.00	$0.00	$0.00	$0.00	
113	Value of Fut Cash Flows (APV Met)	$2,872.03						
114	- Date 0 Project Investment	$360.00						
115	NPV of Project (APV Method)	$2,512.03						
116								
140	(2) Free Cash Flow to Equity (FCFE)							2nd Stage:
141				First Stage: Finite Horizon				Infin Horiz
142	Date	0	1	2	3	4	5	6
143	Inf Horiz Growth Rate of Lev Equity							5.0%
144	Debt + Equity (D+E)	$2,872.03	$3,051.24	$3,239.36	$3,434.30	$3,642.73	$3,860.00	
145	Equity (E)	$2,872.03	$3,051.24	$3,239.36	$3,434.30	$3,642.73	$3,860.00	
146	Levered Cost of Equity Capital		10.0%	10.0%	10.0%	10.0%	10.0%	10.0%
147								
148	Free Cash Flow to Equity (FCFE)		$108.00	$117.00	$129.00	$135.00	$147.00	$193.00
149	Value of Equity (E)	$2,872.03	$3,051.24	$3,239.36	$3,434.30	$3,642.73	$3,860.00	
150	Cash Flow to Debtholders (CFD)		$0.00	$0.00	$0.00	$0.00	$0.00	$0.00
151	Value of Debt (D)	$0.00	$0.00	$0.00	$0.00	$0.00	$0.00	
152	Value of Fut Cash Flows (FCFE Met)	$2,872.03						
153	- Date 0 Project Investment	$360.00						
154	NPV of Project (FCFE Method)	$2,512.03						
155								
181	(3) Free Cash Flow to the Firm (FCFF)							2nd Stage:
182				First Stage: Finite Horizon				Infin Horiz
183	Date	0	1	2	3	4	5	6
184	Inf Horiz Growth Rate of the Firm							5.0%
185	Equity Weight (E / (D+E))	100.0%	100.0%	100.0%	100.0%	100.0%	100.0%	
186	Debt Weight (D / (D+E))	0.0%	0.0%	0.0%	0.0%	0.0%	0.0%	
187	Cost of Firm Capital (WACC)		10.00%	10.00%	10.00%	10.00%	10.00%	10.0%
188								
189	Free Cash Flow to the Firm (FCFF)		$108.00	$117.00	$129.00	$135.00	$147.00	$193.00
190	Value of Fut Cash Flows (FCFF Met)	$2,872.03	$3,051.24	$3,239.36	$3,434.30	$3,642.73	$3,860.00	
191	- Date 0 Project Investment	$360.00						
192	NPV of Project (FCFF Method)	$2,512.03						
193								
211	(4) Dividend Discount Model (DDM)							2nd Stage:
212				First Stage: Finite Horizon				Infin Horiz
213	Year	0	1	2	3	4	5	6
214	Dividend		$108.00	$117.00	$129.00	$135.00	$147.00	$193.00
215	Value of Equity (E)	$2,872.03	$3,051.24	$3,239.36	$3,434.30	$3,642.73	$3,860.00	
216	Cash Flow to Debtholders (CFD)		$0.00	$0.00	$0.00	$0.00	$0.00	$0.00
217	Value of Debt (D)	$0.00	$0.00	$0.00	$0.00	$0.00	$0.00	
218	Value of Fut Cash Flows (DDM Met)	$2,872.03						
219	- Date 0 Project Investment	$360.00						
220	NPV of Project (DDM Method)	$2,512.00						
221								
235	(5) Residual Income (RI) - Incomplete*							2nd Stage:
236				First Stage: Finite Horizon				Infin Horiz
237	Year	0	1	2	3	4	5	6
238	Economic Profit		$12.00	$27.00	$45.00	$57.00	$75.00	$102.00
239	Economic Profit on Salvage Value						($60.00)	
240	Value of the Economic Profit	$748.62	$811.48	$865.63	$907.19	$940.91	$1,020.00	
241	+ Date 0 Book Value of the Firm	$360.00						
242	Value of Fut Cash Flows (RI Method)	$1,108.62						
243	- Date 0 Project Investment	$360.00						
244	NPV of Project (RI Method)	$748.62						

The first four valuation methods produce the same results. The Value of Future Cash Flows is $2,872.03. After subtracting the cost of the Date 0 Project Investment, the Net Present Value of the Project is $2,512.03, so the project should be accepted. In principle, the Residual Income valuation should match the results of the other four valuation methods. However, it does not in the current spreadsheet. Again, I would be grateful for help in how to fix this for the 4th Edition of this book and would be delighted to acknowledge your contribution!

Problems

1. Starting from their historical financial statements, forecast the expected future cash flows for a real firm in two stages correspond to two time periods. Stage one is a finite horizon from years 1 to 5. Stage two is the remaining infinite horizon from year 6 to infinity. Given these forecasted cash flows, compute the current value of the firm and the value added by the firm using five equivalent methods: (1) Adjusted Present Value, (2) Free Cash Flow to Equity, (3) Free Cash Flow to the Firm, (4) Dividend Discount Model, and (5) Residual Income. Given expected future cash flows for a project, compute the present value of future cash flows and the NPV of the project using the same five equivalent methods.

2. Perform instant experiments on whether changing various inputs causes an increase or decrease in the firm's value / share and by how much.

   (a.) What happens when the date 0 firm capital is increased?
   (b.) What happens when the tax rate is increased?
   (c.) What happens when the unlevered cost of equity capital is increased?
   (d.) What happens when the riskfree rate is increased?
   (e.) What happens when the infinite horizon growth rate of unlevered equity is increased?

Appendix: Where did those Two-Stage Formulas for the Cost of Equity Capital and the Cost of Firm Capital come from?

A frequently asked question is where did that two-stage formula in the spreadsheet for the Cost of Levered Equity Capital come from? The Cost of Levered Equity Capital is the discount rate used by the the Free Cash Flows to Equity (FCFE) method. It is obtained by setting

Value of the Firm(FCFE) = Value of the Firm(APV).

Then you just solve for the Cost of Levered Equity Capital. In other words, the formula for the Cost of Levered Equity Capital is precisely what makes the two valuation methods equivalent.

Similarly, the Cost of Firm Capital is the discount rate used by the Free Cash Flows to the Firm (FCFF) method. It is obtained by setting

Value of the Firm(FCFE) = Value of the Firm(FCFF).

Then you just solve for the Cost of Firm Capital. In other words, the formula for the Cost of Firm Capital is precisely what makes the two valuation methods equivalent.

This appendix develops a new, generalized formula for Cost of Levered Equity Capital under a two-stage valuation process, including an infinite horizon growth rate in the second stage. At each stage, it is obtained by equating the value of the firm under FCFE and APV and then solving for the Cost of Levered Equity Capital.

This appendix also develops a new, generalized formula for Cost of Capital to the Firm under a two-stage valuation process, including an infinite horizon growth rate in the second stage. Following a similar approach, the Cost of Firm Capital at each stage is obtained by equating the value of the firm under FCFE and FCFF and then solving for the Cost of Firm Capital.

Define the needed notation:

E_t = Value of Equity on date t

D_t = Value of Debt on date t

V_t^U = Value of an Unlevered Firm on date t

V_t^{TS} = Value of the Tax Shield Benefit on date t

V_t^F = Value of a Levered Firm on date t

CFE_{t+1} = Free Cash Flow to Equity on date t+1

CFD_{t+1} = Free Cash Flow to Debt on date t+1

CFF_{t+1} = Free Cash Flow to the Firm on date t+1

TS_{t+1} = Tax Shield Benefit on date t+1

k_{t+1}^e = Cost of Levered Equity Capital on date t+1

k_{t+1}^d = Cost of Debt on date t+1

k_{t+1}^u = Cost of an Unlevered Firm on date t+1

k_{t+1}^f = Cost of (Levered) Firm Capital on date t+1

g_{T+1}^e = Growth Rate of CFE_{T+1} over the second stage infinite horizon

g_{t+1}^u = Growth Rate of CFF_{T+1} for an unlevered firm over the inf horizon

k_{t+1}^f = Growth Rate of CFF_{T+1} for a levered firm over the infinite horizon

The Cost of Levered Equity Capital in the Second Stage Infinite Horizon.

On date T, equate the value of the firm under FCFE and under APV

$$E_T + D_T = V_T^U + V_T^{TS}.$$

For each term above, substitute using the formula of an infinitely growing perpetuity - namely, (date T+1 cash flow) / (discount rate – growth rate)

$$\frac{CFE_{T+1}}{k_{T+1}^e - g_{T+1}^e} + \frac{CFD_{T+1}}{k_{T+1}^d} = \frac{CFE_{T+1} + CFD_{T+1} - TS_{T+1}}{k_{T+1}^u - g_{T+1}^u} + \frac{TS_{T+1}}{k_{T+1}^d}.$$

Use the relationships $E_T = CFE_{T+1} / \left(k_{T+1}^e - g_{T+1}^e \right)$, $D_T = CFD_{T+1} / k_{T+1}^d$, and $TS_{T+1} = \tau k_{T+1}^d D_T$ to substitute in

$$E_T + D_T = \frac{E_T \left(k_{T+1}^e - g_{T+1}^e \right) + D_T k_{T+1}^d - \tau k_{T+1}^d D_T}{k_{T+1}^u - g_{T+1}^u} + \frac{\tau k_{T+1}^d D_T}{k_{T+1}^d}.$$

Then, just solve for k_{T+1}^e to obtain

$$k_{T+1}^e = k_{T+1}^u - g_{T+1}^u + g_{T+1}^e + \left(\frac{D_T}{E_T}\right)\left(k_{T+1}^u - g_{T+1}^u - k_{T+1}^d\right)(1-\tau).$$

When the infinite growth rates are zero $\left(g_{T+1}^u = 0 \text{ and } g_{T+1}^e = 0\right)$, it simplifies to

$$k_{T+1}^e = k_{T+1}^u + \left(\frac{D_T}{E_T}\right)\left(k_{T+1}^u - k_{T+1}^d\right)(1-\tau),$$

which is the well-known formula from Modigliani and Miller, Proposition II with taxes. Each dollar of growth in CFE_{T+1} under FCFE must be matched by a dollar growth in CFF_{T+1} for the unlevered firm value under APV

$$g_{T+1}^e CFE_{T+1} = g_{T+1}^u CFF_{T+1}.$$

Solving for g_{T+1}^e to obtain

$$g_{T+1}^e = \left(\frac{CFF_{T+1}}{CFE_{T+1}}\right)g_{T+1}^u.$$

The Cost of Levered Equity Capital in the First Stage Finite Horizon.

By dynamic programming, cash flows are recursively discounted backwards. That is, cash flows from date T are discounted back to date T-1, then cash flows from date T-1 are discounted back to date T-2, and so on until cash flows from date 1 are discounted back to date 0. This analysis is for any arbitrary date t along the timeline: 0, 1, 2, ... T-1. The same analysis applies at every date on the timeline.

On date t, equate the value of the firm under FCFE and under APV

$$E_t + D_t = V_t^U + V_t^{TS}.$$

For each term above, substitute the recursive formula for discounting one period backwards - namely, [(date t+1 cash flow) + (date t+1 value of future cash flows)] / (1 + discount rate)

$$\frac{CFE_{t+1} + E_{t+1}}{1+k_{t+1}^e} + \frac{CFD_{t+1} + D_{t+1}}{1+k_{t+1}^d} = \frac{CFE_{t+1} + CFD_{t+1} - TS_{t+1} + V_{t+1}^U}{1+k_{t+1}^u} + \frac{TS_{t+1} + V_{t+1}^{TS}}{1+k_{t+1}^d}.$$

Now use the relationship $E_{t+1} + D_{t+1} = V_{t+1}^U + V_{t+1}^{TS}$ that holds for the future period t+1, as established in the previous step in the dynamic programming, to obtain

$$\frac{CFE_{t+1} + E_{t+1}}{1 + k_{t+1}^e} + \frac{CFD_{t+1} + D_{t+1}}{1 + k_{t+1}^d}$$

$$= \frac{CFE_{t+1} + CFD_{t+1} - TS_{t+1} + \left(E_{t+1} + D_{t+1} - V_{t+1}^{TS}\right)}{1 + k_{t+1}^u} + \frac{TS_{t+1}}{1 + k_{t+1}^d}.$$

Use the relationships $E_t = \left(CFE_{t+1} + E_{t+1}\right)\big/\left(1 + k_{t+1}^e\right)$, $D_t = \left(CFD_{t+1} + D_{t+1}\right)\big/\left(1 + k_{t+1}^d\right)$, and $TS_{t+1} = \tau k_{t+1}^d D_t$ to substitute in

$$E_t + D_t = \frac{E_t\left(1 + k_{t+1}^e\right) + D_t\left(1 + k_{t+1}^d\right) - \tau k_{t+1}^d D_t - V_{t+1}^{TS}}{1 + k_{t+1}^u} + \frac{\tau k_{t+1}^d D_t + V_{t+1}^{TS}}{1 + k_{t+1}^d}.$$

Then, just solve for k_{t+1}^e to obtain

$$k_{t+1}^e = k_{t+1}^u + \left(\frac{k_{t+1}^u - k_{t+1}^d}{E_t\left(1 + k_{t+1}^d\right)}\right)\left[D_t\left(1 + k_{t+1}^d\left(1 - \tau\right)\right) - V_t^{TS}\right].$$

The Cost of Capital to the Firm in the Second Stage Infinite Horizon.

On date T, equate the value of the firm under FCFE and under FCFF

$$E_T + D_T = V_T^F.$$

For each term above, substitute using the formula of an infinitely growing perpetuity - namely, (date T+1 cash flow) / (discount rate – growth rate)

$$\frac{CFE_{T+1}}{k_{T+1}^e - g_{T+1}^e} + \frac{CFD_{T+1}}{k_{T+1}^d} = \frac{CFE_{T+1} + CFD_{T+1} - TS_{T+1}}{k_{T+1}^f - g_{T+1}^f}.$$

Use the relationships $E_T = CFE_{T+1}\big/\left(k_{T+1}^e - g_{T+1}^e\right)$, $D_T = CFD_{T+1}\big/k_{T+1}^d$, and $TS_{T+1} = \tau k_{T+1}^d D_T$ to substitute in

$$E_T + D_T = \frac{E_T\left(k_{T+1}^e - g_{T+1}^e\right) + D_T k_{T+1}^d - \tau k_{T+1}^d D_T}{k_{T+1}^f - g_{T+1}^f}.$$

Then, just solve for k_{T+1}^f to obtain a slightly generalized version of WACC

$$k_{T+1}^f - g_{T+1}^f = \left(\frac{E_T}{E_T + D_T}\right)\left(k_{T+1}^e - g_{T+1}^e\right) + \left(\frac{D_T}{E_T + D_T}\right)k_{T+1}^d\left(1 - \tau\right).$$

When the growth rate terms are zero $\left(g^f_{T+1} = 0 \text{ and } g^e_{T+1} = 0 \right)$, then the familiar version of WACC is obtained

$$k^f_{T+1} = \left(\frac{E_T}{E_T + D_T} \right) k^e_{T+1} + \left(\frac{D_T}{E_T + D_T} \right) k^d_{T+1} (1 - \tau).$$

Each dollar of growth in CFE_{T+1} under FCFE must be matched by a dollar growth in CFF_{T+1} for the unlevered firm value under FCFF

$$g^e_{T+1} CFE_{T+1} = g^f_{T+1} CFF_{T+1}.$$

Solving for g^f_{T+1} and then substitute the previous expression for g^e_{T+1} from the prior infinite horizon section

$$g^f_{T+1} = \left(\frac{CFE_{T+1}}{CFF_{T+1}} \right) g^e_{T+1} = \left(\frac{CFE_{T+1}}{CFF_{T+1}} \right) \left(\frac{CFF_{T+1}}{CFE_{T+1}} \right) g^u_{T+1} = g^u_{T+1}.$$

The Cost of Levered Equity Capital in the First Stage Finite Horizon.

By dynamic programming, cash flows are recursively discounted backwards. This analysis is for any arbitrary date t along the timeline: 0, 1, 2, ... T-1. The same analysis applies at every date on the timeline.

On date t, equate the value of the firm under FCFE and under FCFF

$$E_t + D_t = V^F_t.$$

For each term above, substitute the recursive formula for discounting one period backwards - namely, [(date t+1 cash flow) + (date t+1 value of future cash flows)] / (1 + discount rate)

$$\frac{CFE_{t+1} + E_{t+1}}{1 + k^e_{t+1}} + \frac{CFD_{t+1} + D_{t+1}}{1 + k^d_{t+1}} = \frac{CFF_{t+1} + V^F_{t+1}}{1 + k^f_{t+1}}.$$

Now break CFF_{t+1} out into its components and use the relationship $E_{t+1} + D_{t+1} = V^F_{t+1}$ that holds for the future period t+1, as established in the previous step in the dynamic programming, to obtain

$$\frac{CFE_{t+1} + E_{t+1}}{1 + k^e_{t+1}} + \frac{CFD_{t+1} + D_{t+1}}{1 + k^d_{t+1}} = \frac{\left(CFE_{t+1} + CFD_{t+1} - TS_{t+1} \right) + \left(E_{t+1} + D_{t+1} \right)}{1 + k^f_{t+1}}.$$

Use the relationships $E_t = \left(CFE_{t+1} + E_{t+1} \right) / \left(1 + k^e_{t+1} \right)$, $D_t = \left(CFD_{t+1} + D_{t+1} \right) / \left(1 + k^d_{t+1} \right)$, and and $TS_{t+1} = \tau k^d_{t+1} D_t$ to substitute in

$$E_t + D_t = \frac{E_t\left(1+k_{t+1}^e\right)+D_t\left(1+k_{t+1}^d\right)-\tau k_{t+1}^d D_t}{1+k_{t+1}^f}.$$

Then, just solve for k_{t+1}^f to obtain the traditional WACC formula

$$k_{t+1}^f = \left(\frac{E_t}{E_t+D_t}\right)k_{t+1}^e + \left(\frac{D_t}{E_t+D_t}\right)k_{t+1}^d\left(1-\tau\right).$$

Chapter 10 The Yield Curve

10.1 Obtaining It From Treasury Bills and Strips

Problem. Given bond prices and yields as published by the financial press or other information sources, obtain the U.S. Treasury Yield Curve.

Solution Strategy. Collect maturity date and yield to maturity (e.g., the "ask yield" variable in the *Wall Street Journal Online* at wsj.com) for Treasury Bills and Treasury Strips of a variety of maturity dates. Compute the time to maturity. Graph the yield to maturity of these bonds against their time to maturity.

FIGURE 10.1 Excel Model of The Yield Curve – Obtaining It From Treasury Bills And Strips.

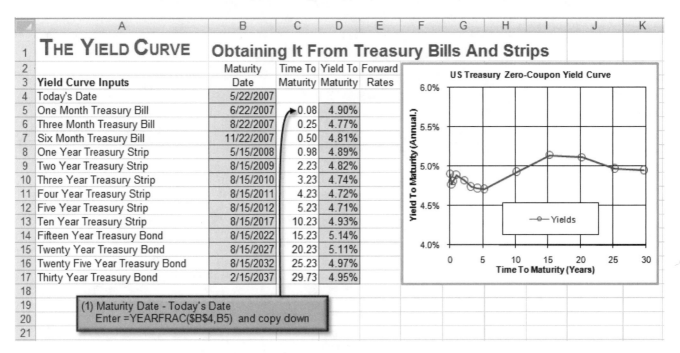

For a given bond, Time To Maturity = Maturity Date - Today's Date. We can calculate the fraction of a year between two calendar dates using the **YEARFRAC** function in Excel's Analysis ToolPak Add-In. Excel's Analysis ToolPak Add-In contains several advanced date functions that are useful in finance. To access any of these functions, you need to install the Analysis ToolPak. Otherwise you will get the error message #NAME?.

Excel 2003 Equivalent

To install the Analysis ToolPak in Excel 2003, click on **Tools**, **Add-Ins**, check the **Analysis TookPak** checkbox on the Add-Ins dialog box, and click on **OK**.

To install the Analysis ToolPak, click on the **Office** button , click on the **Excel Options** button at the bottom of the drop-down window, click on **Add-Ins**, highlight the **Analysis ToolPak** in the list of Inactive Applications, click on **Go**, check the **Analysis ToolPak**, and click on **OK**.

10.2 Using It To Price A Coupon Bond

Problem. Given the yield curve as published by the financial press, consider a coupon bond has a face value of $1,000, an annual coupon rate of 5.0%, makes 2 (semiannual) coupon payments per year, and 8 periods to maturity (or 4 years to maturity). What is price and yield to maturity of this coupon bond based on the Annual Percentage Rate (APR) convention? What is price and yield to maturity of this coupon bond based on the Effective Annual Rate (EAR) convention?

Solution Strategy. We will use the yield curve you entered in **The Yield Curve - Obtaining It From Bond Listings**. We will calculate the bond price as the present value of the bond's cash flows, where each cash flow is discounted based on the correspond yield on the yield curve (e.g., a cash flow in year three will be discounted based on the yield curve's yield at year three). We will use Excel's **RATE** function to determine the yield to maturity of this coupon bond.

FIGURE 10.2 Excel Model of The Yield Curve – Using It To Price A Coupon Bond.

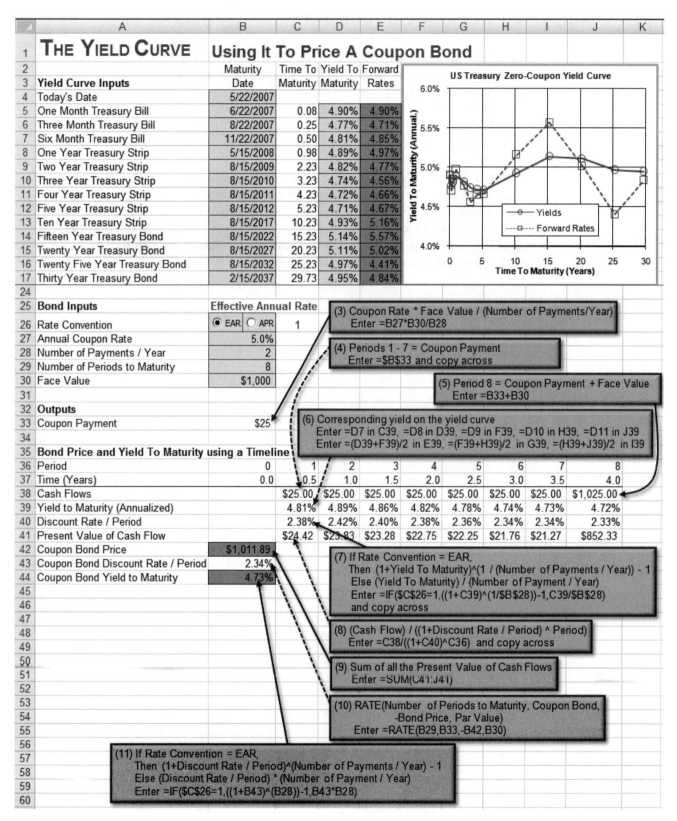

The Coupon Bond's price is $1,093.35 and its Yield To Maturity is 2.53%. Note that this yield is not the same as four year yield or any other point on the yield curve. The yield of the coupon bond is a weighted average of the yields for each of the eight periods. Since the bond's biggest cash flow is on the maturity date, the biggest weight in the weighted average is on the maturity date. Thus the coupon bond's yield is closest to the yield of the maturity date, but it is not the same.

10.3 Using It To Determine Forward Rates

Problem. Given the yield curve as published by the financial press, calculate the implied forward rates at all maturities.

Solution Strategy. We will use the yield curve that you entered in an Excel model for **The Yield Curve - Obtaining It From Bond Listings**. We will calculate the forward rates implied by the yield curve and then graph our results.

FIGURE 10.3 Excel Model of The Yield Curve – Using It To Determine Forward Rates.

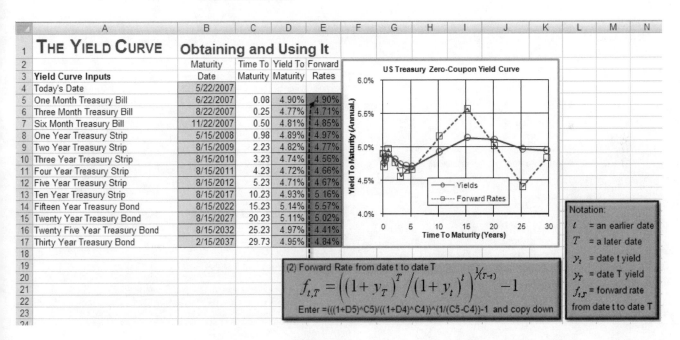

	A	B	C	D	E
1	THE YIELD CURVE	Obtaining and Using It			
2		Maturity	Time To	Yield To	Forward
3	**Yield Curve Inputs**	Date	Maturity	Maturity	Rates
4	Today's Date	5/22/2007			
5	One Month Treasury Bill	6/22/2007	0.08	4.90%	4.90%
6	Three Month Treasury Bill	8/22/2007	0.25	4.77%	4.71%
7	Six Month Treasury Bill	11/22/2007	0.50	4.81%	4.85%
8	One Year Treasury Strip	5/15/2008	0.98	4.89%	4.97%
9	Two Year Treasury Strip	8/15/2009	2.23	4.82%	4.77%
10	Three Year Treasury Strip	8/15/2010	3.23	4.74%	4.56%
11	Four Year Treasury Strip	8/15/2011	4.23	4.72%	4.66%
12	Five Year Treasury Strip	8/15/2012	5.23	4.71%	4.67%
13	Ten Year Treasury Strip	8/15/2017	10.23	4.93%	5.16%
14	Fifteen Year Treasury Bond	8/15/2022	15.23	5.14%	5.57%
15	Twenty Year Treasury Bond	8/15/2027	20.23	5.11%	5.02%
16	Twenty Five Year Treasury Bond	8/15/2032	25.23	4.97%	4.41%
17	Thirty Year Treasury Bond	2/15/2037	29.73	4.95%	4.84%

US Treasury Zero-Coupon Yield Curve

(2) Forward Rate from date t to date T

$$f_{t,T} = \left(\left(1 + y_T\right)^T \Big/ \left(1 + y_t\right)^t \right)^{1/(T-t)} - 1$$

Enter =(((1+D5)^C5)/((1+D4)^C4))^(1/(C5-C4))-1 and copy down

Notation:
t = an earlier date
T = a later date
y_t = date t yield
y_T = date T yield
$f_{t,T}$ = forward rate from date t to date T

Forward rates are an approximate forecast of future interest rates. One difficulty with taking this interpretation literally has to do with market segmentation in the demand for treasury securities. There is significantly more demand for short-term bonds than bonds of other maturities, for their use in short-term cash management. There is also extra demand by institutional bond funds for the newly-issued, longest maturity treasury bond (the so-called, "on-the-run" bond). High demand means high prices, which means low yields. Thus, the yield curve often has lower yields at the short end and the long end due to this segmentation.

Problems

1. Given bond prices and yields as published by the financial press or other information sources, obtain the U.S. Treasury Yield Curve.

2. Given the yield curve as published by the financial press, consider a coupon bond has a face value of $2,000, an annual coupon rate of 4.2%, makes 2 (semiannual) coupon payments per year, and 8 periods to maturity (or 4 years to maturity). Determine the price and yield to maturity of this coupon bond based on the Effective Annual Rate (EAR) convention. Then use it to determine the price and yield to maturity of this coupon bond based on the Annual Percentage Rate (APR) convention.

3. Given the yield curve as published by the financial press, calculate the implied forward rates at all maturities.

Chapter 11 US Yield Curve Dynamics

11.1 Dynamic Chart

How does the US yield curve change over time? What determines the volatility of changes in the yield curve? Are there differences in the volatility of short rates, medium rates, long rates, etc.? You can answer these questions and more using a *Dynamic Chart* of the yield curve, which is based on more than 37 years of monthly US zero-coupon, yield curve data. I update this Excel model each year with the latest yield curve data and make it available for free in the "Free Samples" section of www.excelmodeling.com.

The dynamic chart uses a vertical scroll bar in rows **3** to **5**. Clicking on the right arrow of the scroll bar moves the yield curve forward by one month. Clicking on the left arrow moves back by one month. Clicking right of the position bar, moves the yield curve forward by one *year*. Clicking left of the position bar moves back by one *year*. This allows you to see a dynamic "movie" or animation of the yield curve over time. Thus, you can directly observe the volatility of the yield curve and other dynamic properties. For details of what to look for, see the discussion below on "using the Excel model."

FIGURE 11.1 Excel Model of US Yield Curve Dynamics – Dynamic Chart.

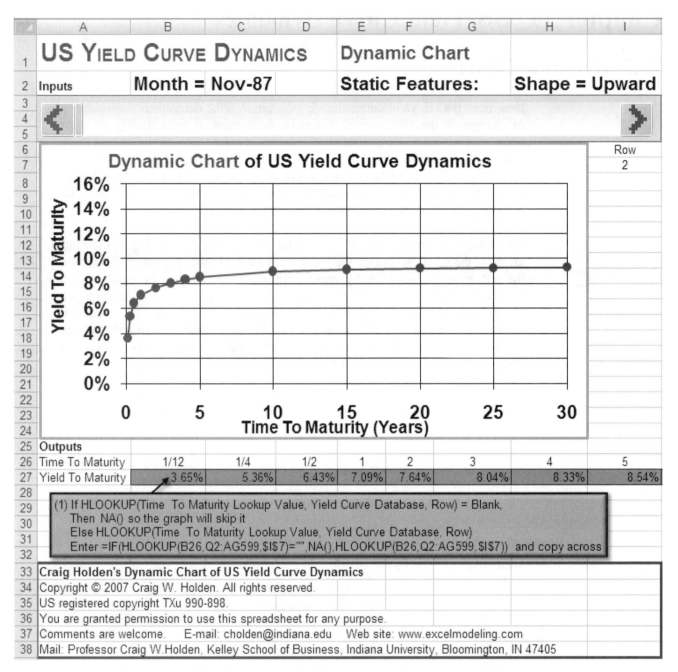

	A	B	C	D	E	F	G	H	I
1	US YIELD CURVE DYNAMICS				Dynamic Chart				
2	Inputs	Month = Nov-87			Static Features:			Shape = Upward	
3									
4	◀								▶
5									
6									Row
7		Dynamic Chart of US Yield Curve Dynamics							2

Chart: Dynamic Chart of US Yield Curve Dynamics. Y-axis: Yield To Maturity (0% to 16%). X-axis: Time To Maturity (Years), 0 to 30.

	A	B	C	D	E	F	G	H	I
25	Outputs								
26	Time To Maturity	1/12	1/4	1/2	1	2	3	4	5
27	Yield To Maturity	3.65%	5.36%	6.43%	7.09%	7.64%	8.04%	8.33%	8.54%

(1) If HLOOKUP(Time To Maturity Lookup Value, Yield Curve Database, Row) = Blank,
Then NA() so the graph will skip it
Else HLOOKUP(Time To Maturity Lookup Value, Yield Curve Database, Row)
Enter =IF(HLOOKUP(B26,Q2:AG599,$I$7)="",NA(),HLOOKUP(B26,Q2:AG599,$I$7)) and copy across

33	**Craig Holden's Dynamic Chart of US Yield Curve Dynamics**
34	Copyright © 2007 Craig W. Holden. All rights reserved.
35	US registered copyright TXu 990-898.
36	You are granted permission to use this spreadsheet for any purpose.
37	Comments are welcome. E-mail: cholden@indiana.edu Web site: www.excelmodeling.com
38	Mail: Professor Craig W.Holden, Kelley School of Business, Indiana University, Bloomington, IN 47405

The yield curve database is located in columns Q to AG. Columns Q, R, and S contain three sets of titles for the dataset. Columns T, U, and V contain yield data for bond maturities of one month, three months, and six months (1/12, 1/4, and 1/2 years, respectively). Columns W through AG contain yield data for bond maturities of 1, 2, 3, 4, 5, 7, 10, 15, 20, 25, and 30 years. Rows **2** through **9** contain examples of static features of the yield curve that can be observed from actual data in a particular month. For example, the yield curve is sometimes upward sloping (as it was in Nov 87) or downward sloping (in Nov 80) or flat (in Jan 70) or hump shaped (in Dec 78). Rows **10** through **457** contain monthly US zero-coupon, yield curve data from January 1970 through March 2007. For the period from January 1970 through December 1991, the database is based on the Bliss (1992) monthly estimates of the zero-coupon, yield curve.[3] For the period from January 1992 to July 2001, the yield curve is directly observed from Treasury Bills and Strips in the *Wall Street Journal*. For the period from August 2001 to March 2007, the data is from the St Louis Fed's free online economic database FRED II at research.stlouisfed.org/fred2.

FIGURE 11.2 Excel Model of the Yield Curve Database.

	P	Q	R	S	T	U	V	W	X	Y
1					Time To Maturity	Time To Maturity	Time To Maturity	Time To Maturity	Time To Maturity	Time To Maturity
2		Title 1	Title 2	Title 3	1/12	1/4	1/2	1	2	3
3		Static Features:	Shape = Upward	11/30/87	3.65%	5.36%	6.43%	7.09%	7.64%	8.04%
4		Static Features:	Shape = Downward	11/28/80	14.83%	14.60%	14.64%	14.17%	13.22%	12.75%
5		Static Features:	Shape = Flat	01/30/70	7.73%	8.00%	8.03%	7.98%	7.95%	7.94%
6		Static Features:	Shape = Hump	12/29/78	8.82%	9.48%	9.99%	10.18%	9.76%	9.40%
7		Static Features:	Level = Low	12/31/70	4.62%	4.91%	4.95%	5.02%	5.40%	5.69%
8		Static Features:	Level = High	10/30/81	12.65%	13.13%	13.53%	13.85%	14.01%	14.06%
9		Static Features:	Curvature = Little	12/29/72	4.93%	5.24%	5.44%	5.62%	5.86%	6.01%
10		Static Features:	Curvature = Lot	09/30/82	6.67%	7.87%	9.05%	10.29%	11.16%	11.43%
11		Monthly Dynamics		01/30/70	7.73%	8.00%	8.03%	7.98%	7.95%	7.94%
12		Monthly Dynamics		02/27/70	6.23%	6.99%	6.97%	6.96%	7.02%	7.04%
13		Monthly Dynamics		03/31/70	6.33%	6.44%	6.53%	6.67%	6.85%	6.95%
14		Monthly Dynamics		04/30/70	6.48%	7.03%	7.35%	7.50%	7.60%	7.67%
15		Monthly Dynamics		05/29/70	6.22%	7.03%	7.28%	7.45%	7.58%	7.63%
16		Monthly Dynamics		06/30/70	6.14%	6.47%	6.81%	7.17%	7.43%	7.53%
17		Monthly Dynamics		07/31/70	6.32%	6.38%	6.55%	6.87%	7.19%	7.31%
18		Monthly Dynamics		08/31/70	6.22%	6.38%	6.57%	6.83%	7.07%	7.18%
19		Monthly Dynamics		09/30/70	5.32%	6.04%	6.49%	6.63%	6.64%	6.77%
20		Monthly Dynamics		10/30/70	5.23%	5.91%	6.23%	6.33%	6.50%	6.69%
21		Monthly Dynamics		11/30/70	4.86%	5.05%	5.11%	5.10%	5.29%	5.59%
22		Monthly Dynamics		12/31/70	4.62%	4.91%	4.95%	5.02%	5.40%	5.69%

Using The US Yield Curve Dynamic Chart.

To run the Dynamic Chart, click on the right arrow of the scroll bar. The movie / animation begins with some background on the yield curve's static features. In the 37 year database we observe:

- four different **shapes**: upward-sloping, downward-sloping, flat, and hump-shaped,
- the overall **level** of the yield curve ranges from low to high, and
- the amount of **curvature** at the short end ranges from a little to a lot.

---

[3] Bliss fits a parsimonious, nonlinear function that is capable of matching all of the empirically observed shapes of the zero-coupon, yield curve. For more details see Bliss, R., 1992, "Testing Term Structure Estimation Methods," Indiana University Discussion Paper #519.

Keep clicking on the right arrow of the scroll bar and you will get to the section of the Dynamic Chart covering 37 years of the US yield curve history. This section shows the yield curve on a month by month basis. For example, the figure below shows the US yield curve in November 1970.

FIGURE 11.3 Excel Model of Month By Month History – Dynamic Chart.

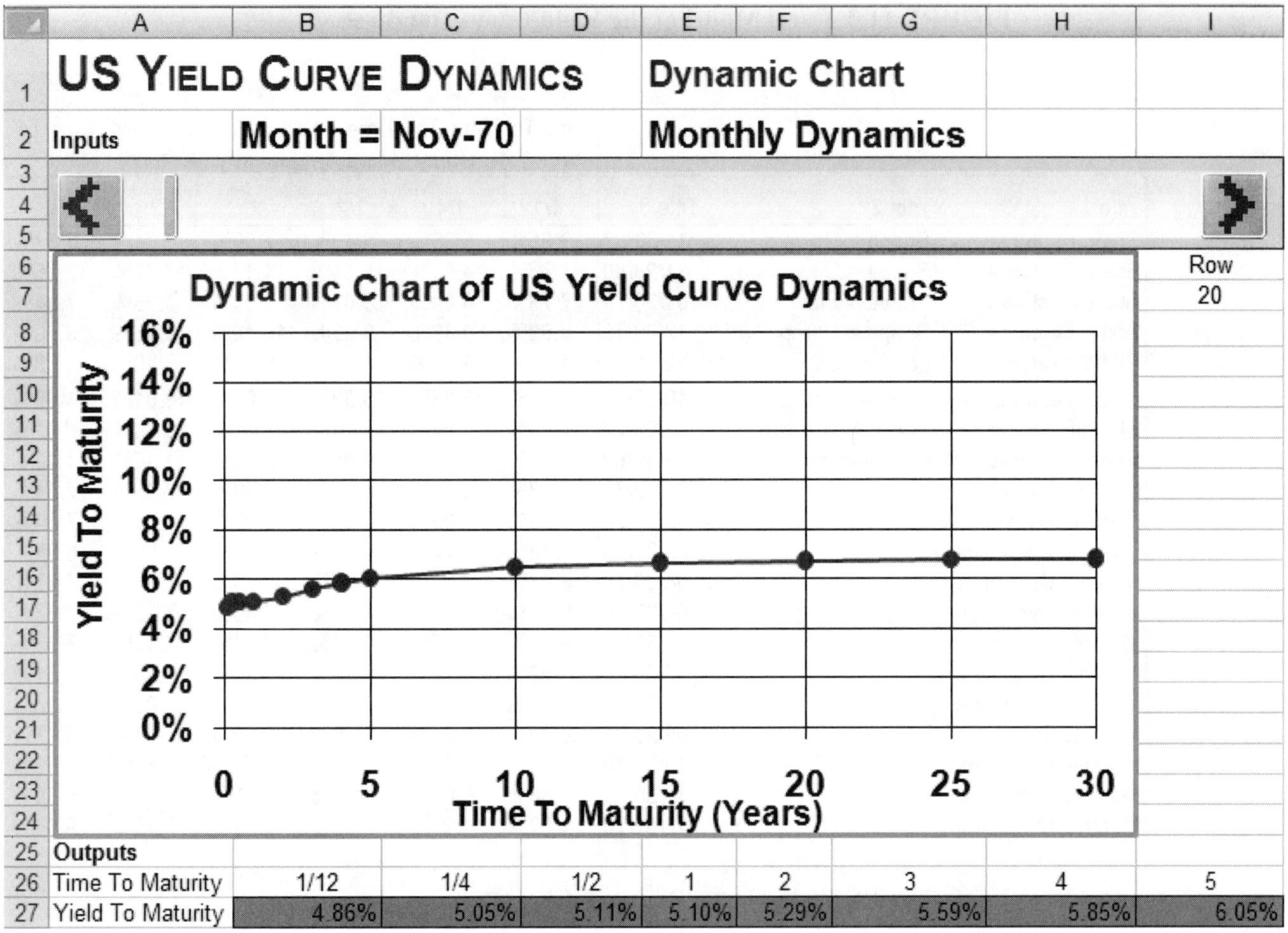

	A	B	C	D	E	F	G	H	I
1	**US YIELD CURVE DYNAMICS**				**Dynamic Chart**				
2	Inputs	**Month = Nov-70**			**Monthly Dynamics**				

Row 20

Dynamic Chart of US Yield Curve Dynamics

25	Outputs								
26	Time To Maturity	1/12	1/4	1/2	1	2	3	4	5
27	Yield To Maturity	4.86%	5.05%	5.11%	5.10%	5.29%	5.59%	5.85%	6.05%

Keep clicking on the right arrow and you will see the yield curve move around over time. By observing this movie / animation, you should be able to recognize the following key **dynamic** properties of the yield curve:

- short rates (the 0 to 5 year piece of the yield curve) are more volatile than long rates (the 15 to 30 year piece),
- the overall volatility of the yield curve is higher when the level is higher (especially in the early 80's), and
- sometimes there are sharp reactions to government intervention.

As an example of the later, consider what happened in 1980. The figure below shows the yield curve in January 1980.

FIGURE 11.4 Excel Model Showing The Yield Curve in January 1980.

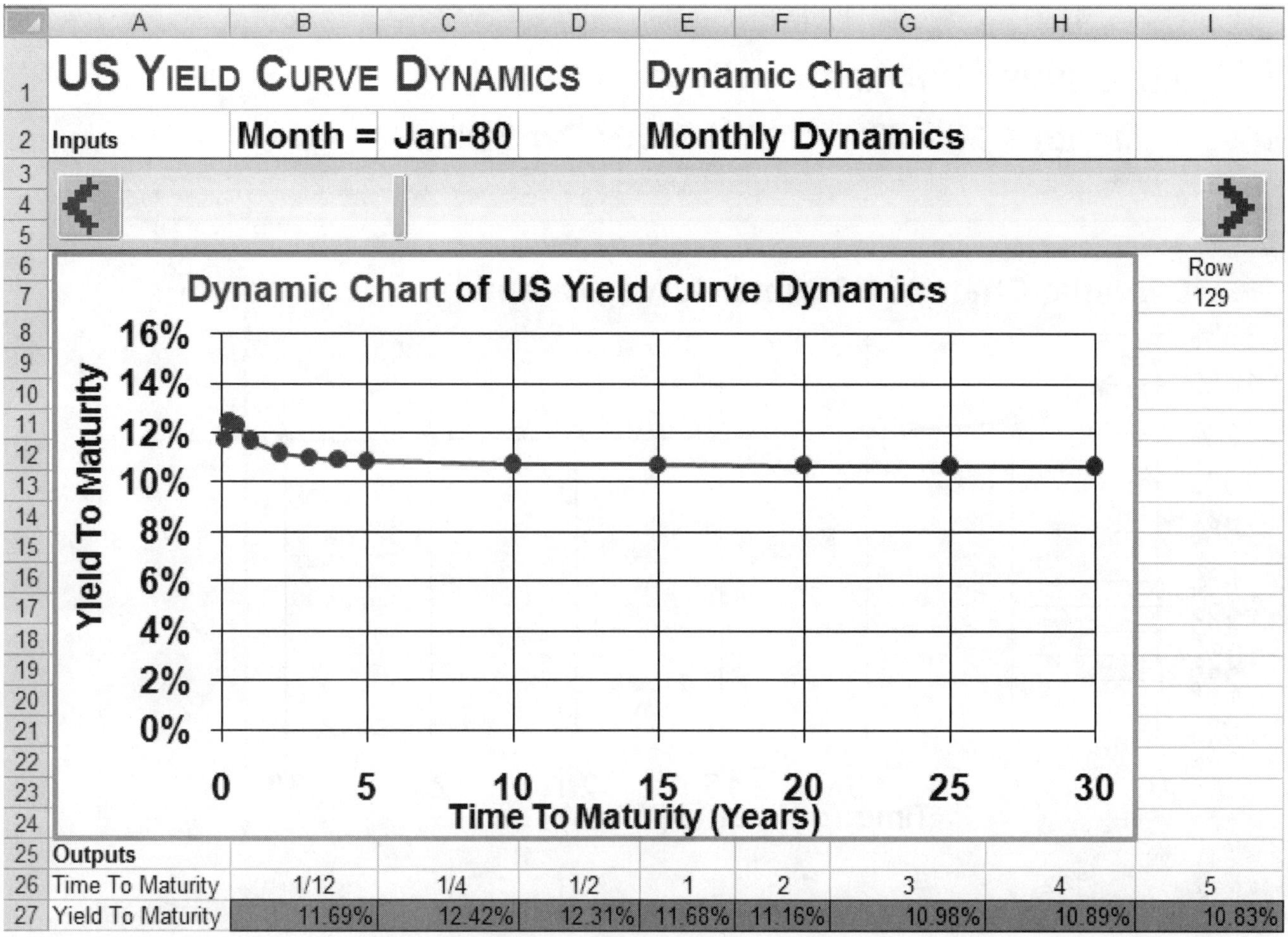

	A	B	C	D	E	F	G	H	I
1	US YIELD CURVE DYNAMICS				Dynamic Chart				
2	Inputs	Month =	Jan-80		Monthly Dynamics				
3									
4	◄								►
5									
6									Row
7	Dynamic Chart of US Yield Curve Dynamics								129

	A	B	C	D	E	F	G	H	I
25	Outputs								
26	Time To Maturity	1/12	1/4	1/2	1	2	3	4	5
27	Yield To Maturity	11.69%	12.42%	12.31%	11.68%	11.16%	10.98%	10.89%	10.83%

Short rates were around 12% and long rates were at 10.7%. President Jimmy Carter was running for re-election. He wished to manipulate the election year economy to make it better for his re-election bid. His strategy for doing this was to impose credit controls on the banking system. Click on the right arrow to see what the reaction of the financial market was.

FIGURE 11.5 Excel Model Showing The Yield Curve in March 1980.

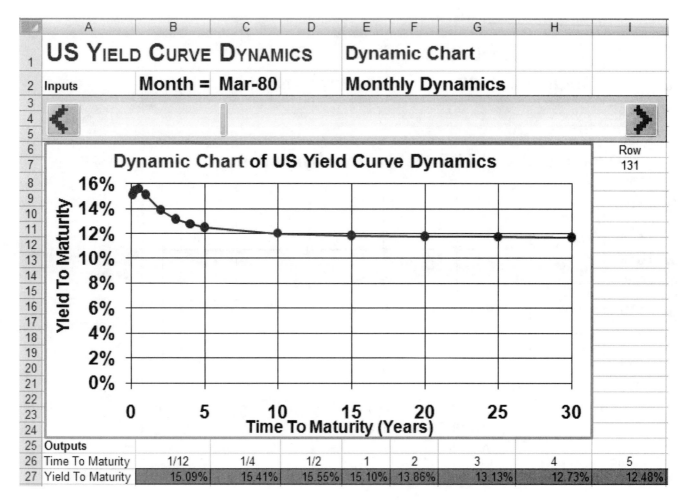

In two months time, the short rate when up to 15.5%, an increase of 3.5%! What a disaster! This was the opposite of the reaction the Carter had intended. Notice that long rates when up to 11.7%, an increase of only 1%. Apparently, the market expected that this intervention would only be a short-lived phenomenon. Carter quickly realized what a big political mistake he had made and announced that the credit controls were being dropped. Click on the right arrow to see what the reaction of the financial market was.

FIGURE 11.6 Excel Model Showing The Yield Curve in April 1980.

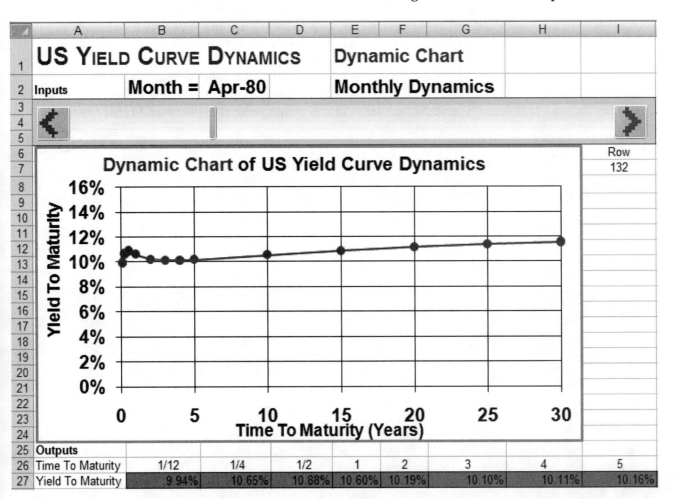

	A	B	C	D	E	F	G	H	I
1	US Yield Curve Dynamics				Dynamic Chart				
2	Inputs	Month = Apr-80			Monthly Dynamics				
7									Row 132
25	Outputs								
26	Time To Maturity	1/12	1/4	1/2	1	2	3	4	5
27	Yield To Maturity	9.94%	10.65%	10.88%	10.60%	10.19%	10.10%	10.11%	10.16%

Short rates dropped to 10.9%! A drop of 4.6% in one month! The high interest rates went away, but the political damage was done. This is the single biggest one month change in the yield curve in 37 years.

Problems

1. How volatile are short rates versus medium rates versus long rates?

   (a.) Get a visual sense of the answer to this question by clicking on the right arrow of the scroll bar to run through all of the years of US Yield Curve history in the database.

   (b.) Calculate the variance of the time series of: (i) one-month yields, (ii) five-year yields, (iii) fifteen-year yields, and (iv) thirty year yields. Use Excel's VAR function to calculate the variance of the yields in columns **T**, **AA**, **AD**, and **AG**.

2. Determine the relationship between the volatility of the yield curve and the level of the yield curve. Specifically, for each five year time period (70-74,

75-79, 80-84, etc.) calculate the variance and the average level of the time series of: (i) one-month yields, (ii) five-year yields, (iii) fifteen-year yields, and (iv) thirty year yields. Use Excel's VAR and AVERAGE functions to calculate the variance and the average of five-year ranges of the yields in columns **T**, **AA**, **AD**, and **AG**. For example:

o   The 70-74 time series of one-month yields is in the range **T11-T69**.
o   The 75-79 time series of one-month yields is in the range **T70-T129**.
o   The 80-84 time series of one-month yields is in the range **T130-T189**.
o   And so on.

Summarize what you have learned from this analysis.

PART 3 CAPITAL BUDGETING

Chapter 12 Project NPV

12.1 Basics

Problem. Suppose a firm is considering the following project, where all of the dollar figures are in thousands of dollars. In year 0, the project requires $11,350 investment in plant and equipment, is depreciated using the straight-line method over seven years, and there is a salvage value of $1,400 in year 7. The project is forecast to generate sales of 2,000 units in year 1, rising to 7,400 units in year 5, declining to 1,800 units in year 7, and dropping to zero in year 8. The inflation rate is forecast to be 2.0% in year 1, rising to 4.0% in year 5, and then leveling off. The real cost of capital is forecast to be 11.0% in year 1, rising to 12.2% in year 7. The tax rate is forecast to be a constant 35.0%. Sales revenue per unit is forecast to be $9.70 in year 1 and then grow with inflation. Variable cost per unit is forecast to be $7.40 in year 1 and then grow with inflation. Cash fixed costs are forecast to be $5,280 in year 1 and then grow with inflation. What is the project NPV?

Solution Strategy. Forecast key assumptions, discounting, sales revenue per unit, variable costs per unit, and fixed costs over the seven year horizon. Then, forecast the project income and expense items. Calculate the net cash flows. Discount each cash flow back to the present and sum to get the NPV.

Modeling Issue. The inflation rate is forecast separately and explicitly enters into the calculation of: (1) the discount rate (= cost of capital) and (2) price or cost / unit items. This guarantees that we are *consistent* in the way we are treating the inflation component of cash flows in the numerator of the NPV calculation and the inflation component of the discount rate in the denominator of the NPV calculation. This avoids a common error in practice that people often treat the cash flows and discount rates *as if* they were unrelated to each other and thus they are *inconsistent* in way that they implicitly treat the inflation component of each.

FIGURE 12.1 Excel Model for Project NPV - Basics.

	A	B	C	D	E	F	G	H	I
1	**PROJECT NPV**	**Basics**							
2	(in thousands of $)								
3		Year 0	Year 1	Year 2	Year 3	Year 4	Year 5	Year 6	Year 7
4	**Key Assumptions**								
5	Unit Sales		2000	4000	5600	6800	7400	3700	1800
6	Inflation Rate		2.0%	2.5%	3.0%	3.5%	4.0%	4.0%	4.0%
7	Real Cost of Capital		11.0%	11.2%	11.4%	11.6%	11.8%	12.0%	12.2%
8	Tax Rate		35.0%	35.0%	35.0%	35.0%	35.0%	35.0%	35.0%
9									
10	**Discounting**								
11	Discount Rate = Cost of Capital		13.2%	14.0%	14.7%	15.5%	16.3%	16.5%	16.7%
12	Cumulative Discount Factor	0.0%	13.2%	29.0%	48.1%	71.0%	98.9%	131.6%	170.3%
13									
14	**Price or Cost / Unit**								
15	Sales Revenue / Unit		$9.70	$9.94	$10.24	$10.60	$11.02	$11.46	$11.92
16	Variable Cost / Unit		$7.40	$7.59	$7.81	$8.09	$8.41	$8.75	$9.10
17	Cash Fixed Costs		$5,280	$5,412	$5,574	$5,769	$6,000	$6,240	$6,490

(1) (1 + Inflation Rate) * (1 + Real Discount Rate) - 1
    Enter =(1+C6)*(1+C7)-1 and copy across

(2) (1 + Last Year's Cumulative Discount Factor)
    * (1 + This Year's Discount Rate) - 1
    Enter =(1+B12)*(1+C11)-1 and copy across

(3) (Last Year's Price/Cost) * (1 + This Year's Inflation Rate)
    Enter =C15*(1+D$6) and copy to the range D15:I17

FIGURE 12.2 Excel Model for Project NPV – Basics (Continued).

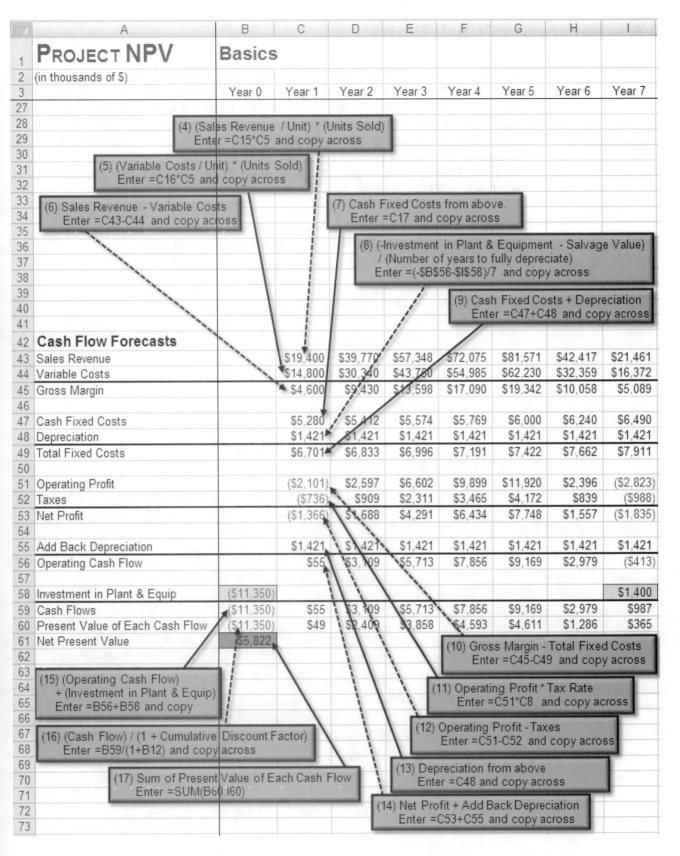

The Net Present Value of the project is $5,822. The project should be accepted.

12.2 Forecasting Cash Flows

Problem. Consider the same project as Project NPV - Basics. Let's examine the details of how you forecast the project cash flows. Suppose that Direct Labor, Materials, Selling Expenses, and Other Variable Costs are forecast to be $3.50, $2.00, $1.20, and $0.70, respectively, in year 1 and then grow with inflation. Lease Payment, Property Taxes, Administration, Advertising, and Other cash fixed costs are forecast to be $2,800, $580, $450, $930, and $520, respectively, in year 1 and then grow with inflation. What is the Total Variable Cost / Unit and the Total Cash Fixed Costs?

Solution Strategy. Forecast the variable cost / unit and cash fixed costs in more detail. Then sum up all of the items in each category to get the total.

FIGURE 12.3 Excel Model for Project NPV – Forecasting Cash Flows.

	A	B	C	D	E	F	G	H	I	J
1	**PROJECT NPV**	**Forecasting Cash Flows**								
2	(in thousands of $)									
3		Year 0	Year 1	Year 2	Year 3	Year 4	Year 5	Year 6	Year 7	
4	**Key Assumptions**									
5	Base Case Unit Sales		2000	4000	5600	6800	7400	3700	1800	
6	Unit Sales Scale Factor		100.0%							
7	Unit Sales		2000	4000	5600	6800	7400	3700	1800	
8	Inflation Rate		2.0%	2.5%	3.0%	3.5%	4.0%	4.0%	4.0%	
9	Real Cost of Capital Increment			0.2%	0.4%	0.6%	0.8%	1.0%	1.2%	
10	Real Cost of Capital		11.0%	11.2%	11.4%	11.6%	11.8%	12.0%	12.2%	
11	Tax Rate		35.0%	35.0%	35.0%	35.0%	35.0%	35.0%	35.0%	
12										
13	**Discounting**									
14	Discount Rate = Cost of Capital		13.2%	14.0%	14.7%	15.5%	16.3%	16.5%	16.7%	
15	Cumulative Discount Factor	0.0%	13.2%	29.0%	48.1%	71.0%	98.9%	131.6%	170.3%	
16										
17	**Price or Cost / Unit**									
18	Sales Revenue / Unit		$9.70	$9.94	$10.24	$10.60	$11.02	$11.46	$11.92	
19										
20	Variable Costs / Unit:									
21	Direct Labor		$3.50	$3.59	$3.70	$3.82	$3.98	$4.14	$4.30	
22	Materials		$2.00	$2.05	$2.11	$2.19	$2.27	$2.36	$2.46	
23	Selling Expenses		$1.20	$1.23	$1.27	$1.31	$1.36	$1.42	$1.47	
24	Other		$0.70	$0.72	$0.74	$0.76	$0.80	$0.83	$0.86	
25	Total Variable Cost / Unit		$7.40	$7.59	$7.81	$8.09	$8.41	$8.75	$9.10	
26										
27	Cash Fixed Costs:									
28	Lease Payment		$2,800	$2,870	$2,956	$3,060	$3,182	$3,309	$3,442	
29	Property Taxes		$580	$595	$612	$634	$659	$685	$713	
30	Administration		$450	$461	$475	$492	$511	$532	$553	
31	Advertising		$930	$953	$982	$1,016	$1,057	$1,099	$1,143	
32	Other		$520	$533	$549	$568	$591	$615	$639	
33	Total Cash Fixed Costs		$5,280	$5,412	$6,574	$5,769	$6,000	$6,240	$6,490	

(3) (Last Year's Cost / Unit) * (1 + This Year's Inflation Rate)
Enter =C21*(1+D$8) and copy to the ranges D21:I24 and D28:I32

(4) Sum the components of Variable Cost / Unit
Enter =SUM(C21:C24) and copy across

(5) Sum the components of Cash Fixed Costs
Enter =SUM(C28:C32) and copy across

12.3 Working Capital

Problem. Consider the same project as above. Suppose we add that the project will require working capital in the amount of $0.87 in year 0 for every unit of next year's forecasted sales and this amount will grow with inflation going forward. What is the project NPV?

FIGURE 12.4 Excel Model for Project NPV – Working Capital.

	A	B	C	D	E	F	G	H	I
1	**PROJECT NPV**	**Working Capital**							
2	(in thousands of $)								
3		Year 0	Year 1	Year 2	Year 3	Year 4	Year 5	Year 6	Year 7
43									
44	(7) (This Year's Work Cap / Next Yr Unit Sales)		(6) (Last Year's Work Cap / Next Yr Unit Sales)						
45	* (Next Yr Unit Sales)		* (1 + This Year's Inflation Rate)						
46	Enter =B48*C7 and copy across		Enter =B48*(1+C$8) and copy across						
47	**Working Capital**								
48	Work Cap / Next Yr Unit Sales	$0.87	$0.89	$0.91	$0.94	$0.97	$1.01	$1.05	$1.09
49	Working Capital	$1,740	$3,550	$5,094	$6,371	$7,176	$3,731	$1,888	$0
50									
51	**Cash Flow Forecasts**								
52	Sales Revenue		$19,400	$39,770	$57,348	$72,075	$81,571	$42,417	$21,461
53	Variable Costs		$14,800	$30,340	$43,750	$54,985	$62,230	$32,359	$16,372
54	Gross Margin		$4,600	$9,430	$13,598	$17,090	$19,342	$10,058	$5,089
55									
56	Cash Fixed Costs		$5,280	$5,412	$5,574	$5,769	$6,000	$6,240	$6,490
57	Depreciation		$1,421	$1,421	$1,421	$1,421	$1,421	$1,421	$1,421
58	Total Fixed Costs		$6,701	$6,833	$6,996	$7,191	$7,422	$7,662	$7,911
59									
60	Operating Profit		($2,101)	$2,597	$6,602	$9,899	$11,920	$2,396	($2,823)
61	Taxes		($736)	$909	$2,311	$3,465	$4,172	$839	($988)
62	Net Profit		($1,366)	$1,688	$4,291	$6,434	$7,748	$1,557	($1,835)
63									
64	Add Back Depreciation		$1,421	$1,421	$1,421	$1,421	$1,421	$1,421	$1,421
65	Operating Cash Flow		$55	$3,109	$5,713	$7,856	$9,169	$2,979	($413)
66									
67	Investment in Working Capital	($1,740)	($1,810)	($1,544)	($1,277)	($805)	$3,444	$1,843	$1,888
68	Investment in Plant & Equip	($11,350)							$1,400
69	Investment Cash Flow	($13,090)	($1,810)	($1,544)	($1,277)	($805)	$3,444	$1,843	$3,288
70									
71	Cash Flows	($13,090)	($1,754)	$1,565	$4,436	$7,051	$12,614	$4,822	$2,875
72	Present Value of Each Cash Flow	($13,090)	($1,549)	$1,213	$2,996	$4,123	$6,343	$2,082	$1,063
73	Net Present Value	$3,180							
74				(8) (Last Year's Working Capital) - (This Year's Working Capital)					
75				Enter =-B49 in cell B67 and					
76				enter =B49-C49 in cell C67 and copy across					
77									
78	(9) (Investment in Working Capital) + (Investment in Plant & Equipment)								
79	Enter =SUM(B67:B68) and copy across								
80	(10) (Operating Cash Flow) + (Investment Cash Flow)								
81	Enter =B65+B69 and copy across								

Solution Strategy. Forecast the working capital amount per next year's unit sales. Then multiply by the forecasted unit sales to determine the required working capital each year. Include the investment in working capital to the total investment cash flows and calculate the project NPV.

The Net Present Value of the project drops to $3,180, because of the additional investment in working capital.

12.4 Sensitivity Analysis

Problem. Consider the same project as above. Assume that the product life-cycle of seven years is viewed as a safe bet, but that the scale of demand for the product is highly uncertain. Analyze the sensitivity of the project NPV to the units sales scale factor and to the cost of capital.

Solution Strategy. Copy the pattern of unit sales in the base case to a new location and multiply this pattern by a scale factor to get the new unit sales scenario. Assume that the real cost of capital is constant. Thus, forecast the future cost of capital by taking the year 1 cost of capital and adding the change in the inflation rate. Create a two-way data table using a range of input values for units sales scale factor and a range of input values for the year 1 cost of capital. Using the data table results, create a 3-D surface chart.

FIGURE 12.5 Excel Model for Sensitivity Analysis.

	A	B	C	D	E	F	G	H	I
1	**PROJECT NPV**	**Sensitivity Analysis**							
2	(in thousands of $)								
3		Year 0	Year 1	Year 2	Year 3	Year 4	Year 5	Year 6	Year 7
4	**Key Assumptions**								
5	Base Case Unit Sales		2000	4000	5600	6800	7400	3700	1800
6	Unit Sales Scale Factor		100.0%						
7	Unit Sales		2000	4000	5600	6800	7400	3700	1800
8	Inflation Rate		2.0%	2.5%	3.0%	3.5%	4.0%	4.0%	4.0%
9	Real Cost of Capital Increment			0.2%	0.4%	0.6%	0.8%	1.0%	1.2%
10	Real Cost of Capital		11.0%	11.2%	11.4%	11.6%	11.8%	12.0%	12.2%
11	Tax Rate		35.0%	35.0%	35.0%	35.0%	35.0%	35.0%	35.0%
12									
13	**Discounting**								
14	Discount Rate = Cost of Capital		13.2%	14.0%	14.7%	15.5%	16.3%	16.5%	16.7%
15	Cumulative Discount Factor	0.0%	13.2%	29.0%	48.1%	71.0%	98.9%	131.6%	170.3%
16									
17	**Price or Cost / Unit**								
18	Sales Revenue / Unit		$9.70	$9.94	$10.24	$10.60	$11.02	$11.46	$11.92
19									
20	Variable Costs / Unit:								
21	Direct Labor		$3.50	$3.59	$3.70	$3.82	$3.98	$4.14	$4.30
22	Materials		$2.00	$2.05	$2.11	$2.19	$2.27	$2.36	$2.46
23	Selling Expenses		$1.20	$1.23	$1.27	$1.31	$1.36	$1.42	$1.47
24	Other		$0.70	$0.72	$0.74	$0.76	$0.80	$0.83	$0.86
25	Total Variable Cost / Unit		$7.40	$7.59	$7.81	$8.09	$8.41	$8.75	$9.10
26									
27	Cash Fixed Costs:								
28	Lease Payment		$2,800	$2,870	$2,956	$3,060	$3,182	$3,309	$3,442
29	Property Taxes		$580	$595	$612	$634	$659	$685	$713
30	Administration		$450	$461	$475	$492	$511	$532	$553
31	Advertising		$930	$953	$982	$1,016	$1,057	$1,099	$1,143
32	Other		$520	$533	$549	$568	$591	$615	$639
33	Total Cash Fixed Costs		$5,280	$5,412	$5,574	$5,769	$6,000	$6,240	$6,490
34	(1) (Base Case Unit Sales)								
35	* (Unit Sales Scale Factor)								
36	Enter =C5*$C$6 and copy across								
37									
38	(2) (Date 0 Real Cost of Capital) + (Increment on date t)								
39	Enter =$C$10+D9 and copy across								

FIGURE 12.6 Excel Model for Two-Way Data Table and 3-D Surface Chart.

	A	B	C	D	E	F	G	H	I	J
1	**PROJECT NPV**	**Sensitivity Analysis**								
2	(in thousands of $)									
3		Year 0	Year 1	Year 2	Year 3	Year 4	Year 5	Year 6	Year 7	

(11) Enter the input values for Unit Sales Scale Factor Enter 80%, 90%, etc. in range C93:G93

(12) Enter the input values for Date 0 Real Cost of Capital Enter 9.0%, 11.0%, etc. in range B94:B98

(13) Enter the output formula Enter =B73

(14) Create the net present value Data Table. Select the range B93:G98, click on Data | Data Tools | What-If Analysis | Data Table, enter C6 in the Row Input Cell and C10 in the Column Input Cell, and click on OK.

Data Table
Row input cell: C6
Column input cell: C10
OK   Cancel

	A	B	C	D	E	F	G
91	Data Table: Sensitivity of the Net Present Value to Unit Sales and Date 0 Real Cost of Capital						
92			Input Values for Unit Sales Scale Factor				
93	Out Formula: Net Present Value	$3,180	80%	90%	100%	110%	120%
94		9.0%	($1,324)	$1,667	$4,658	$7,649	$10,640
95	Input Values for	11.0%	($2,336)	$422	$3,180	$5,938	$8,696
96	Date 0 Real Cost of Capital	13.0%	($3,246)	($698)	$1,851	$4,399	$6,947
97		15.0%	($4,065)	($1,706)	$652	$3,010	$5,369
98		17.0%	($4,804)	($2,617)	($431)	$1,755	$3,941

Sensitivity of Project NPV to Unit Sales and Cost of Capital

$15,000

Project NPV

$10,000

$5,000

■ $10,000 -$15,000

$0

■ $5,000 -$10,000

($5,000)

■ $0 -$5,000

■ ($5,000)-$0

Unit Sales Scale Factor

120% 110% 100% 90% 80%

17.0% 15.0% 13.0% 11.0% 9.0%

Real Cost of Capital

Excel 2003 Equivalent

To call up a Data Table in Excel 2003, click on **Data | Table**

The sensitivity analysis shows that the Project NPV is highly sensitive to the Unit Sales Scale Factor and the Cost of Capital. If the sales forecast is overly optimistic and/or cost of capital estimate is too low, then the project might actually have a negative NPV. Hence, it is worth spending extra resources to verify the accuracy of the sales forecast and the cost of capital estimate.

Problems

1. Suppose a firm is considering the following project, where all of the dollar figures are in thousands of dollars. In year 0, the project requires $37,500 investment in plant and equipment, is depreciated using the straight-line method over seven years, and there is a salvage value of $5,600 in year 7. The project is forecast to generate sales of 5,700 units in year 1, rising to 24,100 units in year 5, declining to 8,200 units in year 7, and dropping to zero in year 8. The inflation rate is forecast to be 1.5% in year 1, rising to 2.8% in year 5, and then leveling off. The real cost of capital is forecast to be 9.3% in year 1, rising to 10.6% in year 7. The tax rate is forecast to be a constant 42.0%. Sales revenue per unit is forecast to be $15.30 in year 1 and then grow with inflation. Variable cost per unit is forecast to be $9.20 in year 1 and then grow with inflation. Cash fixed costs are forecast to be $7,940 in year 1 and then grow with inflation. What is the project NPV?

2. Consider the same project as problem 1, but modify it as follows. Suppose that Direct Labor, Materials, Selling Expenses, and Other Variable Costs are forecast to be $5.20, $3.70, $2.30, and $0.80, respectively, in year 1 and then grow with inflation. Lease Payment, Property Taxes, Administration, Advertising, and Other cash fixed costs are forecast to be $4,100, $730, $680, $1,120, and $730, respectively, in year 1 and then grow with inflation. What are the Total Variable Cost / Unit and the Total Cash Fixed Costs?

3. Consider the same project as problem 2, but modify it as follows. Suppose we add that the project will require working capital in the amount of $1.23 in year 0 for every unit of next year's forecasted sales and this amount will grow with inflation going forward. What is the project NPV?

4. Consider the same project as problem 3. Assume that the product life-cycle of seven years is viewed as a safe bet, but that the scale of demand for the product is highly uncertain. Analyze the sensitivity of the project NPV to the units sales scale factor and to the cost of capital.

Chapter 13 Cost-Reducing Project

13.1 Basics

Problem. Suppose a firm is considering a labor-saving investment. In year 0, the project requires a $6,300 investment in equipment (all figures are in thousands of dollars). This investment is depreciated using the straight-line method over five years and there is salvage value in year 5 of $1,200. With or without the cost-reducing investment, all cash flows start in year 1 and end in year 5. The inflation rate is 3.0% in year 2 and declines to 2.0% in year 5. The real growth rate is 16.0% in year 2 and declines to 7.0% in year 5. The tax rate is 38.0% in all years. The real cost of capital is 9.5% in year 1 and declines to 8.9% in year 5. Without the cost-reducing investment, the firm's existing investments will generate year 1 revenue, labor costs, other cash expenses, and depreciation of $11,500, $3,200, $4,500, and $1,800, respectively. With the cost-reducing investment, the firm's year 1 labor costs will be $1,300 and revenues and other cash expenses will remain the same. What is the cost-reducing project NPV?

Solution Strategy. Forecast revenues and expenses both without the cost-reducing investment and with it. Calculate the Net Cash Flow both without and with the cost-reducing investment. Subtract one from the other to obtain the incremental Difference Due to Investment. Discount the project net cash flows back to the present and determine the NPV.

FIGURE 13.1 Excel Model for Cost-Reducing Project - Basics.

	A	B	C	D	E	F	G	H	I	J
1	**COST-REDUCING PROJECT**			**Basics**						
2	**(in thousands of $)**									
3		Year 0	Year 1	Year 2	Year 3	Year 4	Year 5			
4	**Key Assumptions**									
5	Inflation Rate		3.0%	2.8%	2.5%	2.2%	2.0%			
6	Real Cost of Capital		9.5%	9.3%	9.1%	9.0%	8.9%			
7	Real Growth Rate			16.0%	13.0%	9.0%	7.0%	(1) (1 + Inflation Rate) *		
8	Tax Rate		38.0%	38.0%	38.0%	38.0%	38.0%	(1 + Real Discount Rate) - 1 Enter =(1+C5)*(1+C6)-1 and copy across		
9										
10	**Discounting**									
11	Discount Rate = Cost of Capital		12.8%	12.4%	11.8%	11.4%	11.1%	(2) (1 + Last Year's Cumulative Discount Factor) *		
12	Cumulative Discount Factor	0.0%	12.8%	26.7%	41.7%	57.9%	75.4%	(1 + This Year's Discount Rate) - 1		
13								Enter =(1+B12)*(1+C11)-1 and copy across		
14	**Without Investment**									
15	Revenue		$11,500	$13,714	$15,884	$17,694	$19,311	(3) (Last Year's Revenue/Exp)		
16	Labor Costs		$3,200	$3,816	$4,420	$4,924	$5,374	* (1 + Inflation Rate)		
17	Other Cash Expenses		$4,500	$5,366	$6,215	$6,924	$7,557	* (1 + Real Growth Rate)		
18	Gross Margin		$3,800	$4,531	$5,249	$5,847	$6,381	Enter =C15*(1+D$5)*(1+D$7) and copy to the range D15:G17		
19										
20	Depreciation		$1,800	$1,800	$1,800	$1,800	$1,800			
21	Pretax Profit		$2,000	$2,731	$3,449	$4,047	$4,581			
22										
23	Income Taxes		$760	$1,038	$1,310	$1,538	$1,741			
24	After-tax Profit		$1,240	$1,693	$2,138	$2,509	$2,840			
25										
26	Add Back Depreciation		$1,800	$1,800	$1,800	$1,800	$1,800			
27	Cash Flows		$3,040	$3,493	$3,938	$4,309	$4,640			

(7) Operating Income * Tax Rate
   Enter =C21*C$8 and copy across

(8) Pretax Profit - Income Taxes
   Enter =C21-C23 and copy across

(9) Depreciation from above
   Enter =C20 and copy across

(10) After-tax Profit + Add Back Depreciation
   Enter =C24+C26 and copy across

(4) Revenue - (Labor Costs) - (Other Cash Expenses)
   Enter =C15-C16-C17 and copy across

(5) Depreciation is constant due to the use of the straight line method
   Enter =C20 and copy across

(6) (Gross Margin) - Depreciation
   Enter =C18-C20 and copy across

FIGURE 13.2 Excel Model for Cost-Reducing Project – Basics (Continued).

	A	B	C	D	E	F	G	H
1	**COST-REDUCING PROJECT**			**Basics**				
2	**(in thousands of $)**							
3			Year 0	Year 1	Year 2	Year 3	Year 4	Year 5
38	(11) Set "With Investment" formulas = "Without Investment" formulas							
39	Copy the range C15:G27 to the cell C45							
40								
41	(12) Change "With Investment" Labor Costs			(13) "Without Investment" Depreciation				
42	Enter 1300			+(-New Investment - Salvage Value)				
43				/ (Number of Years to Depreciate)				
44	**With Investment**			Enter =C20+(-$B$61-$G$61)/5				
45	Revenue		$11,500	$13,714	$15,884	$17,694	$19,311	
46	Labor Costs		$1,300	$1,550	$1,796	$2,000	$2,183	
47	Other Cash Expenses		$4,500	$5,366	$6,215	$6,924	$7,557	
48	Gross Margin		$5,700	$6,797	$7,873	$8,770	$9,572	
49								
50	Depreciation		$2,820	$2,820	$2,820	$2,820	$2,820	
51	Pretax Profit		$2,880	$3,977	$5,053	$5,950	$6,752	
52								
53	Income Taxes		$1,094	$1,511	$1,920	$2,261	$2,566	
54	After-tax Profit		$1,786	$2,466	$3,133	$3,689	$4,186	
55								
56	Add Back Depreciation		$2,820	$2,820	$2,820	$2,820	$2,820	
57	Cash Flows		$4,606	$5,286	$5,953	$6,509	$7,006	
58								
59	**Project Difference**							
60	Difference Due to Investment		$1,566	$1,792	$2,015	$2,200	$2,366	
61	Investment and Salvage Value	($6,300)					$1,200	
62	Project Cash Flows	($6,300)	$1,566	$1,792	$2,015	$2,200	$3,566	
63	Present Value of Each Cash Flow	($6,300)	$1,388	$1,414	$1,422	$1,394	$2,033	
64	Project Net Present Value	$1,351						
65					(14) With Investment Cash Flows			
66					- Without Investment Cash Flows			
67					Enter =C57-C27 and copy across			
68					(15) (Difference Due to Investment)			
69					+ (Investment and Salvage Value)			
70					Enter =B60+B61 and copy across			
71					(16) (Cash Flow) / (1 + Cumulative Discount Factor)			
72					Enter =B62/(1+B12) and copy across			
73					(17) Sum of Present Value of Cash Flows			
74					Enter =SUM(B63:G63)			
75								

The Net Present Value of this Cost-reducing Project is $1,351. The project should be accepted.

13.2 Sensitivity Analysis

Problem. For the same cost-reducing project as the previous section, analyze the sensitivity of the Project NPV to the assumed With Investment Labor Costs.

Solution Strategy. Create a Data Table using With Investment Labor Costs as the input variable and Project NPV as the output variable. Then graph the relationship.

FIGURE 13.3 Excel Model for Cost-Reducing Project - Sensitivity Analysis.

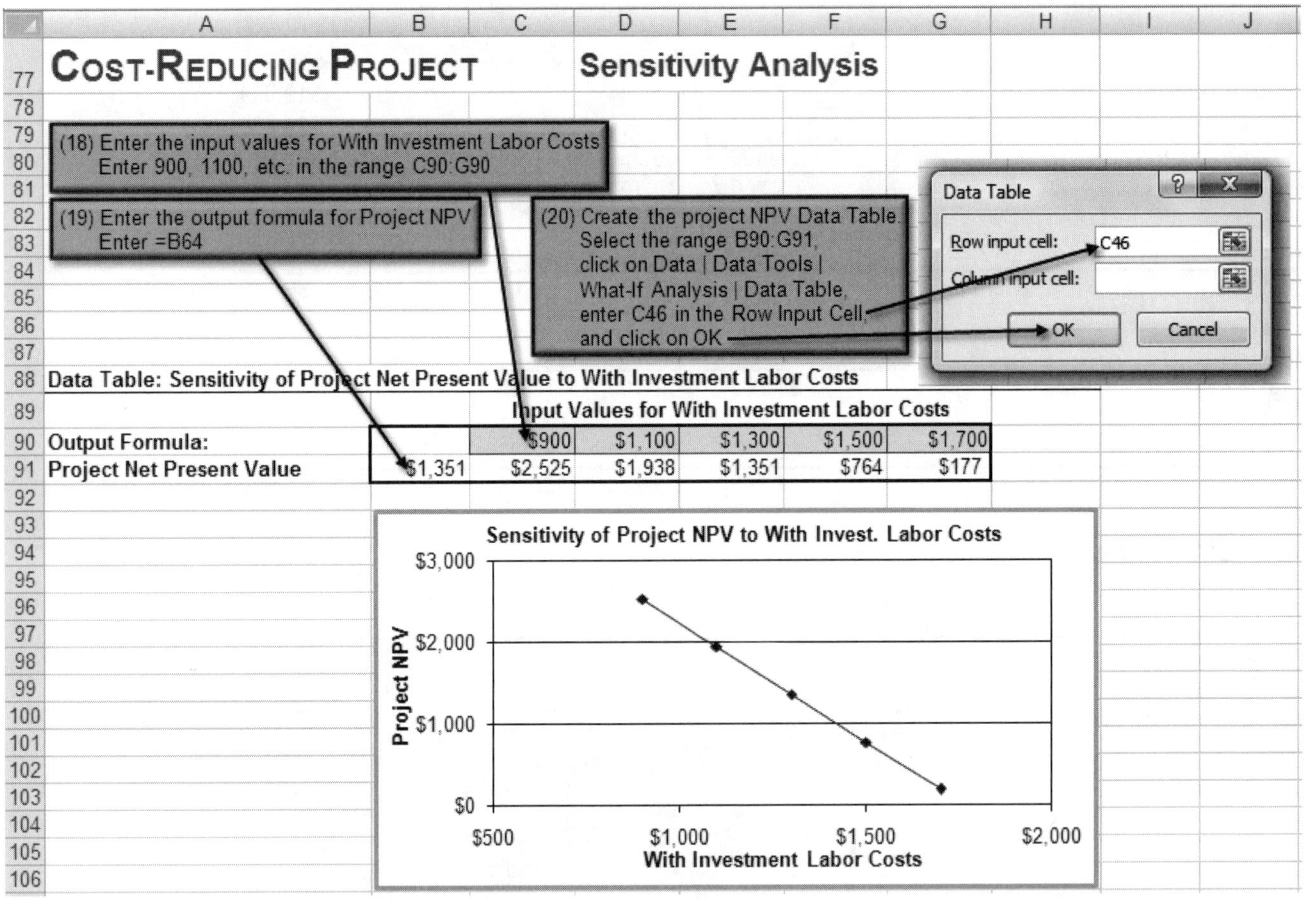

Excel 2003 Equivalent

To call up a Data Table in Excel 2003, click on **Data | Table**

The sensitivity analysis indicates that the Project NPV is not very sensitive to a wide range of values of With Investment Labor Costs. It all cases the project has a positive NPV. This provides confidence that the project's positive NPV is robust to any reasonable error in estimating the labor cost savings.

Problems

1. Suppose a firm is considering a labor-saving investment. In year 0, the project requires a $11,700 investment in equipment (all figures are in thousands of dollars). This investment is depreciated using the straight-line

method over five years and there is salvage value in year 5 of $4,500. With or without the cost-reducing investment, all cash flows start in year 1 and end in year 5. The inflation rate is 2.6% in year 2 and declines to 1.4% in year 5. The real growth rate is 21.3% in year 2 and declines to 9.5% in year 5. The tax rate is 41.0% in all years. The real cost of capital is 8.7% in year 1 and declines to 7.5% in year 5. Without the cost-reducing investment, the firm's existing investments will generate year 1 revenue, labor costs, other cash expenses, and depreciation of $15,200, $4,100, $5,300, and $3,300, respectively. With the cost-reducing investment, the firm's year 1 labor costs will be $1,600 and revenues and other cash expenses will remain the same. What is the cost-reducing project NPV?

2. For the same cost-reducing project as problem 1, analyze the sensitivity of the Project NPV to the assumed With Investment Labor Costs.

Chapter 14 Break-Even Analysis

14.1 Based On Accounting Profit

Problem. A project has a fixed cost of $30,000, variable costs of $4.00 per unit, and generates sales revenue of $6.00 per unit. What is the break-even point in unit sales, where accounting profit exactly equals zero, and what is the intuition for it?

Solution Strategy. First, we solve for the break-even point in unit sales using the formula. Second, we use Excel's Solver to back solve for the break-even point using the income statement. Lastly, we will determine the sensitivity of costs, revenues, and accounting profits to unit sales. This will allow us to graphically illustrate the intuition of the break-even point.

FIGURE 14.1 Excel Model for Break-Even Analysis - Based On Acct Profit.

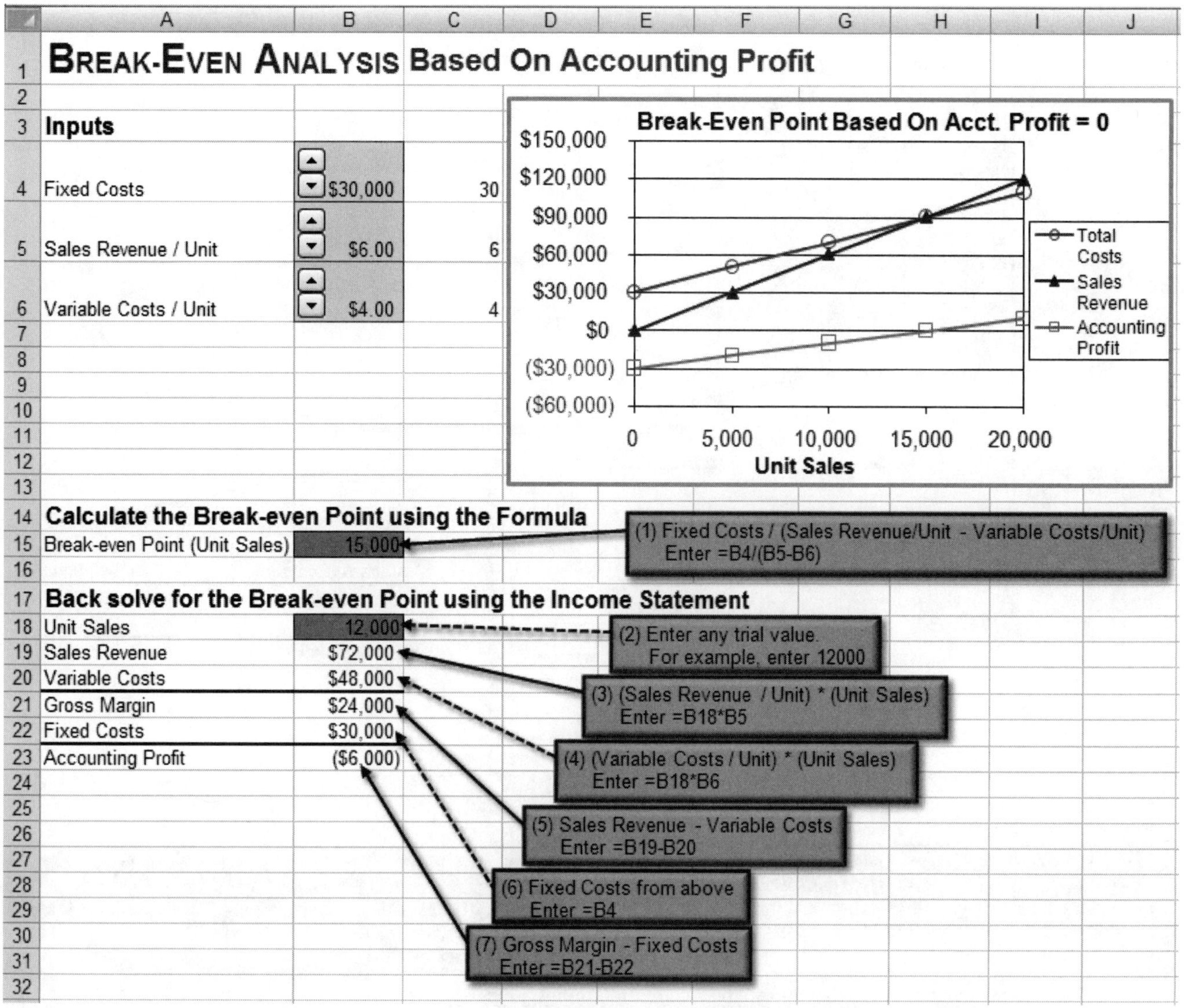

The formula and the graph show that the Break-Even Point is 15,000 units. The graph illustrates two equivalent intuitions for this result. First, the Break-Even Point is where the Sales Revenue line (in blue) crosses Total Costs line (in red). Second, the Break-Even Point is where Accounting Profit (in orange) hits zero and thus decisively switches from negative to positive.

FIGURE 14.2 Excel Model for Break-Even Analysis - Based On Acct Profit.

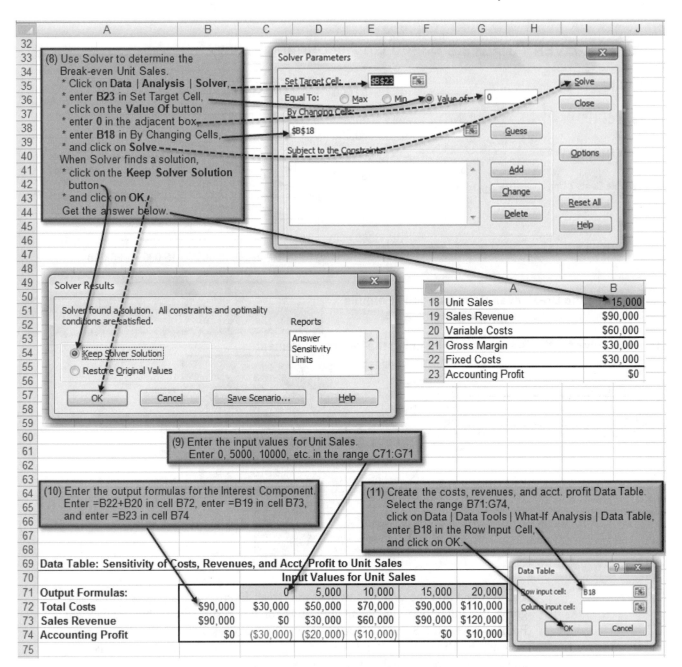

If you don't see **Solver** on the **Data** Tab in the **Analysis** Group, then you need to install the Solver. To install the Solver, click on the **Office** button, click on the **Excel Options** button at the bottom of the drop-down window, click on **Add-Ins**, highlight **Solver** in the list of Inactive Applications, click on **Go**, check **Solver**, and click on **OK**.

By trial and error, the Solver adjusts the value of Unit Sales in cell **B18** until the Accounting Profit in cell **B23** equals zero (within a very small error tolerance). This results in a Break-even Point of 15,000, where Accounting Profit equals zero. Your results may differ by a slight amount depending on the level of precision specified for Solver's error tolerance.

14.2 Based On NPV

Problem. Suppose a firm is considering the following project, where all of the dollar figures are in thousands of dollars. In year 0, the project requires $11,350 investment in plant and equipment, is depreciated using the straight-line method over seven years, and there is a salvage value of $1,400 in year 7. The project is forecast to generate sales of 2,100 units in year 1 and grow at a sales growth rate of 55.0% in year 2. The sales growth rate is forecast to decline by 15.0% in years 3 and 4, to decline by 20.0% in year 5, to decline by 25.0% in year 6, to decline by 30.0% in year 7. Unit sales will drop to zero in year 8. The inflation rate is forecast to be 2.0% in year 1, rising to 4.0% in year 5, and then leveling off. The real cost of capital is forecast to be 11.0% in year 1, rising to 12.2% in year 5, and then leveling off. The tax rate is forecast to be a constant 35.0%. Sales revenue per unit is forecast to be $9.70 in year 1 and then grow with inflation. Variable cost per unit is forecast to be $7.40 in year 1 and then grow with inflation. Cash fixed costs are forecast to be $5,280 in year 1 and then grow with inflation. What is the project NPV? What is the NPV Break-Even Point in Year 1 Unit Sales, where NPV equals zero? What is the NPV Break-Even Point in the Year 2 Sales Growth Rate, where NPV equals zero? What is the NPV Break-Even Contour in the two-dimensional space of Year 1 Unit Sales and Year 2 Sales Growth Rate?

Solution Strategy. Start with the Project NPV - Basics Excel model. Move the Unit Sales line out of the Key Assumptions area, since that is what we are going to solve for. Restructure the Unit Sales forecast to depend on the Sales Growth Rate, which will be a key variable. Structure the Sales Grow Rate forecast over the entire period to depend on how fast the growth rate is initially. This will make it easy to use Solver and to create a Data Table later on. Project the cash flows of the project and calculate the NPV. Use Solver to determine the amount of year 1 unit sales that will cause the NPV to equal zero, when the sales growth rate is at the base case level of 5% per year. Use Solver to determine the sales growth rate that will cause the NPV to equal zero, when the year 1 unit sales is at the base case level of 39,000. Create a two-variable data table using two input variables (year 1 unit sales and sales growth rate) and the output variable: NPV. Use the data table to create a three-dimensional graph showing the NPV Break-Even Contour.

FIGURE 14.3 Excel Model for Break-Even Analysis Based On NPV.

	A	B	C	D	E	F	G	H	I
1	**BREAK-EVEN ANALYSIS**		**Based On NPV**						
2	(in thousands of $)								
3		Year 0	Year 1	Year 2	Year 3	Year 4	Year 5	Year 6	Year 7
4	**Key Assumptions**								
5	Sales Growth Rate			55.0%	40.0%	25.0%	5.0%	-20.0%	-50.0%
6	Change in Sales Growth Rate				-15.0%	-15.0%	-20.0%	-25.0%	-30.0%
7	Inflation Rate		2.0%	2.5%	3.0%	3.5%	4.0%	4.0%	4.0%
8	Real Cost of Capital		11.0%	11.2%	11.4%	11.6%	11.8%	12.0%	12.2%
9	Tax Rate		35.0%	35.0%	35.0%	35.0%	35.0%	35.0%	35.0%
10									
11	**Discounting**								
12	Discount Rate = Cost of Capital		13.2%	14.0%	14.7%	15.5%	16.3%	16.5%	16.7%
13	Cumulative Discount Factor	0.0%	13.2%	29.0%	48.1%	71.0%	98.9%	131.6%	170.3%
14									
15	**Price or Cost / Unit**								
16	Unit Sales		2,100	3255	4557	5696	5981	4785	2392
17	Sales Revenue / Unit		$9.70	$9.94	$10.24	$10.60	$11.02	$11.46	$11.92
18	Variable Cost / Unit		$7.40	$7.59	$7.81	$8.09	$8.41	$8.75	$9.10
19	Cash Fixed Costs		$5,280	$5,412	$5,574	$5,769	$6,000	$6,240	$6,490
20									
21									
22									
23									
24	**Cash Flow Forecasts**								
25	Sales Revenue		$20,370	$32,363	$46,667	$60,376	$65,930	$54,854	$28,524
26	Variable Costs		$15,540	$24,689	$35,602	$46,060	$50,297	$41,847	$21,761
27	Gross Margin		$4,830	$7,674	$11,065	$14,316	$15,633	$13,007	$6,763
28									
29	Cash Fixed Costs		$5,280	$5,412	$5,574	$5,769	$6,000	$6,240	$6,490
30	Depreciation		$1,421	$1,421	$1,421	$1,421	$1,421	$1,421	$1,421
31	Total Fixed Costs		$6,701	$6,833	$6,996	$7,191	$7,422	$7,662	$7,911
32									
33	Operating Profit		($1,871)	$840	$4,070	$7,125	$8,211	$5,345	($1,148)
34	Taxes		($655)	$294	$1,424	$2,494	$2,874	$1,871	($402)
35	Net Profit		($1,216)	$546	$2,645	$4,631	$5,337	$3,474	($746)
36									
37	Add Back Depreciation		$1,421	$1,421	$1,421	$1,421	$1,421	$1,421	$1,421
38	Operating Cash Flow		$205	$1,968	$4,067	$6,053	$6,759	$4,896	$675
39									
40	Investment in Plant & Equip	($11,350)							$1,400
41	Cash Flows	($11,350)	$205	$1,968	$4,067	$6,053	$6,759	$4,896	$2,075
42	Present Value of Each Cash Flow	($11,350)	$181	$1,525	$2,746	$3,539	$3,399	$2,114	$768
43	Net Present Value	$2,921							

(2) (Unit Sales on date t-1)
* (1 + Unit Sales Growth Rate)
Enter =C16*(1+D5) and copy across

(1) (Sales Growth Rate on date t-1) +
(Change in Sales Growth Rate on date t)
Enter =D5+E6 and copy across

The project NPV is $2,921 and should be accepted. But how sure are you of this result? How sensitive is this result to small changes in the assumptions? The Break-Even Point gives you an idea of the robustness of this result.

FIGURE 14.4 Excel Model for Break-Even Analysis Based On NPV (Cont.).

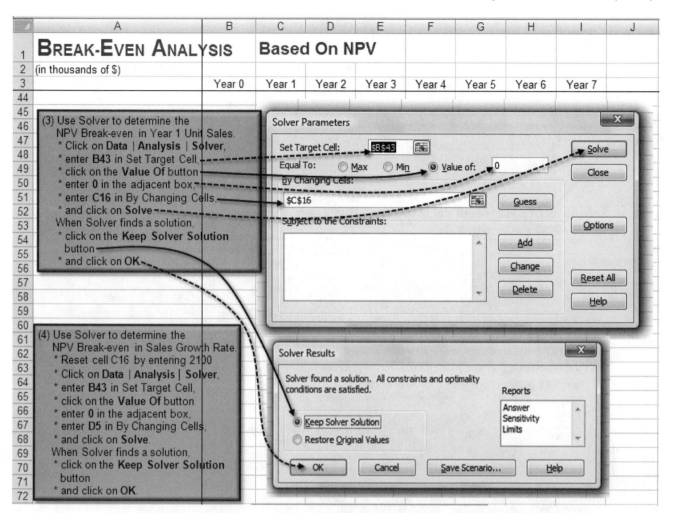

By trial and error, the Solver adjusts the value of the Year 1 Unit Sales in cell **C16** until the Net Present Value in cell **B40** equals zero (within a very small error tolerance). This results in a NPV Break-Even Point in Year 1 Unit Sales (shown in cell **C16**) of 1,875.

By trial and error, the Solver adjusts the value of the Sales Growth Rate in cell **D5** until the Net Present Value in cell **B40** equals zero. This results in a NPV Break-Even Point in Sales Growth Rate (shown in cell **D5**) of 50.1%.

FIGURE 14.5 Two Way Data Table and 3D Graph.

	A	B	C	D	E	F	G	H	I	J
1	**BREAK-EVEN ANALYSIS**		**Based On NPV**							
2	(in thousands of $)									
3			Year 0	Year 1	Year 2	Year 3	Year 4	Year 5	Year 6	Year 7
73										
74			(5) Enter the input values for Year 1 Unit Sales. Enter 1700, 1900, etc. in the range C85:F85							
75										
76	(6) Enter the input values for Year 2 Unit Sales Growth Rate. Enter 45.0%, 50.0%, etc. in the range B86:B90				(8) Create the net present value Data Table. Select the range B85:F90, click on Data | Data Tools | What-If Analysis | Data Tools, enter C16 in the Row Input Cell, enter D5 in the Column Input Cell, and click on OK.					
77										
78		(7) Enter the output formula for the Net Present Value Enter =B43								
79										
80										
81										
82	**Data Table: Sensitivity of Net Present Value to Year 1 Unit Sales**						Data Table			
83	**and Year 2 Sales Growth Rate**									
84	**Output Formula:**			**Input Values for Year 1 Unit Sales**			Row input cell:	C16		
85	**Net Present Value**	$2,921	1,700	1,900	2,100	2,300	Column input cell:	D5		
86		45.0%	($6,767)	($4,692)	($2,618)	($543)				
87	**Input Values for Year 2**	50.0%	($4,673)	($2,352)	($31)	$2,290	OK	Cancel		
88	**Sales Growth Rate**	55.0%	($2,283)	$319	$2,921	$5,523				
89		60.0%	$442	$3,365	$6,288	$9,210				
90		65.0%	$3,548	$6,836	$10,124	$13,412				
91										

NPV Break-Even Contour (Based On NPV = 0) Across Year 1 Unit Sales And Year 2 Sales Growth Rate

NPV Break-Even Contour

The 3-D Graph shows the Net Present Value of the project for combinations of Year 1 Unit Sales and Year 2 Sales Growth Rate. The multi-color surface illustrates various ranges of NPV. In the top corner, the dark purple color is for NPV > $10,000. Below it, a medium green section is for a NPV of $5,000 to $10,000. And so on. At the intersection of the very light pink section ($0 to $5,000) and the medium purple section (-$5,000 to $0) is a contour highlighted by the arrow. This is the NPV Break-Even Contour, where NPV = 0. Every point on this contour represents a combination of Year 1 Unit Sales and Year 2 Sales

Growth Rate for which the NPV = 0. The 3-D Graph shows that project's positive NPV is *very sensitive*. If the Year 1 Unit Sales are a little bit lower than assumed or if the year 2 Sale Growth Rate is a little bit lower than assumed, then the whole project could have a negative NPV.

Problems

1. A project has a fixed cost of $73,000, variable costs of $9.20 per unit, and generates sales revenue of $15.40 per unit. What is the break-even point in unit sales, where accounting profit exactly equals zero, and what is the intuition for it?

2. Suppose a firm is considering the following project, where all of the dollar figures are in thousands of dollars. In year 0, the project requires $24,490 investment in plant and equipment, is depreciated using the straight-line method over seven years, and there is a salvage value of $5,800 in year 7. The project is forecast to generate sales of 4,800 units in year 1 and grow at a sales growth rate of 72.0% in year 2. The sales growth rate is forecast to decline by 12.0% in years 3, to decline by 15.0% in year 4, to decline by 18.0% in year 5, to decline by 23.0% in year 6, to decline by 29.0% in year 7. Unit sales will drop to zero in year 8. The inflation rate is forecast to be 2.7% in year 1 and rising to 3.5% in year 7. The real cost of capital is forecast to be 10.2% in year 1, rising to 11.9% in year 7. The tax rate is forecast to be a constant 38.0%. Sales revenue per unit is forecast to be $12.20 in year 1 and then grow with inflation. Variable cost per unit is forecast to be $7.30 in year 1 and then grow with inflation. Cash fixed costs are forecast to be $6,740 in year 1 and then grow with inflation. What is the project NPV? What is the NPV Break-Even Point in Year 1 Unit Sales, where NPV equals zero? What is the NPV Break-Even Point in the Year 2 Sales Growth Rate, where NPV equals zero? What is the NPV Break-Even Contour in the two-dimensional space of Year 1 Unit Sales and Year 2 Sales Growth Rate?

PART 4 FINANCIAL PLANNING

Chapter 15 Corporate Financial Planning

15.1 Actual

Problem. Construct actual (historical) financial statements for **Cutting Edge B2B Inc.** in preparation for forecasting their financial statements.

Solution Strategy. Enter actual values in the yellow input sections. Enter appropriate additions and subtractions to complete the Income Statement and Balance sheet. Then calculate the Key Assumptions over the actual years.

FIGURE 15.1 Actual Income Statement for Cutting Edge B2B Inc.

	A	B	C	D	E	F	G	H	I	J
1	**CORPORATE FINANCIAL PLANNING**				**Actual**					
2	**Cutting Edge B2B Inc.**	2003	2004	2005	2006	2007	2008	2009	Ave Hist.	
3	**Financial Plan**	Actual	Actual	Actual	Actual	Forecast	Forecast	Forecast	% of Sales	
24										
25	(1) Sales - Cost of Goods Sold									
26	Enter =B34-B35 and copy across									
27										
28	(2) Gross Margin									
29	- SG&A Expense									
30	- Depreciation									
31	Enter =B36-B38-B39									
32	and copy across									
33	**Income Statement (Mil.$)**									
34	Sales	$73.84	$93.28	$115.93	$138.84					
35	Cost of Goods Sold	$41.83	$58.39	$75.49	$89.83					
36	Gross Margin	$32.01	$34.89	$40.44	$49.01					
37										
38	Selling, Gen & Adm Expenses	$6.58	$7.28	$8.56	$10.21					
39	Depreciation	$5.91	$6.37	$7.31	$9.86					
40	EBIT	$19.52	$21.24	$24.57	$28.94					
41										
42	Interest Expense	$4.76	$5.23	$6.69	$8.88					
43	Taxes	$6.21	$6.96	$7.52	$7.60					
44	Net Income	$8.55	$9.05	$10.36	$12.46					
45	Shares Outstanding (Millions)	39.60	40.36	44.93	53.91					
46	Earnings Per Share	$0.22	$0.22	$0.23	$0.23					
47										
48	Allocation of Net Income:									
49	Dividends	$2.90	$3.17	$3.63	$4.36					
50	Change in Equity	$5.65	$5.88	$6.73	$8.10					
51										
52	(3) EBIT - Interest Expense		(4) Net Income							
53	- Taxes		/ Shares Outstanding							
54	Enter =B40-B42-B43		Enter =B44/B45							
55	and copy across		and copy across							
56		(5) Net Income - Dividends								
57		Enter =B44-B49 and copy across								

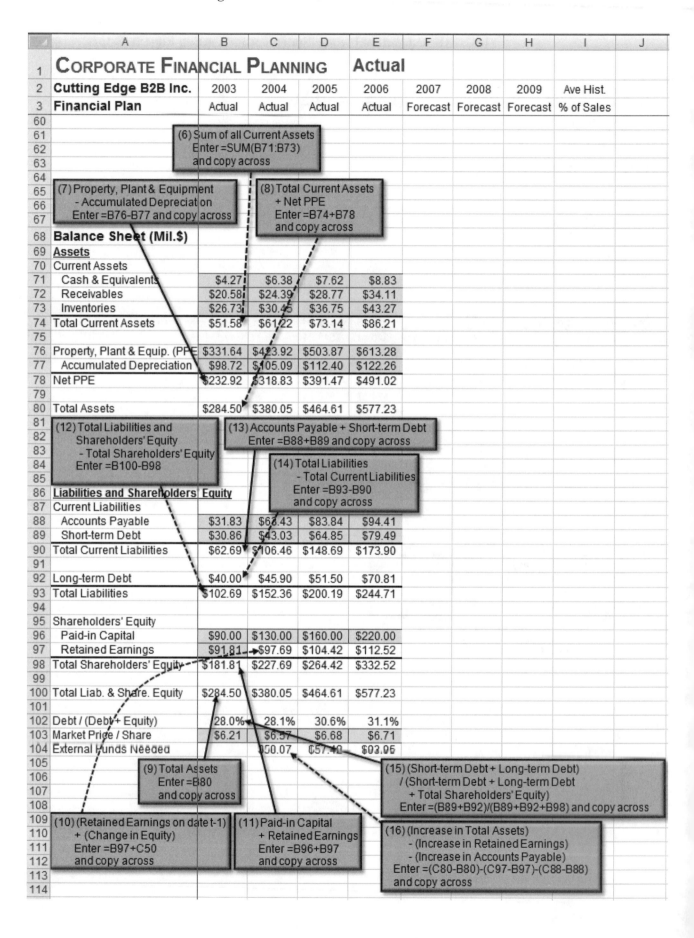

	A	B	C	D	E	F	G	H	I	J
1	**CORPORATE FINANCIAL PLANNING**				**Actual**					
2	**Cutting Edge B2B Inc.**	2003	2004	2005	2006	2007	2008	2009	Ave Hist.	
3	**Financial Plan**	Actual	Actual	Actual	Actual	Forecast	Forecast	Forecast	% of Sales	
60										
61		(6) Sum of all Current Assets								
62		Enter =SUM(B71:B73)								
63		and copy across								
64										
65	(7) Property, Plant & Equipment		(8) Total Current Assets							
66	- Accumulated Depreciation		+ Net PPE							
67	Enter =B76-B77 and copy across		Enter =B74+B78							
68	**Balance Sheet (Mil.$)**		and copy across							
69	**Assets**									
70	Current Assets									
71	Cash & Equivalents	$4.27	$6.38	$7.62	$8.83					
72	Receivables	$20.58	$24.39	$28.77	$34.11					
73	Inventories	$26.73	$30.45	$36.75	$43.27					
74	Total Current Assets	$51.58	$61.22	$73.14	$86.21					
75										
76	Property, Plant & Equip. (PPE	$331.64	$423.92	$503.87	$613.28					
77	Accumulated Depreciation	$98.72	$105.09	$112.40	$122.26					
78	Net PPE	$232.92	$318.83	$391.47	$491.02					
79										
80	Total Assets	$284.50	$380.05	$464.61	$577.23					
81	(12) Total Liabilities and		(13) Accounts Payable + Short-term Debt							
82	Shareholders' Equity		Enter =B88+B89 and copy across							
83	- Total Shareholders' Equity									
84	Enter =B100-B98		(14) Total Liabilities							
85			- Total Current Liabilities							
86	**Liabilities and Shareholders Equity**		Enter =B93-B90							
87	Current Liabilities		and copy across							
88	Accounts Payable	$31.83	$63.43	$83.84	$94.41					
89	Short-term Debt	$30.86	$43.03	$64.85	$79.49					
90	Total Current Liabilities	$62.69	$106.46	$148.69	$173.90					
91										
92	Long-term Debt	$40.00	$45.90	$51.50	$70.81					
93	Total Liabilities	$102.69	$152.36	$200.19	$244.71					
94										
95	Shareholders' Equity									
96	Paid-in Capital	$90.00	$130.00	$160.00	$220.00					
97	Retained Earnings	$91.81	$97.69	$104.42	$112.52					
98	Total Shareholders' Equity	$181.81	$227.69	$264.42	$332.52					
99										
100	Total Liab. & Share. Equity	$284.50	$380.05	$464.61	$577.23					
101										
102	Debt / (Debt + Equity)	28.0%	28.1%	30.6%	31.1%					
103	Market Price / Share	$6.21	$6.57	$6.68	$6.71					
104	External Funds Needed		$50.07	$57.40	$63.95					
105		(9) Total Assets								
106		Enter =B80			(15) (Short-term Debt + Long-term Debt)					
107		and copy across			/ (Short-term Debt + Long-term Debt					
108					+ Total Shareholders' Equity)					
109	(10) (Retained Earnings on date t-1)		(11) Paid-in Capital	Enter =(B89+B92)/(B89+B92+B98) and copy across						
110	+ (Change in Equity)		+ Retained Earnings	(16) (Increase in Total Assets)						
111	Enter =B97+C50		Enter =B96+B97	- (Increase in Retained Earnings)						
112	and copy across		and copy across	- (Increase in Accounts Payable)						
113				Enter =(C80-B80)-(C97-B97)-(C88-B88)						
114				and copy across						

FIGURE 15.3 Actual Key Assumptions for Cutting Edge B2B Inc.

	A	B	C	D	E	F	G	H	I	J
1	**CORPORATE FINANCIAL PLANNING** **Actual**									
2	**Cutting Edge B2B Inc.**	2003	2004	2005	2006	2007	2008	2009	Ave Hist.	
3	**Financial Plan**	Actual	Actual	Actual	Actual	Forecast	Forecast	Forecast	% of Sales	
4	**Key Assumptions**									
5	Sales Growth Rate		26.3%	24.3%	19.8%					
6	Tax Rate	42.1%	43.5%	42.1%	37.9%					
7	Int Rate on Short-Term Debt	6.5%	6.7%	6.9%	7.1%					
8	Int Rate on Long-Term Debt	7.7%	7.9%	8.1%	8.3%					
9	Dividend Payout Rate	33.9%	35.0%	35.0%	35.0%					
10	Price / Earnings	28.8	29.3	29.0	29.0					
11										
12				(17) (Sales (date t) - Sales (date t-1)) / Sales (date t-1) Enter =(C34-B34)/B34 and copy across						
13										
14				(18) Taxes / (Before-tax Income) = Taxes / (EBIT - Interest Expense) Enter =B43/(B40-B42) and copy across						
15										
16										
17				(19) Dividend Payout Rate = Dividends / Net Income Enter =B49/B44 and copy across						
18										
19				(20) Price / Earnings = (Market Price per Share) / (Earnings per Share) Enter =B103/B46 and copy across						
20										

Now you are ready to Forecast the Financial Statements.

15.2 Forecast

Problem. Given actual financial statements for **Cutting Edge B2B Inc.**, forecast their financial statements for the next three years. Explore the impact of the financing *choice variables*: debt or equity.

Solution Strategy. Analyze the historical financial statements to determine which income statement and balance sheet items are close to being a constant percentage of sales and which items are not. Then, forecast sales as accurately as possible. Then, apply the average historical percentage of sales to generate most of the income statement and balance sheet items. Forecast other key assumptions to generate most of the rest and work out the implications for additional financing. Make the Balance Sheet balance by calculating long-term debt as the plug item. Raise (or lower) the portion of equity relative to the portion of debt by raising (or lowering) paid-in capital.

	A	B	C	D	E	F	G	H	I	J
1	**CORPORATE FINANCIAL PLANNING**				**Forecast**					
2	**Cutting Edge B2B Inc.**	2003	2004	2005	2006	2007	2008	2009	Ave Hist.	
3	**Financial Plan**	Actual	Actual	Actual	Actual	Forecast	Forecast	Forecast	% of Sales	
116	(21) (Each Income Statement item) / Sales				(24) Average of historical (actual) Percent of Sales					
117	Enter =B34/B$34 and copy to the range B121:H137				Enter =AVERAGE(B121:E121) and copy to range I121:I167					
118	Delete ranges that should be blank (B124:H124, etc.)				Delete cells that should be blank (I124, I128, etc.)					
119										
120	**Income Statement (% of Sales)**									
121	Sales	100.0%	100.0%	100.0%	100.0%	100.0%	100.0%	100.0%	100.0%	
122	Cost of Goods Sold	56.6%	62.6%	65.1%	64.7%	62.3%	62.3%	62.3%	62.3%	
123	Gross Margin	43.4%	37.4%	34.9%	35.3%	37.7%	37.7%	37.7%	37.7%	
124										
125	Selling, Gen & Adm Expenses	8.9%	7.8%	7.4%	7.4%	7.9%	7.9%	7.9%	7.9%	
126	Depreciation	8.0%	6.8%	6.3%	7.1%	7.1%	7.1%	7.1%	7.1%	
127	EBIT	26.4%	22.8%	21.2%	20.8%	22.8%	22.8%	22.8%	22.8%	
128										
129	Interest Expense	6.4%	5.6%	5.8%	6.4%	7.1%	6.8%	6.7%	6.1%	
130	Taxes	8.4%	7.5%	6.5%	5.5%	6.3%	6.4%	6.4%	7.0%	
131	Net Income	11.6%	9.7%	8.9%	9.0%	9.5%	9.6%	9.6%	9.8%	
132	Shares Outstanding (Millions	53.6%	43.3%	38.8%	38.8%	37.2%	35.8%	34.2%	43.6%	
133	Earnings Per Share	0.3%	0.2%	0.2%	0.2%	0.2%	0.1%	0.1%	0.2%	
134										
135	Allocation of Net Income:									
136	Dividends	3.9%	3.4%	3.1%	3.1%	3.3%	3.4%	3.4%	3.4%	
137	Change in Equity	7.7%	6.3%	5.8%	5.8%	6.1%	6.3%	6.3%	6.4%	
138										
139	**Balance Sheet (% of Sales)**		(22) (Each Balance Sheet Asset item) / Sales							
140	**Assets**		Enter =B71/B$34 and copy to range B142:H151							
141	Current Assets		Delete ranges that should be blank (B146:H146, etc.)							
142	Cash & Equivalents	5.8%	6.8%	6.6%	6.4%	6.4%	6.4%	6.4%	6.4%	
143	Receivables	27.9%	26.1%	24.8%	24.6%	25.9%	25.9%	25.9%	25.9%	
144	Inventories	36.2%	32.6%	31.7%	31.2%	32.9%	32.9%	32.9%	32.9%	
145	Total Current Assets	69.9%	65.6%	63.1%	62.1%	65.2%	65.2%	65.2%	65.2%	
146										
147	Property, Plant & Equip. (PPE	449.1%	454.5%	434.6%	441.7%	420.1%	417.6%	416.7%	445.0%	
148	Accum Depreciation	133.7%	112.7%	97.0%	88.1%	83.0%	80.5%	79.6%	107.8%	
149	Net PPE	315.4%	341.8%	337.7%	353.7%	337.1%	337.1%	337.1%	337.1%	
150										
151	Total Assets	385.3%	407.4%	400.8%	415.8%	402.3%	402.3%	402.3%	402.3%	
152					(23) (Each Balance Sheet Liab. & Equity item) / Sales					
153	**Liabilities and Shareholders' Equity**				Enter =B88/B$34 and copy to range B155:H167					
154	Current Liabilities				Delete ranges that should be blank (B158:H158, etc.)					
155	Accounts Payable	43.1%	68.0%	72.3%	68.0%	62.9%	62.9%	62.9%	62.9%	
156	Short-term Debt	41.8%	46.1%	55.9%	57.3%	50.3%	50.3%	50.3%	50.3%	
157	Total Current Liabilities	84.9%	114.1%	128.3%	125.3%	113.1%	113.1%	113.1%	113.1%	
158										
159	Long-term Debt	54.2%	49.2%	44.4%	51.0%	51.7%	50.8%	53.3%	49.7%	
160	Total Liabilities	139.1%	163.3%	172.7%	176.3%	164.9%	164.0%	166.5%	162.8%	
161										
162	Shareholders' Equity									
163	Paid-in Capital	121.9%	139.4%	138.0%	158.5%	161.4%	164.8%	163.4%	139.4%	
164	Retained Earnings	124.3%	104.7%	90.1%	81.0%	76.0%	73.5%	72.5%	100.0%	
165	Total Shareholders' Equity	246.2%	244.1%	228.1%	239.5%	237.4%	238.4%	235.9%	239.5%	
166										
167	Total Liabilities and Equity	385.3%	407.4%	400.8%	415.8%	402.3%	402.3%	402.3%	402.3%	

CORPORATE FINANCIAL PLANNING Forecast

	A	B	C	D	E	F	G	H	I	J
2	**Cutting Edge B2B Inc.**	2003	2004	2005	2006	2007	2008	2009	Ave Hist.	
3	**Financial Plan**	Actual	Actual	Actual	Actual	Forecast	Forecast	Forecast	% of Sales	
4	**Key Assumptions**									
5	Sales Growth Rate		26.3%	24.3%	19.8%	16.0%	13.0%	11.0%		
6	Tax Rate	42.1%	43.5%	42.1%	37.9%	40.0%	40.0%	40.0%		
7	Int Rate on Short-Term Debt	6.5%	6.7%	6.9%	7.1%	7.0%	6.9%	6.8%		
8	Int Rate on Long-Term Debt	7.7%	7.9%	8.1%	8.3%	8.2%	8.1%	8.0%		
9	Dividend Payout Rate	33.9%	35.0%	35.0%	35.0%	35.0%	35.0%	35.0%		
10	Price / Earnings	28.8	29.3	29.0	29.0	29.4	29.4	29.4		

(25) Forecast key assumptions Enter forecast values in the range F5:H10 (done for you)

CORPORATE FINANCIAL PLANNING Forecast

	A	B	C	D	E	F	G	H	I	J
2	**Cutting Edge B2B Inc.**	2003	2004	2005	2006	2007	2008	2009	Ave Hist.	
3	**Financial Plan**	Actual	Actual	Actual	Actual	Forecast	Forecast	Forecast	% of Sales	
33	**Income Statement (Mil.$)**									
34	Sales	$73.84	$93.28	$115.93	$138.84	$161.05	$181.99	$202.01		
35	Cost of Goods Sold	$41.83	$58.39	$75.49	$89.83	$100.28	$113.32	$125.78		
36	Gross Margin	$32.01	$34.89	$40.44	$49.01	$60.77	$68.67	$76.23		
37										
38	Selling, Gen & Adm Expenses	$6.58	$7.28	$8.56	$10.21	$12.66	$14.31	$15.88		
39	Depreciation	$5.91	$6.37	$7.31	$9.86	$11.37	$12.85	$14.26		
40	EBIT	$19.52	$21.24	$24.57	$28.94	$36.74	$41.51	$46.08		
41										
42	Interest Expense	$4.76	$5.23	$6.69	$8.88	$11.37	$12.34	$13.62		
43	Taxes	$6.21	$6.96	$7.52	$7.60	$10.15	$11.67	$12.98		
44	Net Income	$8.55	$9.05	$10.36	$12.46	$15.22	$17.51	$19.48		
45	Shares Outstanding (Millions)	39.60	40.36	44.93	53.91	59.87	65.22	69.02		
46	Earnings Per Share	$0.22	$0.22	$0.23	$0.23	$0.25	$0.27	$0.28		
47										
48	Allocation of Net Income:									
49	Dividends	$2.90	$3.17	$3.63	$4.36	$5.33	$6.13	$6.82		
50	Change in Equity	$5.65	$5.88	$6.73	$8.10	$9.89	$11.38	$12.66		

(26) (Sales on date t-1) * (1 + Sales Growth Rate) Enter =E34*(1+F5) and copy across

(27) (Ave. Hist. Goods Sold / Sales) * Sales Enter =$I122*F$34 and copy across

(28) (Ave. Hist. SG&A / Sales) * Sales Copy cell F35 to the range F38:H39

(29) (Interest Rate on Short-term Debt) * (Prior Year Short-term Debt Amount) + (Interest Rate on Long-term Debt) * (Prior Year Long-term Debt Amount) Enter =F7*E89+F8*E92 and copy across

(30) (EBIT - Interest Expense) * (Tax Rate) Enter =(F40-F42)*F6 and copy across

(31) (Shares Outstanding on date t-1) + (Paid in Capital on date t - Paid in Capital on date t-1) / (Market Price / Share on date t-1) Enter =E45+(F96-E96)/E103 and copy across

(32) (Net Income) * (Dividend Payout Rate) Enter =F44*F9 and copy across

(33) Net Income - Dividends Enter =F44-F49 and copy across

FIGURE 15.7 Forecast Balance Sheet Assets for Cutting Edge B2B Inc.

	A	B	C	D	E	F	G	H	I	J
1	**CORPORATE FINANCIAL PLANNING**					**Forecast**				
2	**Cutting Edge B2B Inc.**	2003	2004	2005	2006	2007	2008	2009	Ave Hist.	
3	**Financial Plan**	Actual	Actual	Actual	Actual	Forecast	Forecast	Forecast	% of Sales	
60										
61										
62										
63										
64										
65										
66										
67										
68	**Balance Sheet (Mil.$)**									
69	Assets									
70	Current Assets									
71	Cash & Equivalents	$4.27	$6.38	$7.62	$8.83	$10.29	$11.63	$12.91		
72	Receivables	$20.58	$24.39	$28.77	$34.11	$41.63	$47.05	$52.22		
73	Inventories	$26.73	$30.45	$36.75	$43.27	$53.03	$59.92	$66.52		
74	Total Current Assets	$51.58	$61.22	$73.14	$86.21	$104.95	$118.60	$131.64		
75										
76	Property, Plant & Equip. (PPE	$331.64	$423.92	$503.87	$613.28	$676.62	$760.05	$841.81		
77	Accumulated Depreciation	$98.72	$105.09	$112.40	$122.26	$133.63	$146.48	$160.74		
78	Net PPE	$232.92	$318.83	$391.47	$491.02	$542.98	$613.57	$681.07		
79										
80	Total Assets	$284.50	$380.05	$464.61	$577.23	$647.94	$732.17	$812.71		
81										
82										
83										
84										
85										
86	Liabilities and Shareholders' Equity									
87	Current Liabilities									
88	Accounts Payable	$31.83	$63.43	$83.84	$94.41	$101.23	$114.39	$126.98		
89	Short-term Debt	$30.86	$43.03	$64.85	$79.49	$80.98	$91.50	$101.57		
90	Total Current Liabilities	$62.69	$106.46	$148.69	$173.90	$182.21	$205.90	$228.54		
91										
92	Long-term Debt	$40.00	$45.90	$51.50	$70.81	$83.32	$92.48	$107.71		
93	Total Liabilities	$102.69	$152.36	$200.19	$244.71	$265.53	$298.38	$336.26		
94										
95	Shareholders' Equity									
96	Paid-in Capital	$90.00	$130.00	$160.00	$220.00	$260.00	$300.00	$330.00		
97	Retained Earnings	$91.81	$97.69	$104.42	$112.52	$122.41	$133.79	$146.45		
98	Total Shareholders' Equity	$181.81	$227.69	$264.42	$332.52	$382.41	$433.79	$476.45		
99										
100	Total Liab. & Share. Equity	$284.50	$380.05	$464.61	$577.23	$647.94	$732.17	$812.71		
101										
102	Debt / (Debt + Equity)	28.0%	28.1%	30.6%	31.1%	30.1%	29.8%	30.5%		
103	Market Price / Share	$6.21	$6.57	$6.68	$6.71	$7.47	$7.89	$8.30		
104	External Funds Needed		$58.07	$57.42	$93.95	$53.99	$59.69	$55.30		

Callout notes:

(34) (Ave. Hist. Current Asset Item / Sales) * Sales
Enter =$I142*F$34 and copy to the range F71:H73

(35) Accumulated Depreciation + Net PPE
Enter =F77+F78 and copy across

(36) Accumulated Depreciation (t-1)
+ Depreciation
Enter =E77+F39 and copy across

(37) (Ave. Hist. PPE / Sales) * Sales
Copy F71 to the range F78:H78

(38) (Ave. Hist. Liab. & Equity Item / Sales) * Sales
Enter =$I155*F$34 and copy to the range F88:H89

(39) Adjust Paid-in Capital to keep Debt / (Debt + Equity) in row 102 near the target level, which is 30% in this case (done for you)

(40) (Price / Earnings) * (Earnings / Share)
Enter =F10*F46 and copy across

After all of the forecasting is done, it is important to check Long-term Debt to make sure that it isn't growing explosively or dropping rapidly (perhaps going negative!). If it is going wild, then backtrack to identify the source of sharp up or down movements and check for errors.

The forecast for the next three years is a steady increase in Earnings Per Share from $0.25 to $0.27 to $0.28.

15.3 Cash Flow

Problem. Given historical and forecasted Income Statements and Balance Sheets for **Cutting Edge B2B Inc.**, create the historical and forecasted Cash Flow Statement.

Solution Strategy. Construct the cash flow statement by starting with Net Income from the Income Statement and then picking up the year to year changes from the Balance Sheets.

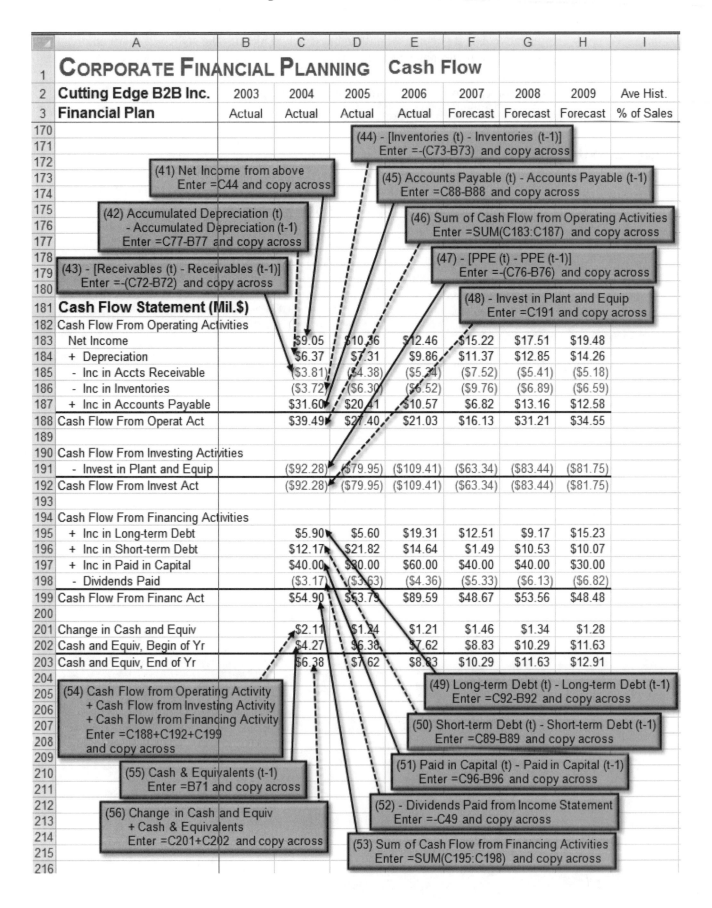

	A	B	C	D	E	F	G	H	I
1	**CORPORATE FINANCIAL PLANNING**				Cash Flow				
2	**Cutting Edge B2B Inc.**	2003	2004	2005	2006	2007	2008	2009	Ave Hist.
3	**Financial Plan**	Actual	Actual	Actual	Actual	Forecast	Forecast	Forecast	% of Sales
170									
171					(44) - [Inventories (t) - Inventories (t-1)] Enter =-(C73-B73) and copy across				
172									
173		(41) Net Income from above Enter =C44 and copy across			(45) Accounts Payable (t) - Accounts Payable (t-1) Enter =C88-B88 and copy across				
174									
175		(42) Accumulated Depreciation (t) - Accumulated Depreciation (t-1) Enter =C77-B77 and copy across			(46) Sum of Cash Flow from Operating Activities Enter =SUM(C183:C187) and copy across				
176									
177									
178					(47) - [PPE (t) - PPE (t-1)] Enter =-(C76-B76) and copy across				
179		(43) - [Receivables (t) - Receivables (t-1)] Enter =-(C72-B72) and copy across							
180					(48) - Invest in Plant and Equip Enter =C191 and copy across				
181	**Cash Flow Statement (Mil.$)**								
182	Cash Flow From Operating Activities								
183	Net Income		$9.05	$10.36	$12.46	$15.22	$17.51	$19.48	
184	+ Depreciation		$6.37	$7.31	$9.86	$11.37	$12.85	$14.26	
185	- Inc in Accts Receivable		($3.81)	($4.38)	($5.34)	($7.52)	($5.41)	($5.18)	
186	- Inc in Inventories		($3.72)	($6.30)	($6.52)	($9.76)	($6.89)	($6.59)	
187	+ Inc in Accounts Payable		$31.60	$20.41	$10.57	$6.82	$13.16	$12.58	
188	Cash Flow From Operat Act		$39.49	$27.40	$21.03	$16.13	$31.21	$34.55	
189									
190	Cash Flow From Investing Activities								
191	- Invest in Plant and Equip		($92.28)	($79.95)	($109.41)	($63.34)	($83.44)	($81.75)	
192	Cash Flow From Invest Act		($92.28)	($79.95)	($109.41)	($63.34)	($83.44)	($81.75)	
193									
194	Cash Flow From Financing Activities								
195	+ Inc in Long-term Debt		$5.90	$5.60	$19.31	$12.51	$9.17	$15.23	
196	+ Inc in Short-term Debt		$12.17	$21.82	$14.64	$1.49	$10.53	$10.07	
197	+ Inc in Paid in Capital		$40.00	$30.00	$60.00	$40.00	$40.00	$30.00	
198	- Dividends Paid		($3.17)	($3.63)	($4.36)	($5.33)	($6.13)	($6.82)	
199	Cash Flow From Financ Act		$54.90	$53.79	$89.59	$48.67	$53.56	$48.48	
200									
201	Change in Cash and Equiv		$2.11	$1.24	$1.21	$1.46	$1.34	$1.28	
202	Cash and Equiv, Begin of Yr		$4.27	$6.38	$7.62	$8.83	$10.29	$11.63	
203	Cash and Equiv, End of Yr		$6.38	$7.62	$8.83	$10.29	$11.63	$12.91	
204									
205	(54) Cash Flow from Operating Activity + Cash Flow from Investing Activity + Cash Flow from Financing Activity Enter =C188+C192+C199 and copy across				(49) Long-term Debt (t) - Long-term Debt (t-1) Enter =C92-B92 and copy across				
206									
207					(50) Short-term Debt (t) - Short-term Debt (t-1) Enter =C89-B89 and copy across				
208									
209									
210		(55) Cash & Equivalents (t-1) Enter =B71 and copy across			(51) Paid in Capital (t) - Paid in Capital (t-1) Enter =C96-B96 and copy across				
211									
212		(56) Change in Cash and Equiv + Cash & Equivalents Enter =C201+C202 and copy across			(52) - Dividends Paid from Income Statement Enter =-C49 and copy across				
213									
214					(53) Sum of Cash Flow from Financing Activities Enter =SUM(C195:C198) and copy across				
215									
216									

Notice that the $6.38 Cash and Equivalents at the End of Year 2004, which was obtained by summing all of the cash flows from operations, investments, and financing together with the Beginning of the Year balance for 2004, does indeed equal the $6.38 Cash and Equivalents at the Beginning of Year 2005. Thus, the sum of the cash flows from operations, investments, and financing does equal the Change in Cash and Equivalents. This balancing of the Cash Flow Statement is a direct consequence of the balancing of the Balance Sheet. It is also a good way to check for possible errors in your Excel model.

15.4 Ratios

Problem. Given historical and forecasted financial statements for **Cutting Edge B2B Inc.**, create the historical and forecasted financial ratios.

Solution Strategy. Calculate the financial ratios by referencing the appropriate items on the Income Statement or Balance Sheet.

FIGURE 15.9 Historical and Forecasted Financial Ratios for Cutting Edge B2B Inc.

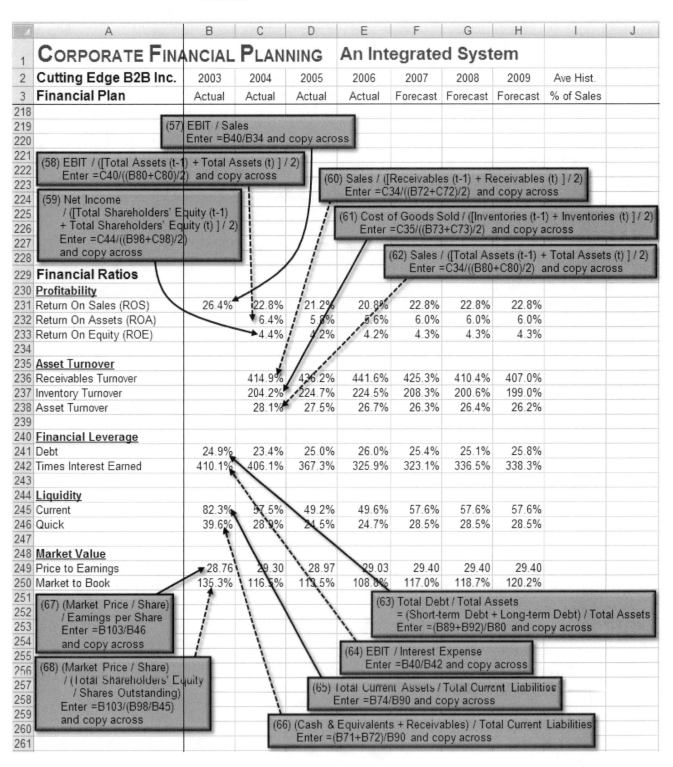

The financial ratios are very useful in interpreting the financial condition of the firm.

15.5 Sensitivity

Problem. Given historical and forecasted financial statements for **Cutting Edge B2B Inc.**, analyze the sensitivity of the 2007 External Funds Needed to the assumed 2007 Sales Growth Rate.

Solution Strategy. Create a Data Table using Sales Growth Rate as the input variable and External Funds Needed as the output variable. Then graph the relationship.

FIGURE 15.10 Sensitivity Analysis for Cutting Edge B2B Inc.

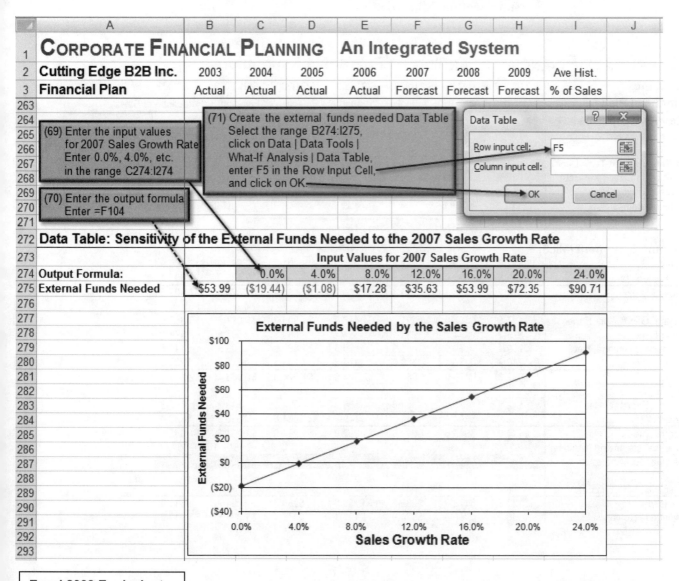

The sensitivity analysis indicates that 2007 External Funds Needed is very sensitive to the assumption about 2007 Sales Growth Rate. Further, there is a linear relationship between 2007 Sales Growth Rate and 2007 External Funds Needed.

15.6 Full-Scale Estimation

Problem. Given historical 10K financial statements for **Nike, Inc.**, forecast their financial statements over the next three years.

Solution Strategy. Modify the financial statement Excel model developed for the fictional firm **Cutting Edge B2B Inc.** by adding an additional level of detail found in the actual 10K financial statements of **Nike, Inc.** Then forecast the financial statements in the same way as before.

FIGURE 15.11 Historical and Forecasted Assumptions and Income Statement for Nike, Inc.

	A	B	C	D	E	F	G	H	I	J
1	CORPORATE FINANCIAL PLANNING				Full-Scale Estimation					
2	Nike, Inc.	5/31/2003	5/31/2004	5/31/2005	5/31/2006	5/31/2007	5/31/2008	5/31/2009	Ave. %	
3	Financial Plan	Actual	Actual	Actual	Actual	Forecast	Forecast	Forecast	of Sales	
4	Key Assumptions									
5	Sales Growth Rate		14.5%	12.1%	8.8%	7.0%	6.0%	5.0%		
6	Tax Rate	44.7%	34.8%	34.9%	35.0%	35.0%	35.0%	35.0%		
7	Int Rate on Short-Term Debt	1.0%	2.1%	3.4%	5.1%	4.5%	4.5%	4.5%		
8	Int Rate on Long-Term Debt	2.3%	3.9%	3.8%	5.1%	5.5%	5.5%	5.5%		
9	Dividend Payout Rate	29.1%	19.0%	19.5%	20.9%	21.0%	22.0%	23.0%		
10	Price / Earnings	62.3	39.6	35.4	29.5	30.0	31.0	32.0		
11										
12										
13	Income Statement (Mil.$)									
14	Sales	$10,697.0	$12,253.1	$13,739.7	$14,954.9	$16,001.7	$16,961.8	$17,809.9		
15	Cost of Goods Sold	$6,072.8	$6,824.0	$7,596.3	$8,190.7	$8,901.8	$9,435.9	$9,907.7		
16	Gross Margin	$4,624.2	$5,429.1	$6,143.4	$6,764.2	$7,100.0	$7,526.0	$7,902.3		
17										
18	Selling, Gen & Adm Expenses	$3,137.6	$3,702.0	$4,221.7	$4,477.8	$4,809.0	$5,097.6	$5,352.5		
19	Other Expense	$79.9	$74.7	$29.1	$4.4	$63.9	$67.8	$71.1		
20	Accounting Change, Net	$266.1	$0.0	$0.0	$0.0	$99.5	$105.5	$110.8		
21	Depreciation	$240.8	$177.4	$28.0	$177.2	$203.5	$215.7	$226.5		
22	EBIT	$899.8	$1,475.0	$1,864.6	$2,104.8	$1,924.0	$2,039.4	$2,141.4		
23										
24	Interest Expense, Net	$42.9	$25.0	$4.8	($36.8)	$24.5	$48.3	$55.8		
25	Taxes	$382.9	$504.4	$648.2	$749.6	$664.8	$696.9	$730.0		
26	Net Income	$474.0	$945.6	$1,211.6	$1,392.0	$1,234.6	$1,294.3	$1,355.6		
27	Shares Outstanding (Millions)	527.2	526.2	522.2	512.0	512.0	512.0	512.0		
28	Earnings Per Share	$0.90	$1.80	$2.32	$2.72	$2.41	$2.53	$2.65		
29										
30	Allocation of Net Income:									
31	Dividends	$137.8	$179.2	$236.7	$290.9	$259.3	$284.7	$311.8		
32	Change in Equity	$336.2	$766.4	$974.9	$1,101.1	$975.4	$1,009.5	$1,043.0		

(1) Forecast key assumptions Enter forecast values in the range F5:H10 (done for you)

(2) Gross Margin - Sum of Expenses Enter =B16-SUM(B18:B21) and copy across

FIGURE 15.12 Historical and Forecasted Balance Sheet for Nike, Inc.

	A	B	C	D	E	F	G	H	I	J
1	**CORPORATE FINANCIAL PLANNING**				**Full-Scale Estimation**					
2	**Nike, Inc.**	5/31/2003	5/31/2004	5/31/2005	5/31/2006	5/31/2007	5/31/2008	5/31/2009	Ave. %	
3	**Financial Plan**	Actual	Actual	Actual	Actual	Forecast	Forecast	Forecast	of Sales	
34	**Balance Sheet (Mil.$)**	(3) Sum of Current Assets items Enter =SUM(B37:B42) and copy across				(4) Total Current Assets + Sum of Rest of Assets Enter =B43+SUM(B45:B48) and copy across				
35	**Assets**									
36	Current Assets									
37	Cash & Equivalents	$634.0	$828.0	$1,388.1	$954.2	$1,110.0	$1,260.6	$1,415.4		
38	Short-term Investments	$0.0	$400.8	$436.6	$1,348.8	$618.8	$655.9	$688.7		
39	Receivables	$2,101.1	$2,120.2	$2,262.1	$2,395.9	$2,777.5	$2,944.2	$3,091.4		
40	Inventories	$1,514.9	$1,633.6	$1,811.1	$2,076.7	$2,182.7	$2,313.7	$2,429.4		
41	Deferred Income Taxes	$163.7	$165.0	$110.2	$203.3	$201.6	$213.7	$224.3		
42	Prepaid Expenses	$266.2	$364.4	$343.0	$380.1	$420.1	$445.3	$467.5		
43	Total Current Assets	$4,679.9	$5,512.0	$6,351.1	$7,359.0	$7,310.6	$7,833.3	$8,316.7		
44										
45	Property, Plant & Equip., Net	$1,620.8	$1,586.9	$1,605.8	$1,657.7	$2,035.2	$2,157.3	$2,265.2		
46	Intangible Assets, Net	$118.2	$366.3	$406.1	$405.5	$390.5	$413.9	$434.6		
47	Goodwill	$65.6	$135.4	$135.4	$130.8	$143.2	$151.7	$159.3		
48	Deferred Inc. Taxes & Other	$229.4	$291.0	$295.2	$316.6	$351.4	$372.5	$391.2		
49	Total Assets	$6,713.9	$7,891.6	$8,793.6	$9,869.6	$10,230.9	$10,928.8	$11,567.0		
50										
51	**Liabilities and Shareholders' Equity**	(5) Sum of Current Liabilities items Enter =SUM(B53:B57) and copy across				(6) Total Liab -Total Cur Liab -Def ITO -RedPS Enter =F63-F58-F61-F62 and copy across				
52	Current Liabilities									
53	Current Portion of L.T. Debt	$205.7	$6.6	$6.2	$255.3	$149.2	$158.1	$166.0		
54	Notes Payable	$75.4	$146.0	$69.8	$43.4	$107.8	$114.3	$120.0		
55	Accounts Payable	$572.7	$763.8	$843.9	$952.2	$964.0	$1,021.8	$1,072.9		
56	Accrued Liabilities	$1,054.2	$974.4	$984.3	$1,286.9	$1,343.2	$1,423.8	$1,495.0		
57	Income Taxes Payable	$107.2	$118.2	$95.0	$85.5	$129.2	$137.0	$143.8		
58	Total Current Liabilities	$2,015.2	$2,009.0	$1,999.2	$2,623.3	$2,693.4	$2,855.0	$2,997.7		
59										
60	Long-term Debt	$551.6	$682.4	$687.3	$410.7	$789.2	$921.5	$371.6		
61	Deferred Inc. Taxes & Other	$156.1	$418.2	$462.6	$550.1	$476.8	$505.4	$530.6		
62	Redeemable Preferred Stock	$0.3	$0.3	$0.3	$0.3	$0.4	$0.4	$0.4		
63	Total Liabilities	$2,723.2	$3,109.9	$3,149.4	$3,584.4	$3,959.7	$4,282.2	$3,900.4		
64										
65		(7) Sum of Shareholders' Equity Items Enter =SUM(B67:B72) and copy across								
66	Shareholders' Equity									
67	Common Stock Class A	$0.2	$0.1	$0.1	$0.1	$0.2	$0.2	$0.2		
68	Common Stock Class B	$2.6	$2.7	$2.7	$2.7	$2.6	$2.6	$2.6		
69	Capital in Excess of Stated	$589.0	$887.8	$1,182.9	$1,451.4	$650.0	$20.0	$0.0		
70	Unearned Stock Compen.	($0.6)	($5.5)	($11.4)	($4.1)	($6.4)	($6.8)	($7.2)	(8) Adjust Capital in Excess of	
71	Accum. Other Comp. Loss	($239.7)	($86.3)	$73.4	$121.7	($63.9)	($67.7)	($71.1)	Stated to keep	
72	Retained Earnings	$3,639.2	$3,982.9	$4,396.5	$4,713.4	$5,688.8	$6,698.3	$7,742.1	Debt / (Debt +	
73	Total Shareholders' Equity	$3,990.7	$4,781.7	$5,644.2	$6,285.2	$6,271.2	$6,646.6	$7,666.7	Equity) in row 77	
74									near the target	
75	Total Liab. & Share. Equity	$6,713.9	$7,891.6	$8,793.6	$9,869.6	$10,230.9	$10,928.8	$11,567.0	level, which is	
76									15% in this case	
77	Debt / (Debt + Equity)	17.3%	14.9%	11.9%	10.1%	14.3%	15.2%	7.9%	(done for you)	
78	Market Price / Share	$55.99	$71.15	$82.20	$80.31	$72.34	$78.36	$84.73		
79	External Funds Needed		$642.9	$408.3	$650.8	($626)	($369.5)	($456.7)		

FIGURE 15.13 Historical and Forecasted Income Statement Percent of Sales for Nike, Inc.

	A	B	C	D	E	F	G	H	I	J
1	CORPORATE FINANCIAL PLANNING				Full-Scale Estimation					
2	Nike, Inc.	5/31/2003	5/31/2004	5/31/2005	5/31/2006	5/31/2007	5/31/2008	5/31/2009	Ave. %	
3	Financial Plan	Actual	Actual	Actual	Actual	Forecast	Forecast	Forecast	of Sales	
80										
81	(9) (Each Income Statement item) / Sales				(11) Average of historical (actual) Percent of Sales					
82	Enter =B14/B$14 and copy to the range B86:H104				Enter =AVERAGE(B86:E86) and copy to range I86:I147					
83	Delete ranges that should be blank (B89:H89, etc.)				Delete cells that should be blank (I89, I95, etc.)					
84	(done for you)				(done for you)					
85	**Income Statement (% of Sales)**									
86	Sales	100.0%	100.0%	100.0%	100.0%	100.0%	100.0%	100.0%	100.0%	
87	Cost of Goods Sold	56.8%	55.7%	55.3%	54.8%	55.6%	55.6%	55.6%	55.6%	
88	Gross Margin	43.2%	44.3%	44.7%	45.2%	44.4%	44.4%	44.4%	44.4%	
89										
90	Selling, Gen & Adm Expenses	29.3%	30.2%	30.7%	29.9%	30.1%	30.1%	30.1%	30.1%	
91	Other Expense	0.7%	0.6%	0.2%	0.0%	0.4%	0.4%	0.4%	0.4%	
92	Accounting Change, Net	2.5%	0.0%	0.0%	0.0%	0.6%	0.6%	0.6%	0.6%	
93	Depreciation	2.3%	1.4%	0.2%	1.2%	1.3%	1.3%	1.3%	1.3%	
94	EBIT	8.4%	12.0%	13.6%	14.1%	12.0%	12.0%	12.0%	12.0%	
95										
96	Interest Expense, Net	0.4%	0.2%	0.0%	-0.2%	0.2%	0.3%	0.3%	0.1%	
97	Taxes	3.6%	4.1%	4.7%	5.0%	4.2%	4.1%	4.1%	4.4%	
98	Net Income	4.4%	7.7%	8.8%	9.3%	7.7%	7.6%	7.6%	7.6%	
99	Shares Outstanding (Millions)	4.9%	4.3%	3.8%	3.4%	3.2%	3.0%	2.9%	4.1%	
100	Earnings Per Share	0.0%	0.0%	0.0%	0.0%	0.0%	0.0%	0.0%	0.0%	
101										
102	Allocation of Net Income:	0.0%	0.0%	0.0%	0.0%	0.0%	0.0%	0.0%	0.0%	
103	Dividends	1.3%	1.5%	1.7%	1.9%	1.6%	1.7%	1.8%	1.6%	
104	Change in Equity	3.1%	6.3%	7.1%	7.4%	6.1%	6.0%	5.9%	6.0%	

FIGURE 15.14 Historical and Forecasted Balance Sheet Percent of Sales for Nike, Inc.

	A	B	C	D	E	F	G	H	I
1	**CORPORATE FINANCIAL PLANNING**				**Full-Scale Estimation**				
2	**Nike, Inc.**	5/31/2003	5/31/2004	5/31/2005	5/31/2006	5/31/2007	5/31/2008	5/31/2009	Ave. %
3	**Financial Plan**	Actual	Actual	Actual	Actual	Forecast	Forecast	Forecast	of Sales
105									
106			(10) (Each Balance Sheet Asset item) / Sales						
107	**Balance Sheet (% of Sales)**		Enter =B37/B$14 and copy to range B110:H147						
108	Assets		Delete ranges that should be blank (B117:H117, etc.)						
109	Current Assets		(done for you)						
110	Cash & Equivalents	5.9%	6.8%	10.1%	6.4%	6.9%	7.4%	7.9%	7.3%
111	Short-term Investments	0.0%	3.3%	3.2%	9.0%	3.9%	3.9%	3.9%	3.9%
112	Receivables	19.6%	17.3%	16.5%	16.0%	17.4%	17.4%	17.4%	17.4%
113	Inventories	14.2%	13.3%	13.2%	13.9%	13.6%	13.6%	13.6%	13.6%
114	Deferred Income Taxes	1.5%	1.3%	0.8%	1.4%	1.3%	1.3%	1.3%	1.3%
115	Prepaid Expenses	2.5%	3.0%	2.5%	2.5%	2.6%	2.6%	2.6%	2.6%
116	Total Current Assets	43.7%	45.0%	46.2%	49.2%	45.7%	46.2%	46.7%	46.0%
117									
118	Property, Plant & Equip., Net	15.2%	13.0%	11.7%	11.1%	12.7%	12.7%	12.7%	12.7%
119	Intangible Assets, Net	1.1%	3.0%	3.0%	2.7%	2.4%	2.4%	2.4%	2.4%
120	Goodwill	0.6%	1.1%	1.0%	0.9%	0.9%	0.9%	0.9%	0.9%
121	Deferred Inc. Taxes & Other	2.1%	2.4%	2.1%	2.1%	2.2%	2.2%	2.2%	2.2%
122	Total Assets	62.8%	64.4%	64.0%	66.0%	63.9%	64.4%	64.9%	64.3%
123									
124	Liabilities and Shareholders' Equity								
125	Current Liabilities								
126	Current Portion of L.T. Debt	1.9%	0.1%	0.0%	1.7%	0.9%	0.9%	0.9%	0.9%
127	Notes Payable	0.7%	1.2%	0.5%	0.3%	0.7%	0.7%	0.7%	0.7%
128	Accounts Payable	5.4%	6.2%	6.1%	6.4%	6.0%	6.0%	6.0%	6.0%
129	Accrued Liabilities	9.9%	8.0%	7.2%	8.6%	8.4%	8.4%	8.4%	8.4%
130	Income Taxes Payable	1.0%	1.0%	0.7%	0.6%	0.8%	0.8%	0.8%	0.8%
131	Total Current Liabilities	18.8%	16.4%	14.6%	17.5%	16.8%	16.8%	16.8%	16.8%
132									
133	Long-term Debt	5.2%	5.6%	5.0%	2.7%	4.9%	5.4%	2.1%	4.6%
134	Deferred Inc. Taxes & Other	1.5%	3.4%	3.4%	3.7%	3.0%	3.0%	3.0%	3.0%
135	Redeemable Preferred Stock	0.0%	0.0%	0.0%	0.0%	0.0%	0.0%	0.0%	0.0%
136	Total Liabilities	25.5%	25.4%	22.9%	24.0%	24.7%	25.2%	21.9%	24.4%
137									
138	Shareholders' Equity								
139	Common Stock Class A	0.0%	0.0%	0.0%	0.0%	0.0%	0.0%	0.0%	0.0%
140	Common Stock Class B	0.0%	0.0%	0.0%	0.0%	0.0%	0.0%	0.0%	0.0%
141	Capital in Excess of Stated	5.5%	7.2%	8.6%	9.7%	4.1%	0.1%	0.0%	7.8%
142	Unearned Stock Compen.	0.0%	0.0%	-0.1%	0.0%	0.0%	0.0%	0.0%	0.0%
143	Accum. Other Comp. Loss	-2.2%	-0.7%	0.5%	0.8%	-0.4%	-0.4%	-0.4%	-0.4%
144	Retained Earnings	34.0%	32.5%	32.0%	31.5%	35.6%	39.5%	43.5%	32.5%
145	Total Shareholders' Equity	37.3%	39.0%	41.1%	42.0%	39.2%	39.2%	43.0%	39.9%
146									
147	Total Liab. & Share. Equity	62.8%	64.4%	64.0%	66.0%	63.9%	64.4%	64.9%	64.3%

FIGURE 15.15 Historical and Forecasted Cash Flow Statement for Nike, Inc.

	A	B	C	D	E	F	G	H	I	J
1	CORPORATE FINANCIAL PLANNING				Full-Scale Estimation					
2	Nike, Inc.	5/31/2003	5/31/2004	5/31/2005	5/31/2006	5/31/2007	5/31/2008	5/31/2009	Ave. %	
3	Financial Plan	Actual	Actual	Actual	Actual	Forecast	Forecast	Forecast	of Sales	
149	Cash Flow Statement (Mil.$)									
150	Cash Provided (Used) By Operating Activities									
151	Net Income	$474.0	$945.6	$1,211.6	$1,392.0	$1,234.6	$1,294.3	$1,355.6		
152	Income Charges (Credits) Not Affecting Cash:									
153	Depreciation	$239.3	$252.1	$257.2	$282.0	$322.1	$341.4	$358.5		
154	Cum Effect of Acct Change	$266.1	$0.0	$0.0	$0.0	$99.5	$105.5	$110.8		
155	Deferred Income Taxes	$50.4	$19.0	$21.3	($26.0)	$24.3	$25.8	$27.0		
156	Amortization and other	$23.2	$58.3	$30.5	$8.9	$39.0	$41.3	$43.4		
157	Inc Tax Ben Exer Options	$12.5	$47.2	$63.1	$54.2	$53.0	$56.1	$58.9		
158	Changes in Certain Working Capital Components:									
159	(Inc) dec in Inventories	($102.8)	($55.9)	($103.3)	($200.3)	($140.4)	($148.8)	($156.2)		
160	(Inc) dec in Accounts Rec.	($136.3)	$82.5	($93.5)	($85.1)	($74.0)	($78.5)	($82.4)		
161	Dec (inc) in Prepd & Ot CA	$60.9	($103.5)	$71.4	($37.2)	($0.2)	($0.2)	($0.2)		
162	Inc (dec.) in Account Pay,									
163	Accr Liab., & Inc Tax Pay.	$30.1	$269.1	$112.4	$279.4	$206.6	$219.0	$229.9		
164	Cash Provided By Operations	$917.4	$1,514.4	$1,570.7	$1,667.9	$1,764.5	$1,855.9	$1,945.4		
165										
166				(12) Sum of Cash Provided By Operations items						
				Enter =SUM(B151:B163) and copy across						
167	Cash Provided (Used) By Investing Activities									
168	Purch of short-term invest	$0.0	($400.8)	($1,527.2)	($2,619.7)	($1,276.3)	($1,352.9)	($1,420.5)		
169	Matur of short-term invest	$0.0	$0.0	$1,491.9	$1,709.8	$891.8	$945.3	$992.5		
170	Additions to PP & E	($185.9)	($213.9)	($257.1)	($333.7)	($303.5)	($321.7)	($337.8)		
171	Disposals of PP & E	$14.8	$11.6	$7.2	$1.6	$11.8	$12.6	$13.2		
172	Increase in Other Assets	($46.3)	($53.4)	($39.1)	($30.3)	($54.2)	($57.5)	($60.4)		
173	Inc (dec.) in Other Liab	$1.8	($0.9)	$11.1	($4.3)	$2.5	$2.6	$2.7		
174	Acq of subs-net assets acq	$0.0	($289.1)	($47.2)	$0.0	($108.1)	($114.6)	($120.3)		
175	Cash Used By Investing Act	($215.6)	($946.5)	($360.4)	($1,276.6)	($836.1)	($886.2)	($930.5)		
176										
177				(13) Sum of Cash Provided by Investing items						
				Enter =SUM(B168:B174) and copy across						
178	Cash Provided (Used) By Financing Activities									
179	Proc from Long-term Debt	$90.4	$153.8	$0.0	$0.0	$84.0	$89.1	$93.5		
180	Reduct in Long-term Debt	($55.9)	($206.6)	($9.2)	($6.0)	($92.6)	($98.2)	($103.1)		
181	Inc (dec.) in Notes Payable	($349.8)	($0.3)	($81.7)	($18.2)	($159.6)	($169.1)	($177.6)		
182	Proc from Exer of Options	$44.2	$253.6	$226.8	$225.3	$225.6	$239.2	$251.1		
183	Repurchase of stock	($196.3)	($419.8)	($556.2)	($761.1)	($576.0)	($610.6)	($641.1)		
184	Dividends - common & pref	($137.8)	($179.2)	($236.7)	($290.9)	($256.8)	($272.2)	($285.8)		
185	Cash Used By Financing Act	($605.2)	($398.5)	($657.0)	($850.9)	($775.3)	($821.9)	($863.0)		
186										
187	Effect of Exch. Rate Chgs	($38.1)	$24.6	$6.8	$25.7	$2.6	$2.8	$2.9		
188	Net Inc (Dec.) Cash & Equiv.	$58.5	$194.0	$560.1	($433.9)	$155.8	$150.6	$154.8		
189										
190	Cash and Equiv. Beg of Year	$575.5	$634.0	$828.0	$1,300.1	$961.2	$1,110.0	$1,260.6		
191	Cash and Equiv. End of Year	$634.0	$828.0	$1,388.1	$954.2	$1,110.0	$1,260.6	$1,415.4		
192		(14) Sum of Cash Provided by Financing items			(15) Cash By Op + Cash By Invest + Cash By Financing + Exch Rate Chgs					
193		Enter =SUM(B179:B184) and copy across			Enter =B164+B175+B185+B187 and copy across					
194										

FIGURE 15.16 Historical and Forecasted Cash Flow Statement Percent of Sales for Nike, Inc.

	A	B	C	D	E	F	G	H	I
1	**CORPORATE FINANCIAL PLANNING**				**Full-Scale Estimation**				
2	Nike, Inc.	5/31/2003	5/31/2004	5/31/2005	5/31/2006	5/31/2007	5/31/2008	5/31/2009	Ave. %
3	Financial Plan	Actual	Actual	Actual	Actual	Forecast	Forecast	Forecast	of Sales
195	(16) (Each Income Statement item) / Sales				(17) Average of historical (actual) Percent of Sales				
196	Enter =B151/B$14 and copy to the range B201:H239				Enter =AVERAGE(B201:E201) and copy to range I201:I239				
197	Delete ranges that should be blank (B202:H202, etc.)				Delete cells that should be blank (I202, I208, etc.)				
198	(done for you)				(done for you)				
199	**Cash Flow Statement (% of Sales)**								
200	**Cash Provided (Used) By Operating Activities**								
201	Net Income	4.4%	7.7%	8.8%	9.3%	7.7%	7.6%	7.6%	7.6%
202	Income Charges (Credits) Not Affecting Cash:								
203	Depreciation	2.2%	2.1%	1.9%	1.9%	2.0%	2.0%	2.0%	2.0%
204	Cum Effect of Acct Change	2.5%	0.0%	0.0%	0.0%	0.6%	0.6%	0.6%	0.6%
205	Defered Income Taxes	0.5%	0.2%	0.2%	-0.2%	0.2%	0.2%	0.2%	0.2%
206	Amortization and other	0.2%	0.5%	0.2%	0.1%	0.2%	0.2%	0.2%	0.2%
207	Inc Tax Ben Exer Options	0.1%	0.4%	0.5%	0.4%	0.3%	0.3%	0.3%	0.3%
208	Changes in Certain Working Capital Components:								
209	(Inc) dec in Inventories	-1.0%	-0.5%	-0.8%	-1.3%	-0.9%	-0.9%	-0.9%	-0.9%
210	(Inc) dec in Accounts Rec.	-1.3%	0.7%	-0.7%	-0.6%	-0.5%	-0.5%	-0.5%	-0.5%
211	Dec (inc) in Prepd & Ot CA	0.6%	-0.8%	0.5%	-0.2%	0.0%	0.0%	0.0%	0.0%
212	Inc (dec.) in Account Pay,	0.0%	0.0%	0.0%	0.0%	0.0%	0.0%	0.0%	0.0%
213	Accr Liab., & Inc Tax Pay.	0.3%	2.2%	0.8%	1.9%	1.3%	1.3%	1.3%	1.3%
214	Cash Provided By Operations	8.6%	12.4%	11.4%	11.2%	11.0%	10.9%	10.9%	10.9%
215									
216	**Cash Provided (Used) By Investing Activities**								
217	Purch of short-term invest	0.0%	-3.3%	-11.1%	-17.5%	-8.0%	-8.0%	-8.0%	-8.0%
218	Matur of short-term invest	0.0%	0.0%	10.9%	11.4%	5.6%	5.6%	5.6%	5.6%
219	Additions to PP & E	-1.7%	-1.7%	-1.9%	-2.2%	-1.9%	-1.9%	-1.9%	-1.9%
220	Disposals of PP & E	0.1%	0.1%	0.1%	0.0%	0.1%	0.1%	0.1%	0.1%
221	Increase in Other Assets	-0.4%	-0.4%	-0.3%	-0.2%	-0.3%	-0.3%	-0.3%	-0.3%
222	Inc (dec.) in Other Liab	0.0%	0.0%	0.1%	0.0%	0.0%	0.0%	0.0%	0.0%
223	Acq of subs-net assets acq	0.0%	-2.4%	-0.3%	0.0%	-0.7%	-0.7%	-0.7%	-0.7%
224	Cash Used By Investing Act	-2.0%	-7.7%	-2.6%	-8.5%	-5.2%	-5.2%	-5.2%	-5.2%
225									
226	**Cash Provided (Used) By Financing Activities**								
227	Proc from Long-term Debt	0.8%	1.3%	0.0%	0.0%	0.5%	0.5%	0.5%	0.5%
228	Reduct in Long-term Debt	-0.5%	-1.7%	-0.1%	0.0%	-0.6%	-0.6%	-0.6%	-0.6%
229	Inc (dec.) in Notes Payable	-3.3%	0.0%	-0.6%	-0.1%	-1.0%	-1.0%	-1.0%	-1.0%
230	Proc from Exer of Options	0.4%	2.1%	1.7%	1.5%	1.4%	1.4%	1.4%	1.4%
231	Repurchase of stock	-1.8%	-3.4%	-4.0%	-5.1%	-3.6%	-3.6%	-3.6%	-3.6%
232	Dividends - common & pref	-1.3%	-1.5%	-1.7%	-1.9%	-1.6%	-1.6%	-1.6%	-1.6%
233	Cash Used By Financing Act	-5.7%	-3.3%	-4.8%	-5.7%	-4.8%	-4.8%	-4.8%	-4.8%
234									
235	Effect of Exch. Rate Chgs	-0.4%	0.2%	0.0%	0.2%	0.0%	0.0%	0.0%	0.0%
236	Net Inc (Dec.) Cash & Equiv.	0.5%	1.6%	4.1%	-2.9%	1.0%	0.9%	0.9%	0.8%
237									
238	Cash and Equiv. Beg of Year	5.4%	5.2%	6.0%	9.3%	6.0%	6.5%	7.1%	6.5%
239	Cash and Equiv. End of Year	5.9%	6.8%	10.1%	6.4%	6.9%	7.4%	7.9%	7.3%

FIGURE 15.17 Historical and Forecasted Financial Ratios for Nike, Inc.

	A	B	C	D	E	F	G	H	I
1	CORPORATE FINANCIAL PLANNING				Full-Scale Estimation				
2	Nike, Inc.	5/31/2003	5/31/2004	5/31/2005	5/31/2006	5/31/2007	5/31/2008	5/31/2009	Ave. %
3	Financial Plan	Actual	Actual	Actual	Actual	Forecast	Forecast	Forecast	of Sales
240									
241	**Financial Ratios**	(18) (Current Portion of L.T. Debt + Notes Payable + Long-term Debt) / (Total Assets)							
242	Profitability	Enter =(B53+B54+B60)/B49 and copy across							
243	Return On Sales (ROS)	8.4%	12.0%	13.6%	14.1%	12.0%	12.0%	12.0%	
244	Return On Assets (ROA)		20.2%	22.4%	22.6%	19.1%	19.3%	19.0%	
245	Return On Equity (ROE)		21.6%	23.2%	23.3%	19.7%	20.0%	18.9%	
246									
247	**Asset Turnover**								
248	Receivables Turnover		5.8	6.3	6.4	6.2	5.9	5.9	
249	Inventory Turnover		4.3	4.4	4.2	4.2	4.2	4.2	
250	Asset Turnover		1.7	1.6	1.6	1.6	1.6	1.6	
251									
252	**Financial Leverage**								
253	Debt	12.4%	10.6%	8.7%	7.2%	10.2%	10.9%	5.7%	
254	Times Interest Earned	21.0	59.0	388.5	-57.2	78.4	42.3	38.4	
255									
256	**Liquidity**								
257	Current	232.2%	274.4%	317.7%	280.5%	271.4%	274.4%	277.4%	
258	Quick	135.7%	146.7%	182.6%	127.7%	144.3%	147.3%	150.3%	
259									
260	**Market Value**								
261	Price to Earnings	62.3	39.6	35.4	29.5	30.00	31.00	32.00	
262	Market to Book	739.7%	783.0%	760.5%	654.2%	590.6%	603.7%	565.8%	

The percentage of sales method does a good job for most purposes. Additional refinements would increase accuracy of the forecast. For example, some items may be better projected as a trend, rather than an average. Other items, such as the Accounting Change, may have unique patterns. The bottom line of this forecast is steady growth in Earnings Per Share from $2.41 to $2.53 to $2.65.

Problems

1. Given historical financial statements for **Global Impact P2P** on the **Problems** tab, forecast their financial statements for the next three years. Then explore the company's needs for additional financing as expressed by the following *choice variables*: debt and equity (paid-in capital under shareholder's equity).

2. Given historical and forecasted Income Statements and Balance Sheets for **Global Impact P2P**, create the historical and forecasted Cash Flow Statement.

3. Given historical and forecasted financial statements for **Global Impact P2P**, create the historical and forecasted financial ratios.

4. Select a company with publically traded stock. Locate the historical 10K financial statements for that company over the past few years. Forecast your company's financial statements over the next three years.

FIGURE 15.18 Historical Assumptions and Income Statement for Global Impact P2P

	A	B	C	D	E	F
1	CORPORATE FINANCIAL PLANNING				Problems	
2	**Global Impact P2P**	2003	2004	2005	2006	
3	**Financial Plan**	Actual	Actual	Actual	Actual	
4	**Key Assumptions**					
5	Sales Growth Rate			21.4%	19.3%	
6	Tax Rate	40.5%	38.8%	38.2%	36.0%	
7	Int Rate on Short-Term Debt	6.3%	6.3%	6.4%	6.5%	
8	Int Rate on Long-Term Debt	7.4%	7.4%	7.5%	7.6%	
9	Dividend Payout Rate	26.1%	25.9%	26.8%	24.4%	
10	Price / Earnings	8.6	8.4	8.7	9.3	
11						
33	**Income Statement (Mil.$)**					
34	Sales	$185.76	$194.29	$235.84	$281.38	
35	Cost of Goods Sold	$109.81	$112.25	$138.97	$171.57	
36	Gross Margin	$75.95	$82.04	$96.87	$109.81	
37						
38	Selling, Gen & Adm Expenses	$12.73	$13.54	$16.87	$19.94	
39	Depreciation	$11.66	$12.39	$14.58	$18.37	
40	EBIT	$51.56	$56.11	$65.42	$71.50	
41						
42	Interest Expense	$14.23	$15.69	$23.88	$24.55	
43	Taxes	$15.12	$15.68	$15.87	$16.92	
44	Net Income	$22.21	$24.74	$25.67	$30.03	
45	Shares Outstanding (Millions)	2.03	2.10	2.15	2.44	
46	Earnings Per Share	$10.94	$11.78	$11.94	$12.31	
47						
48	Allocation of Net Income:					
49	Dividends	$5.80	$6.41	$6.87	$7.33	
50	Change in Equity	$16.41	$18.33	$18.80	$22.70	

FIGURE 15.19 Historical Balance Sheet for Global Impact P2P

	A	B	C	D	E	F
1	**CORPORATE FINANCIAL PLANNING**				**Problems**	
2	**Global Impact P2P**	2003	2004	2005	2006	
3	**Financial Plan**	Actual	Actual	Actual	Actual	
67						
68	**Balance Sheet (Mil.$)**					
69	**Assets**					
70	Current Assets					
71	Cash & Equivalents	$8.56	$13.97	$15.34	$17.75	
72	Receivables	$41.63	$49.52	$57.37	$68.91	
73	Inventories	$52.11	$60.94	$73.49	$86.32	
74	Total Current Assets	$102.30	$124.43	$146.20	$172.98	
75						
76	Property, Plant & Equip. (PPE	$663.29	$846.39	$910.34	$958.31	
77	Accumulated Depreciation	$189.20	$201.59	$216.17	$234.54	
78	Net PPE	$474.09	$644.80	$694.17	$723.77	
79						
80	Total Assets	$576.39	$769.23	$840.37	$896.75	
81						
82	**Liabilities and Shareholders' Equity**					
83	Current Liabilities					
84	Accounts Payable	$62.46	$90.48	$134.32	$174.57	
85	Short-term Debt	$202.12	$307.87	$304.96	$312.85	
86	Total Current Liabilities	$264.58	$398.35	$439.28	$487.42	
87						
88	Long-term Debt	$40.00	$55.74	$62.15	$17.69	
89	Total Liabilities	$304.58	$454.09	$501.43	$505.11	
90						
91	Shareholders' Equity					
92	Paid-in Capital	$180.00	$205.00	$210.00	$240.00	
93	Retained Earnings	$91.81	$110.14	$128.94	$151.64	
94	Total Shareholders' Equity	$271.81	$315.14	$338.94	$391.64	
95						
96	Total Liab. & Share. Equity	$576.39	$769.23	$840.37	$896.75	
97						
98	Debt / (Debt + Equity)	47.1%	53.6%	52.0%	45.8%	
99	Market Price / Share	$94.58	$99.12	$103.47	$114.95	
100	External Funds Needed		$146.49	$8.50	($6.57)	

Chapter 16 Du Pont System Of Ratio Analysis

16.1 Basics

Problem. A company's Net Profit is $170, Pretax Profit is $260, EBIT is $470, Sales is $4,600, Assets is $4,200, and Equity is $4,300. Calculate the company's ROE and decompose the ROE into its components using the Du Pont System.

FIGURE 16.1   Excel Model of Du Pont System of Ratio Analysis - Basics.

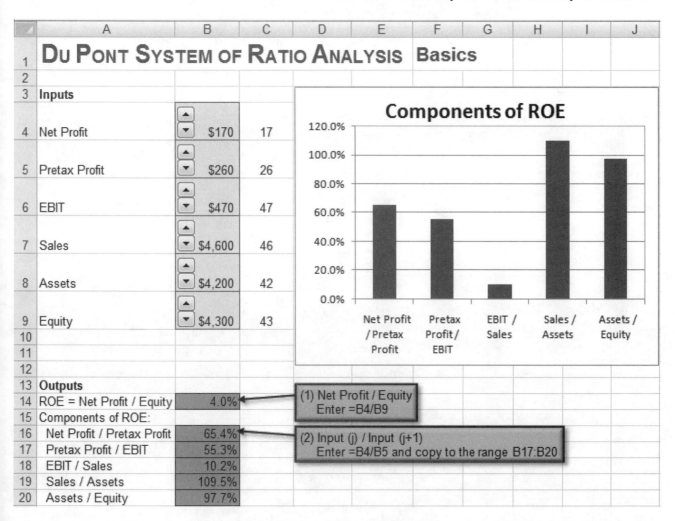

The ROE = 4.0%. The decomposition helps us see where this comes from. Here is an intuitive interpretation of the components:

- Net Profit / Pretax = 65.4% is a tax-burden ratio.
- Pretax Profits / EBIT = 55.3% is an interest-burden ratio.
- EBIT / Sales = 10.2% is the profit margin.
- Sales / Assets = 109.5% is the asset turnover.
- Asset / Equity = 97.7% is the leverage ratio.

Problems

1. A company's Net Profit is $82, Pretax Profit is $153, EBIT is $583, Sales is $3,740, Assets is $5,460, and Equity is $7,230. Calculate the company's ROE and decompose the ROE into its components using the Du Pont System.

2. A company's Net Profit is $265, Pretax Profit is $832, EBIT is $1,045, Sales is $5,680, Assets is $7,620, and Equity is $9,730. Calculate the company's ROE and decompose the ROE into its components using the Du Pont System.

Chapter 17 Life-Cycle Financial Planning

17.1 Basics

Problem. Suppose that you are currently 30 years old and expect to earn a constant real salary of $80,000 starting next year. You are planning to retire at age 70. You currently have $0 in financial capital. You are limited to investing in the riskfree asset. The real riskfree rate is 2.8%. Develop a financial plan for real savings and real consumption over your lifetime.

Solution Strategy. Develop a financial plan on a year-by-year basis over an entire lifetime. During your working years, divide your salary each year between current consumption and savings to provide for consumption during your retirement years. Put savings in a retirement fund that is invested at the riskfree rate. During your retirement years, your salary is zero, but you are able to consume each year by withdrawing money from your retirement fund. Calculate a constant level of real consumption that can be sustained in both working years and retirement years. Since there is substantial uncertainty about how long you will actually live and since it's not a good idea to run out of money, calculate real consumption based on infinite annuity. This level of real consumption can be sustained indefinitely. Finally, analyze human capital, financial capital, and total wealth over your lifetime.

Life Expectancy. How long will you live? For the US in 2004, the average age of death ("life expectancy at birth") was 78. Also in 2004, the average age of death by those 65 or older ("life expectancy at 65") was 84. Life expectancy at birth and at age 65 have both increased by approximately 1 year over the prior 5 years due to medical and health progress. By simply extrapolating this trend into the future, the next 60 years would add 12 years to life expectancy. So life expectancy at birth would rise to 90 and life expectancy at 65 would rise to 96. So averaging between those two figures, today's typical 30 year old might expect to live to 93. This is a very conservative forecast in the sense that medical and health progress is likely to accelerate, rather than just maintain the current rate of improvement.

To determine your individual life expectancy, add to (or subtract from) 93 based on your individual health-conscious practices. Not smoking adds nine years. Aerobic exercising and getting seven to eight hours of sleep per night adds three years. A healthy diet and maintaining a desirable weight based on your height adds three years. A thorough annual medical exam to catch cancer and other health problems early adds two years. The following six items add one year each: (1) daily aspirin to reduce fatal heart attacks, (2) preventing high blood pressure, (3) avoiding accidents, (4) getting immunized against pneumonia and influenza, (5) avoiding suicide and AIDS, and (6) avoiding heavy alcohol consumption. For more information on the factors effecting longevity and the long-run impact of scientific and medical progress, visit George Webster's web site at: www.george-webster.com.

FIGURE 17.1 Excel Model of Life-Cycle Financial Planning - Basics.

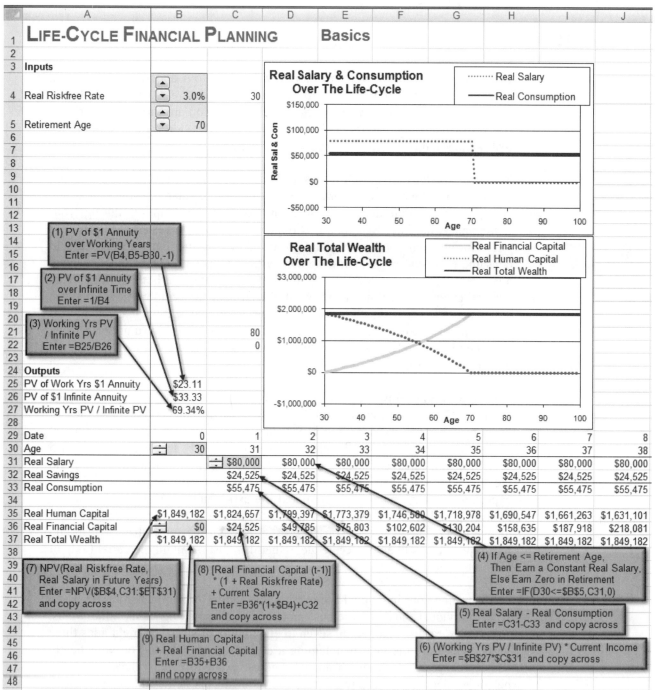

FIGURE 17.2 Transition from Working Years to Retirement Years.

	A	AN	AO	AP	AQ	AR
29	Date	38	39	40	41	42
30	Age	68	69	70	71	72
31	Real Salary	$80,000	$80,000	$80,000	$0	$0
32	Real Savings	$24,525	$24,525	$24,525	-$55,475	-$55,475
33	Real Consumption	$55,475	$55,475	$55,475	$55,475	$55,475
34						
35	Real Human Capital	$153,078	$77,670	$0	$0	$0
36	Real Financial Capital	$1,696,104	$1,771,512	$1,849,182	$1,849,182	$1,849,182
37	Real Total Wealth	$1,849,182	$1,849,182	$1,849,182	$1,849,182	$1,849,182

From the first graph, we see that your Real Salary from working years only is used to support a constant level of Real Consumption over an "infinite" lifetime. By using this approach, the same level of Real Consumption can be sustained even if you end up living much longer than originally anticipated. From the second graph, we see that Real Total Wealth is constant over a lifetime. At date 0, Real Total Wealth comes entirely from Real Human Capital, which is the present value of all future Real Salary. Over time Real Human Capital declines and Real Financial Capital builds up. After retirement, Real Total Wealth comes entirely from Real Financial Capital.

17.2 Full-Scale Estimation

Problem. Suppose that you are currently 30 years old and expect to earn a constant real salary of $80,000 starting next year. You are planning to retire at age 70. You currently have $0 in financial capital. You can invest in the riskfree asset or a broad stock portfolio. The inflation rate is 2.1% and the real riskfree rate is 2.8%. A broad stock portfolio offers an average real return of 6.0% and a standard deviation of 17.0%. Suppose that federal income taxes have six brackets with the following rates: 10.0%, 15.0%, 25.0%, 28.0%, 33.0%, and 35.0%. For current year, the upper cutoffs on the first five brackets are $7,550, $30,650, $74,200, $154,800, and $336,550 and these cutoffs are indexed to inflation. The state tax rate is 3.0%, federal FICA-SSI tax rate on salary up to $97,500 is 6.2%, and the federal FICA-Medicare tax rate on any level of salary is 1.45%. The current level of social security benefits is $34,368 per year and this is indexed to inflation. Develop a financial plan for real savings and real consumption over your lifetime.

Solution Strategy. The full-scale Excel model of life-cycle financial planning adds consideration of inflation, taxes, social security, and the opportunity to invest in a broad stock index. It is assumed that your savings are put in a tax-deferred retirement fund. You pay zero taxes on contributions to the retirement fund during your working years. But you have to pay taxes on withdrawals from the retirement fund during your retirement years. This Excel model includes several *choice variables*. You need to choose your Real Growth Rate in Salary. You need to choose your Taxable Income / Total Wealth. Specifying taxable income as a percentage of total wealth indirectly determines your consumption and savings as a percentage of total wealth. You also need to choose your Asset Allocation: Stock Portfolio %, that is, what percentage of your savings to invest in the broad stock portfolio. Investing in the broad stock portfolio will give you higher average returns than the riskfree asset, but also more risk. The balance of your savings will be invested in the riskfree asset and will grow at the riskfree rate.

FIGURE 17.3 Excel Model of Life-Cycle Fin Plan – Full-Scale Estimation.

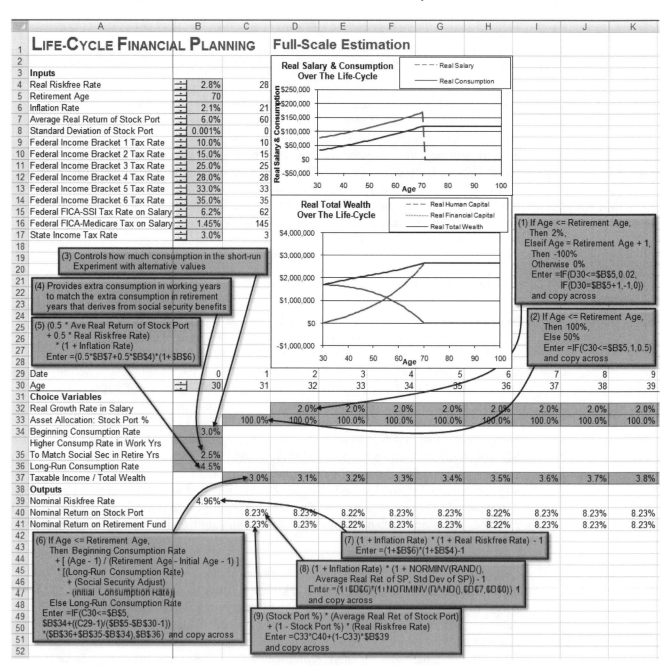

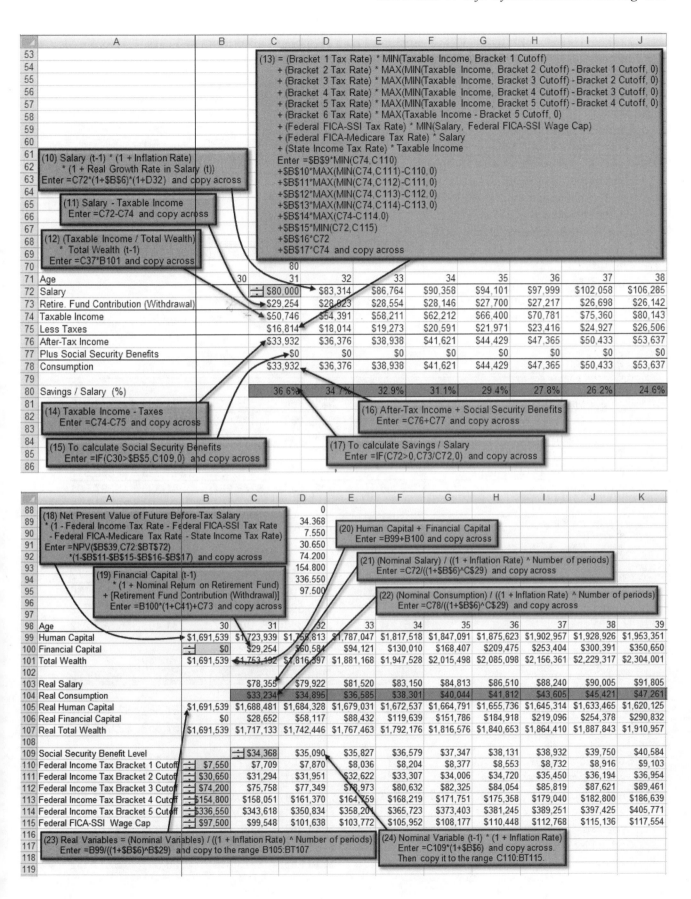

	A	B	C	D	E	F	G	H	I	J
53			(13) = (Bracket 1 Tax Rate) * MIN(Taxable Income, Bracket 1 Cutoff)							
54			+ (Bracket 2 Tax Rate) * MAX(MIN(Taxable Income, Bracket 2 Cutoff) - Bracket 1 Cutoff, 0)							
55			+ (Bracket 3 Tax Rate) * MAX(MIN(Taxable Income, Bracket 3 Cutoff) - Bracket 2 Cutoff, 0)							
56			+ (Bracket 4 Tax Rate) * MAX(MIN(Taxable Income, Bracket 4 Cutoff) - Bracket 3 Cutoff, 0)							
57			+ (Bracket 5 Tax Rate) * MAX(MIN(Taxable Income, Bracket 5 Cutoff) - Bracket 4 Cutoff, 0)							
58			+ (Bracket 6 Tax Rate) * MAX(Taxable Income - Bracket 5 Cutoff, 0)							
59			+ (Federal FICA-SSI Tax Rate) * MIN(Salary, Federal FICA-SSI Wage Cap)							
60			+ (Federal FICA-Medicare Tax Rate) * Salary							
61	(10) Salary (t-1) * (1 + Inflation Rate)		+ (State Income Tax Rate) * Taxable Income							
62	* (1 + Real Growth Rate in Salary (t))		Enter =$B$9*MIN(C74,C110)							
63	Enter =C72*(1+$B$6)*(1+D32) and copy across		+$B$10*MAX(MIN(C74,C111)-C110,0)							
64			+$B$11*MAX(MIN(C74,C112)-C111,0)							
65	(11) Salary - Taxable Income		+$B$12*MAX(MIN(C74,C113)-C112,0)							
66	Enter =C72-C74 and copy across		+$B$13*MAX(MIN(C74,C114)-C113,0)							
67			+$B$14*MAX(C74-C114,0)							
68	(12) (Taxable Income / Total Wealth)		+$B$15*MIN(C72,C115)							
69	* Total Wealth (t-1)		+$B$16*C72							
70	Enter =C37*B101 and copy across		+$B$17*C74 and copy across	80						
71	Age	30	31	32	33	34	35	36	37	38
72	Salary		$80,000	$83,314	$86,764	$90,358	$94,101	$97,999	$102,058	$106,285
73	Retire. Fund Contribution (Withdrawal)		$29,254	$28,823	$28,554	$28,146	$27,700	$27,217	$26,698	$26,142
74	Taxable Income		$50,746	$54,391	$58,211	$62,212	$66,400	$70,781	$75,360	$80,143
75	Less Taxes		$16,814	$18,014	$19,273	$20,591	$21,971	$23,416	$24,927	$26,506
76	After-Tax Income		$33,932	$36,376	$38,938	$41,621	$44,429	$47,365	$50,433	$53,637
77	Plus Social Security Benefits		$0	$0	$0	$0	$0	$0	$0	$0
78	Consumption		$33,932	$36,376	$38,938	$41,621	$44,429	$47,365	$50,433	$53,637
79										
80	Savings / Salary (%)		36.6%	34.7%	32.9%	31.1%	29.4%	27.8%	26.2%	24.6%
81										
82	(14) Taxable Income - Taxes				(16) After-Tax Income + Social Security Benefits					
83	Enter =C74-C75 and copy across				Enter =C76+C77 and copy across					
84										
85	(15) To calculate Social Security Benefits			(17) To calculate Savings / Salary						
86	Enter =IF(C30>$B$5,C109,0) and copy across			Enter =IF(C72>0,C73/C72,0) and copy across						

	A	B	C	D	E	F	G	H	I	J	K
88	(18) Net Present Value of Future Before-Tax Salary			0							
89	* (1 - Federal Income Tax Rate - Federal FICA-SSI Tax Rate			34.368		(20) Human Capital + Financial Capital					
90	- Federal FICA-Medicare Tax Rate - State Income Tax Rate)			7.550		Enter =B99+B100 and copy across					
91	Enter =NPV($B$39,C72:$BT$72)			30.650							
92	*(1-$B$11-$B$15-$B$16-$B$17) and copy across			74.200		(21) (Nominal Salary) / ((1 + Inflation Rate) ^ Number of periods)					
93				154.800		Enter =C72/((1+$B$6)^C$29) and copy across					
94	(19) Financial Capital (t-1)			336.550							
95	* (1 + Nominal Return on Retirement Fund)			97.500		(22) (Nominal Consumption) / ((1 + Inflation Rate) ^ Number of periods)					
96	+ [Retirement Fund Contribution (Withdrawal)]					Enter =C78/((1+$B$6)^C$29) and copy across					
97	Enter =B100*(1+C41)+C73 and copy across										
98	Age		30	31	32	33	34	35	36	37	38	39
99	Human Capital		$1,691,539	$1,723,939	$1,755,813	$1,787,047	$1,817,518	$1,847,091	$1,875,623	$1,902,957	$1,928,926	$1,953,351
100	Financial Capital		$0	$29,254	$60,584	$94,121	$130,010	$168,407	$209,475	$253,404	$300,391	$350,650
101	Total Wealth		$1,691,539	$1,753,192	$1,816,397	$1,881,168	$1,947,528	$2,015,498	$2,085,098	$2,156,361	$2,229,317	$2,304,001
102												
103	Real Salary			$78,355	$79,922	$81,520	$83,150	$84,813	$86,510	$88,240	$90,005	$91,805
104	Real Consumption			$33,234	$34,895	$36,585	$38,301	$40,044	$41,812	$43,605	$45,421	$47,261
105	Real Human Capital		$1,691,539	$1,688,481	$1,684,328	$1,679,031	$1,672,537	$1,664,791	$1,655,736	$1,645,314	$1,633,465	$1,620,125
106	Real Financial Capital		$0	$28,652	$58,117	$88,432	$119,639	$151,786	$184,918	$219,096	$254,378	$290,832
107	Real Total Wealth		$1,691,539	$1,717,133	$1,742,446	$1,767,463	$1,792,176	$1,816,576	$1,840,653	$1,864,410	$1,887,843	$1,910,957
108												
109	Social Security Benefit Level		$34,368	$35,090	$35,827	$36,579	$37,347	$38,131	$38,932	$39,750	$40,584
110	Federal Income Tax Bracket 1 Cutoff	$7,550	$7,709	$7,870	$8,036	$8,204	$8,377	$8,553	$8,732	$8,916	$9,103
111	Federal Income Tax Bracket 2 Cutoff	$30,650	$31,294	$31,951	$32,622	$33,307	$34,006	$34,720	$35,450	$36,194	$36,954
112	Federal Income Tax Bracket 3 Cutoff	$74,200	$75,758	$77,349	$78,973	$80,632	$82,325	$84,054	$85,819	$87,621	$89,461
113	Federal Income Tax Bracket 4 Cutoff	$154,800	$158,051	$161,370	$164,759	$168,219	$171,751	$175,358	$179,040	$182,800	$186,639
114	Federal Income Tax Bracket 5 Cutoff	$336,550	$343,618	$350,834	$358,201	$365,723	$373,403	$381,245	$389,251	$397,425	$405,771
115	Federal FICA-SSI Wage Cap	$97,500	$99,548	$101,638	$103,772	$105,952	$108,177	$110,448	$112,768	$115,136	$117,554
116	(23) Real Variables = (Nominal Variables) / ((1 + Inflation Rate) ^ Number of periods)				(24) Nominal Variable (t-1) * (1 + Inflation Rate)						
117	Enter =B99/((1+$B$6)^B29) and copy to the range B105:BT107				Enter =C109*(1+$B$6) and copy across.						
118						Then copy it to the range C110:BT115.						
119												

FIGURE 17.5 Transition From Working To Retirement Years.

A	AN	AO	AP	AQ	AR
29 Date	38	39	40	41	42
30 Age	68	69	70	71	72
31 **Choice Variables**					
32 Real Growth Rate in Salary	2.0%	2.0%	2.0%	-100.0%	0.0%
33 Asset Allocation: Stock Port %	100.0%	100.0%	100.0%	50.0%	50.0%
34 Beginning Consumption Rate					
35 Higher Consump Rate in Work Yrs To Match Social Sec in Retire Yrs					
36 Long-Run Consumption Rate					
37 Taxable Income / Total Wealth	6.8%	6.9%	7.0%	4.5%	4.5%
38 **Outputs**					
39 Nominal Riskfree Rate					
40 Nominal Return on Stock Port	8.23%	8.23%	8.23%	8.23%	8.22%
41 Nominal Return on Retirement Fund	8.23%	8.23%	8.23%	6.59%	6.59%
42					
70					
71 Age	68	69	70	71	72
72 Salary	$359,128	$374,003	$389,494	$0	$0
73 Retire. Fund Contribution (Withdrawl)	-$15,466	-$19,060	-$23,015	-$274,181	-$279,940
74 Taxable Income	$374,594	$393,063	$412,509	$274,181	$279,940
75 Less Taxes	$123,841	$130,364	$137,242	$71,706	$73,212
76 After-Tax Income	$250,753	$262,698	$275,267	$202,475	$206,727
77 Plus Social Security Benefits	$0	$0	$0	$78,919	$80,577
78 Consumption	$250,753	$262,698	$275,267	$281,395	$287,304
79					
80 Savings / Salary (%)	-4.3%	-5.1%	-5.9%	0.0%	0.0%
81					
97					
98 Age	68	69	70	71	72
99 Human Capital	$456,816	$238,798	$0	$0	$0
100 Financial Capital	$5,247,985	$5,660,592	$6,103,227	$6,231,408	$6,362,232
101 Total Wealth	$5,704,801	$5,899,390	$6,103,227	$6,231,408	$6,362,232
102					
103 Real Salary	$163,031	$166,292	$169,618	$0	$0
104 Real Consumption	$113,833	$116,803	$119,874	$120,022	$120,022
105 Real Human Capital	$207,378	$106,176	$0	$0	$0
106 Real Financial Capital	$2,382,398	$2,516,853	$2,657,846	$2,657,852	$2,657,837
107 Real Total Wealth	$2,589,777	$2,623,029	$2,657,846	$2,657,852	$2,657,837
108					
109 Social Security Benefit Level	$74,149	$75,706	$77,296	$78,919	$80,577
110 Federal Income Tax Bracket 1 Cutoff	$16,631	$16,981	$17,337	$17,701	$18,073
111 Federal Income Tax Bracket 2 Cutoff	$67,516	$68,934	$70,382	$71,860	$73,369
112 Federal Income Tax Bracket 3 Cutoff	$163,449	$166,881	$170,386	$173,964	$177,617
113 Federal Income Tax Bracket 4 Cutoff	$340,996	$348,157	$355,468	$362,933	$370,555
114 Federal Income Tax Bracket 5 Cutoff	$741,358	$756,926	$772,822	$789,051	$805,621
115 Federal FICA-SSI Wage Cap	$214,775	$219,285	$223,890	$228,591	$233,392

As you adapt this model to your own situation, it is not necessary to go from full-time work to zero work. You could consider retiring to part-time work and then gradually tapering off. For example, you could drop to half-time work by setting your Real Growth in Salary to **-50%** in your first retirement year and then set your Real Growth in Salary to **-100.0%** in the year that you stop working entirely.

It is assumed that the Real Return on Broad Stock Portfolio is normally distributed with the average return given in cell **B7** and the standard deviation given in cell **B8**. The Excel function **RAND()** generates a random variable with a uniform distribution over the interval from 0 to 1 (that is, with an equal chance of getting any number between 0 and 1). To transform this uniformly distributed random variable into a normally distributed one, just place **RAND()** inside the Excel function **NORMINV**.[4]

The Human Capital computation make a fairly rough adjustment for taxes, but the year-by-year cash flow analysis has a more sophisticated calculation of taxes. The reason for doing it this way (as opposed to present valuing the After-Tax Income row) is that this approach avoids generating circular references

It doesn't make any sense to live like a king in your working years and the live in poverty in your retirement years. Similarly, it doesn't make sense to live in poverty in your working years and live like a king in your retirement years. The key idea is that you want to have a smooth pattern of real consumption over the life-cycle. Setting Taxable Income as a percentage of Total Wealth does a good job of delivering a smooth pattern. The only tricky part is when social security kicks in. Looking at the graph of Real Consumption, you should see a smooth pattern with no jump up or down at your retirement date. Notice that Taxable Income / Total Wealth is 7.0% in cell **AP37** and 4.5% the next year in cell **AQ37**, which is an adjustment of 2.5%. In other words, the drop in Taxable Income is offset by addition of Social Security Benefits (which are NOT taxable). Notice that Real Consumption transitions smoothly from $119,874 in cell **AP104** to $120,022 in cell **AQ104**. The Higher Consumption in Working Years of 2.5% in cell **B35** works well for the default input values of this Excel model. When you change input values, you may need to change the adjustment. Manually adjust the value in cell **B35** in small increments until the graph of Real Consumption shows a smooth pattern with no jump at the retirement date.

Since the standard deviation (risk) in cell **B8** is virtually zero, the results we see in the two graphs are based on *average returns*. Starting with the second graph, we see that Real Human Capital starts at $1.7 million and declines smoothly to $0 at retirement. Real Financial Capital starts at $0, rises smoothly to $2.7

---

[4] The "Transformation Method" for converting a uniform random variable x into some other random variable y based on a cumulative distribution F is $y(x) = F^{-1}(x)$. See Press, W., B. Flannery, S. Teukolsky, and W. Vetterling, 1987, Numerical Recopies: The Art of Scientific Computing, Cambridge University Press, chapter on Random Numbers, subsection on the Transformation Method, page 201.

million at retirement, and then stays constant at that level. Turning to the first graph, Real Consumption starts at $33,234, rises smoothly to $120,022 at retirement, and then stays constant at that level.

How much saving does it take to reach such a comfortable lifestyle? Savings starts at 36.6% of salary at age 31 and gradually tapers off. Clearly, a lot of saving is required to live so well in retirement.

Now let's consider the risk involved. Change the standard deviation to a realistic figure. Enter **17.000%** in cell **B8**. The random variables in rows **40** and **41** spring to life and the graph of real consumption over the life-cycle reflect the high or low realizations of the broad stock portfolio. Press the function key **F9** and the Excel model is recalculated. You see a new realization of real consumption on the first graph. The three figures below show: (a) a low real consumption case due to low stock returns, (b) a medium real consumption case due to medium stock returns, and (c) a high real consumption case due to high stock returns.

FIGURE 17.6 Low Real Consumption Due To Low Stock Returns.

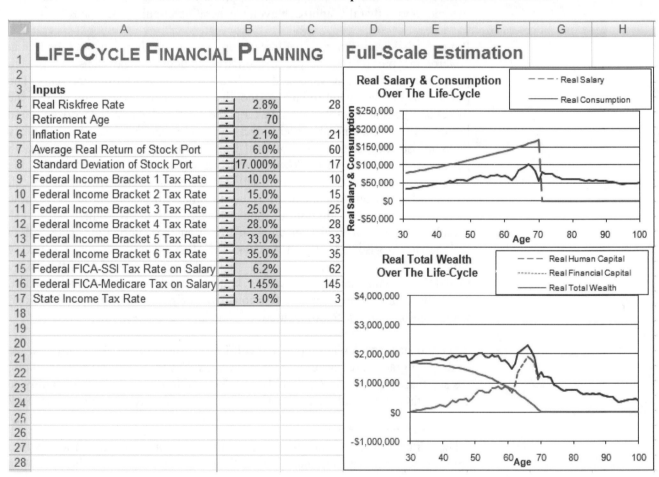

FIGURE 17.7 Medium Real Consumption Due To Medium Stock Returns.

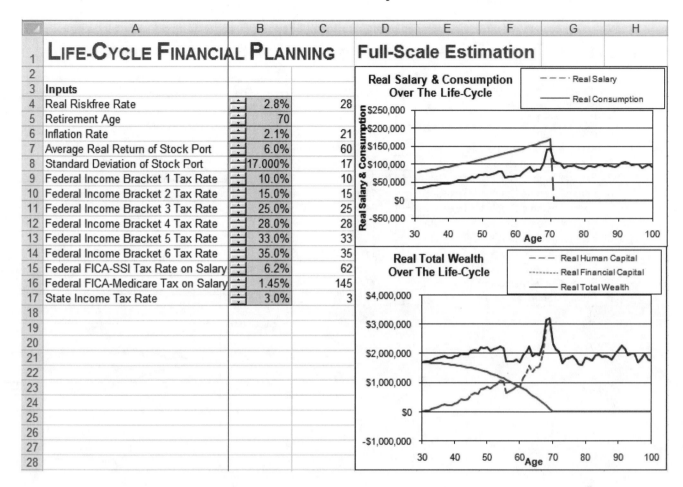

FIGURE 17.8 High Real Consumption Due To High Stock Returns.

	A	B	C	D	E	F	G	H
1	LIFE-CYCLE FINANCIAL PLANNING			Full-Scale Estimation				
2								
3	Inputs							
4	Real Riskfree Rate	2.8%	28					
5	Retirement Age	70						
6	Inflation Rate	2.1%	21					
7	Average Real Return of Stock Port	6.0%	60					
8	Standard Deviation of Stock Port	17.000%	17					
9	Federal Income Bracket 1 Tax Rate	10.0%	10					
10	Federal Income Bracket 2 Tax Rate	15.0%	15					
11	Federal Income Bracket 3 Tax Rate	25.0%	25					
12	Federal Income Bracket 4 Tax Rate	28.0%	28					
13	Federal Income Bracket 5 Tax Rate	33.0%	33					
14	Federal Income Bracket 6 Tax Rate	35.0%	35					
15	Federal FICA-SSI Tax Rate on Salary	6.2%	62					
16	Federal FICA-Medicare Tax on Salary	1.45%	145					
17	State Income Tax Rate	3.0%	3					
18								
19								
20								
21								
22								
23								
24								
25								
26								
27								
28								

These three graphs are "representative" of the risk you face from being heavily investing in the broad stock portfolio. In the low case, real consumption drops to about $50,000. In the medium case, real consumption fluctuates around $100,000. In the high case, real consumption fluctuates between $150,000 and $200,000. Clearly, there is substantial risk from being so heavily exposed to the broad stock portfolio.

Now that we have completed the Excel model, it is time for you to explore. Click on the spin buttons to change the inputs and/or edit the values of the choice variables and see the implications for lifetime real consumption and real total wealth. For example, if you are uncomfortable with the amount of risk implied by the three figures above, consider more conservative strategies. Many investors reduce stock exposure in retirement years to little or nothing.

A key driver in the model is the Beginning Consumption Rate in cell **B34**. Raise this value and there will be more real consumption in early working years and less real consumption retirement years. Lower this value and it will tilt in the opposite direction.

Play around with the choice variables and have fun exploring your lifetime opportunities. Enjoy!

Problems

1. Suppose that you are currently 28 years old and expect to earn a constant real salary of $64,000 starting next year. You are planning to work for 32 years and then retire. You currently have $0 in financial capital. You are limited to investing in the riskfree asset. The real riskfree rate is 2.8%. Develop a financial plan for real savings and real consumption over your lifetime.

2. Suppose that you are currently 32 years old and expect to earn a constant real salary of $85,000 starting next year. You are planning to work for 25 years and then retire. You currently have $10,000 in financial capital. You can invest in the riskfree asset or a broad stock portfolio. The inflation rate is 3.4% and the real riskfree rate is 2.5%. A broad stock portfolio offers an average real return of 7.3% and a standard deviation of 25.0%. Suppose that federal income taxes have six brackets with the following rates: 10.0%, 15.0%, 27.0%, 30.0%, 35.0%, and 38.6%. For current year, the upper cutoffs on the first five brackets are $6,000, $27,950, $67,700, $141,250, and $307,050 and these cutoffs are indexed to inflation. The state tax rate is 4.5%, federal FICA-SSI tax rate on salary up to $87,000 is 6.2%, and the federal FICA-Medicare tax rate on any level of salary is 1.45%. You will start receiving social security benefits at age 66. The current level of social security benefits is $24,204 per year and this is indexed to inflation. Develop a financial plan for real savings and real consumption over your lifetime.

PART 5 OPTIONS AND CORPORATE FINANCE

Chapter 18 Binomial Option Pricing

18.1 Estimating Volatility

The binomial option pricing model can certainly be used to price European calls and puts, but it can do much more. The Binomial Tree / Risk Neutral method can be extended to price *any* type of derivative security (European vs. American vs. other) on any underlying asset(s), with any underlying dividends or cash flows, with any derivative payoffs at maturity and/or payoffs before maturity. Indeed, it is one of the most popular techniques on Wall Street for pricing and hedging derivatives.

Problem. What is the annual standard deviation of Amazon.com stock based on continuous returns?

Solution Strategy. Download three months of Amazon.com's daily stock price. Then calculate continuous returns. Finally, calculate the annual standard deviation of the continuous returns.

FIGURE 18.1 Excel Model of Binomial Option Pricing - Estimating Volatility.

	A	B	C	D	E	F	G	H
1	BINOMIAL OPTION PRICING					Estimating Volatility		
2								
3		(1) Download three months of daily stock price data						
4								
5								
6	Stock:	Amazon			(2) LN[(Price on date t) / (Price on date t-1)] Enter =LN(G11/G12) and copy down			
7	Symbol:	AMZN						
8								
9								
10	Date	Open	High	Low	Close	Volume	Adjusted Close	Continuous Return
11	6/19/2007	$71.55	$71.66	$69.68	$69.81	11,871,000	$69.81	-2.85%
12	6/18/2007	$72.34	$72.64	$71.40	$71.83	7,813,600	$71.83	-0.79%
13	6/15/2007	$72.85	$72.87	$71.19	$72.40	9,833,200	$72.40	0.64%
14	6/14/2007	$70.90	$72.12	$70.80	$71.94	8,245,300	$71.94	1.47%
15	6/13/2007	$70.90	$71.89	$69.25	$70.89	11,917,900	$70.89	1.16%
16	6/12/2007	$70.44	$70.76	$69.42	$70.07	11,829,500	$70.07	-1.56%
17	6/11/2007	$73.00	$73.05	$71.00	$71.17	11,159,100	$71.17	-2.87%
18	6/8/2007	$72.47	$73.24	$71.05	$73.24	10,204,500	$73.24	1.65%
19	6/7/2007	$72.57	$74.72	$70.88	$72.04	24,138,200	$72.04	-0.35%
20	6/6/2007	$73.14	$73.75	$71.86	$72.29	15,591,000	$72.29	-1.86%
21	6/5/2007	$71.10	$74.24	$70.86	$73.65	30,442,500	$73.65	4.48%
69	3/27/2007	$38.82	$39.42	$38.76	$39.37	3,993,600	$39.37	0.92%
70	3/26/2007	$38.98	$39.05	$38.43	$39.01	3,521,100	$39.01	0.08%
71	3/23/2007	$39.56	$39.60	$38.98	$38.98	2,941,500	$38.98	-1.30%
72	3/22/2007	$39.48	$39.72	$38.91	$39.49	5,331,500	$39.49	-0.78%
73	3/21/2007	$38.55	$39.80	$38.31	$39.80	4,996,400	$39.80	3.11%
74	3/20/2007	$38.53	$38.69	$38.23	$38.58	3,801,300	$38.58	
75								
76						Standard Deviation (Daily)		3.75%
77						Standard Deviation (Annual)		71.65%
78								
79		(3) Standard Deviation of the Daily Return Series Enter =STDEV(H11:H73) and copy across						
80								
81								
82		(4) (Daily Standard Deviation) * (Square Root of Days in a Year) Enter =H76*SQRT(365) and copy across						
83								

We find that Amazon.com's annual standard deviation is 71.65%.

18.2 Single Period

Problem. At the close of trading on June 20, 2007, the stock price of Amazon.com was $69.81, the standard deviation of daily returns was 71.65%, the yield on a six-month U.S. Treasury Bill was 4.95%, the exercise price of a January 70 call on Amazon.com was $70.00, the exercise price of a January 70 put on Amazon.com was $70.00, and the time to maturity for both January 18, 2008 maturity options was 0.5777 years. What is the price of a January 70 call and a January 70 put on Amazon.com?

Solution Strategy. First, calculate the binomial tree parameters: time / period, riskfree rate / period, up movement / period, and down movement / period. Second, calculate the date 1, maturity date items: stock up price, stock down price, and the corresponding call and put payoffs. Third, calculate the shares of stock and money borrowed to create a replicating portfolio that replicates the option payoff at maturity. Finally, calculate the price now of the replicating portfolio and, in the absence of arbitrage, this will be the option price now.

FIGURE 18.2 Excel Model of Binomial Option Pricing - Single Period - Call Option.

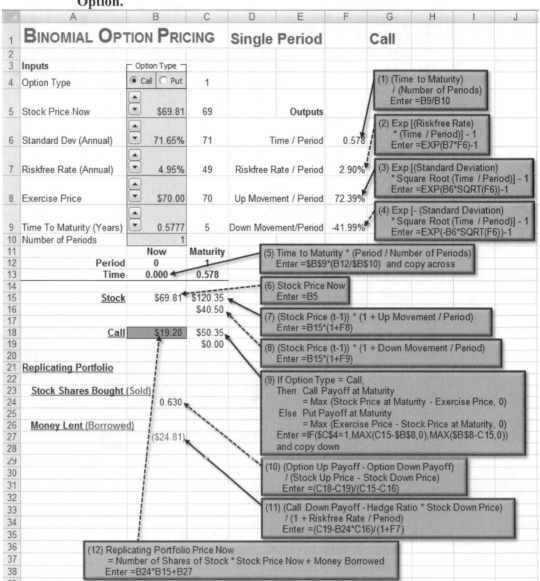

We see that the Binomial Option Pricing model predicts a one-period European call price of $19.20. Now let's check the put.

FIGURE 18.3 Excel Model of Binomial Option Pricing - Single Period - Put

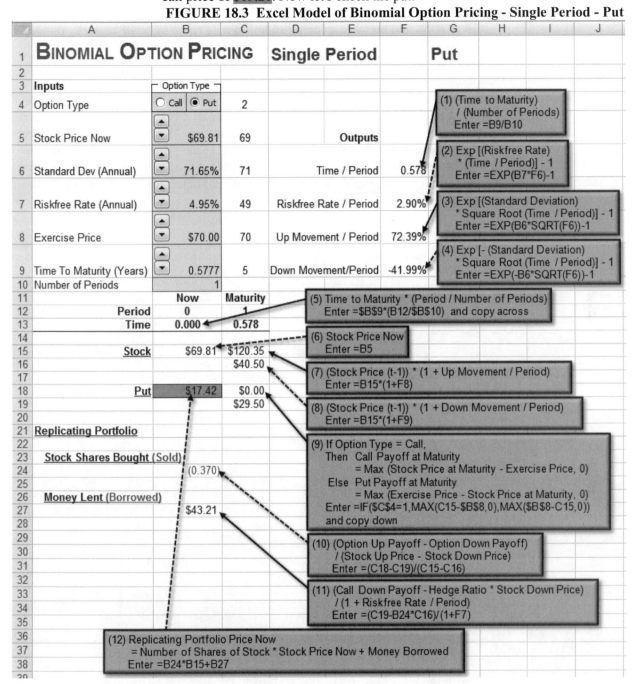

We see that the Binomial Option Pricing model predicts a one-period European put price of $17.42.

18.3 Multi-Period

Problem. Same as before, except we will use an eight-period model to evaluate it. At the close of trading on June 20, 2007, the stock price of Amazon.com was

$69.81, the standard deviation of daily returns is 71.65%, the yield on a six-month U.S. Treasury Bill was 4.95%, the exercise price of a January 70 call on Amazon.com was $70.00, the exercise price of a January 70 put on Amazon.com was $70.00, and the time to maturity for both January 18, 2008 maturity options was 0.5777 years. What is the price of a January 70 call and a January 70 put on Amazon.com?

Solution Strategy. First, copy the binomial tree parameters from the single-period model. Second, build a multi-period tree of stock prices. Third, calculate call and put payoffs at maturity. Fourth, build the multi-period trees of the shares of stock and money borrowed to create a replicating portfolio that replicates the option period by period. Finally, build a multi-period tree of the value of the replicating portfolio and, in the absence of arbitrage, this will be value of the option.

FIGURE 18.4 Binomial Option Pricing - Multi-Period - Call.

	A	B	C	D	E	F	G	H	I	J
1	**BINOMIAL OPTION PRICING**			**Multi-Period**			**Call**			
2										
3	Inputs	Option Type								
4	Option Type	⦿ Call ○ Put	1			(1) Copy the Outputs column from the previous sheet Copy the range F6:F9 from the previous sheet to the range F6:F9 on this sheet				
5	Stock Price Now	$69.81	69		Outputs					
6	Standard Dev (Annual)	71.65%	71	Time / Period		0.072				
7	Riskfree Rate (Annual)	4.95%	49	Riskfree Rate / Period		0.36%				
8	Exercise Price	$70.00	70	Up Movement / Period		21.23%	(2) Time to Maturity * (Period / Number of Periods) Enter =$B$9*(B12/$B$10) and copy across			
9	Time To Maturity (Years)	0.5777	5	Down Movement/Period		-17.51%				
10	Number of Periods	8								
11		**Now**								**Maturity**
12	Period	0	1	2	3	4	5	6	7	8
13	Time	0.000	0.072	0.144	0.217	0.289	0.361	0.433	0.505	0.578
14										
15	**Stock**	$69.81	$84.63	$102.60	$124.39	$150.80	$182.82	$221.63	$268.69	$325.74
16			$57.58	$69.81	$84.63	$102.60	$124.39	$150.80	$182.82	$221.63
17				$47.50	$57.58	$69.81	$84.63	$102.60	$124.39	$150.80
18	(3) Stock Price Now Enter =B5				$39.18	$47.50	$57.58	$69.81	$84.63	$102.60
19						$32.32	$39.18	$47.50	$57.58	$69.81
20							$26.66	$32.32	$39.18	$47.50
21								$21.99	$26.66	$32.32
22	(4) If Cell to the Left = Blank, Then If Cell to the Left & Up One = Blank, Then Blank Else Down Price = (Stock Price to the Left & Up One) * (1+ Down Movement / Period) Else Up Price = (Stock Price to the Left) * (1 + Up Movement / Period) Enter =IF(B15="",IF(B14="","",B14*(1+$F$9)),B15*(1+$F$8)) and copy to the range C15:J23								$18.14	$21.99
23										$14.96
24										
25										
26										
27										
28										
29	(5) If Option Type = Call, Then Call Payoff at Maturity = Max (Stock Price at Maturity - Exercise Price, 0) Else Put Payoff at Maturity = Max (Exercise Price - Stock Price at Maturity, 0) Enter =IF($C$4=1,MAX(J15-$B$8,0),MAX($B$8-J15,0)) and copy to the range J35:J42									
30										
31										
32										
33										
34	**Call**	$15.27	$24.38	$37.81	$56.67	$81.81	$113.56	$152.13	$198.94	$255.74
35			$7.57	$13.06	$21.91	$35.52	$55.16	$81.30	$113.07	$151.63
36				$2.92	$5.56	$10.40	$18.94	$33.16	$54.64	$80.80
37					$0.67	$1.45	$3.17	$6.89	$14.98	$32.60
38						$0.00	$0.00	$0.00	$0.00	$0.00
39							$0.00	$0.00	$0.00	$0.00
40	(8) If Cell to the Right & Down One = Blank, Then Blank Else Set Option Price = Price of the Corresponding Replicating Portfolio = Number of Shares of Stock * Stock Price + Money Borrowed Enter =IF(C35="","",B50*B15+B61) and copy to the range B34:I41 Do NOT copy to column J, which contains the option payoffs at maturity						$0.00	$0.00	$0.00	$0.00
41								$0.00	$0.00	$0.00
42									$0.00	$0.00
43										
44										
45										

We see that the Binomial Option Pricing model predicts an eight-period European call price of $15.27.

FIGURE 18.5 Excel Model of Binomial Option Pricing - Multi-Period - Call (Continued).

	A	B	C	D	E	F	G	H	I	J
1	**BINOMIAL OPTION PRICING**			**Multi-Period**			**Call**			
2										
3	Inputs	Option Type								
4	Option Type	◉ Call ○ Put	1							
5	Stock Price Now	$69.81	69		**Outputs**					
6	Standard Dev (Annual)	71.65%	71		Time / Period	0.072				
7	Riskfree Rate (Annual)	4.95%	49	Riskfree Rate / Period		0.36%				
8	Exercise Price	$70.00	70	Up Movement / Period		21.23%				
9	Time To Maturity (Years)	0.5777	5	Down Movement/Period		-17.51%				
10	Number of Periods	8								
11		**Now**								**Maturity**
12	Period	**0**	**1**	**2**	**3**	**4**	**5**	**6**	**7**	**8**
13	Time	**0.000**	**0.072**	**0.144**	**0.217**	**0.289**	**0.361**	**0.433**	**0.505**	**0.578**
46										
47	**Replicating Portfolio**									
48										
49	**Stock Shares Bought (Sold)**									
50		0.622	0.755	0.874	0.960	0.999	1.000	1.000	1.000	
51			0.454	0.604	0.766	0.911	0.999	1.000	1.000	
52				0.266	0.401	0.583	0.801	0.997	1.000	
53					0.096	0.172	0.309	0.554	0.994	
54						0.000	0.000	0.000	0.000	
55							0.000	0.000	0.000	
56								0.000	0.000	
57									0.000	
58										
59										
60	**Money Lent (Borrowed)**									
61		($28.14)	($39.49)	($51.90)	($62.80)	($68.91)	($69.25)	($69.50)	($69.75)	
62			($18.60)	($29.13)	($42.91)	($57.98)	($69.08)	($69.50)	($69.75)	
63				($9.71)	($17.53)	($30.30)	($48.86)	($69.18)	($69.75)	
64					($3.09)	($6.71)	($14.61)	($31.79)	($69.16)	
65						$0.00	$0.00	$0.00	$0.00	
66							$0.00	$0.00	$0.00	
67								$0.00	$0.00	
68									$0.00	
69										
70										

(6) If Corresponding Option Down Price = Blank, Then Blank
   Else Hedge Ratio = (Option Up Price - Option Down Price)
       / (Stock Up Price - Stock Down Price)
   Enter =IF(C35="","",(C34-C35)/(C15-C16)) and copy to the range B50:I57

(7) If Corresponding Option Down Price = Blank, Then Blank
   Else (Option Down Price - Hedge Ratio * Stock Down Price)
       / (1 + Riskfree Rate / Period)
   Enter =IF(C35="","",(C35-B50*C16)/(1+$F$7)) and copy in range B61:I68

Now let's check the put.

FIGURE 18.6 Binomial Option Pricing - Multi-Period - Put.

	A	B	C	D	E	F	G	H	I	J
1	**BINOMIAL OPTION PRICING**			Multi-Period			**Put**			
2										
3	**Inputs**	Option Type								
4	Option Type	○ Call ● Put	2			(1) Copy the Outputs column from the previous sheet Copy the range F6:F9 from the previous sheet to the range F6:F9 on this sheet				
5	Stock Price Now	$69.81	69		**Outputs**					
6	Standard Dev (Annual)	71.65%	71		Time / Period	0.072				
7	Riskfree Rate (Annual)	4.95%	49		Riskfree Rate / Period	0.36%				
8	Exercise Price	$70.00	70		Up Movement / Period	21.23%	(2) Time to Maturity * (Period / Number of Periods) Enter =$B$9*(B12/$B$10) and copy across			
9	Time To Maturity (Years)	0.5777	5		Down Movement/Period	-17.51%				
10	Number of Periods	8								
11		**Now**								**Maturity**
12	Period	0	1	2	3	4	5	6	7	8
13	Time	0.000	0.072	0.144	0.217	0.289	0.361	0.433	0.505	0.578
14										
15	**Stock**	$69.81	$84.63	$102.60	$124.39	$150.80	$182.82	$221.63	$268.69	$325.74
16			$57.58	$69.81	$84.63	$102.60	$124.39	$150.80	$182.82	$221.63
17	(3) Stock Price Now Enter =B5			$47.50	$57.58	$69.81	$84.63	$102.60	$124.39	$150.80
18					$39.18	$47.50	$57.58	$69.81	$84.63	$102.60
19						$32.32	$39.18	$47.50	$57.58	$69.81
20							$26.66	$32.32	$39.18	$47.50
21								$21.99	$26.66	$32.32
22	(4) If Cell to the Left = Blank, Then If Cell to the Left & Up One = Blank, Then Blank Else Down Price = (Stock Price to the Left & Up One) * (1+ Down Movement / Period) Else Up Price = (Stock Price to the Left) * (1 + Up Movement / Period) Enter =IF(B15="",IF(B14="","",B14*(1+$F$9)),B15*(1+$F$8)) and copy to the range C15:J23								$18.14	$21.99
23										$14.96
24										
25										
26										
27										
28										
29				(5) If Option Type = Call, Then Call Payoff at Maturity = Max (Stock Price at Maturity - Exercise Price, 0) Else Put Payoff at Maturity = Max (Exercise Price - Stock Price at Maturity, 0) Enter =IF($C$4=1,MAX(J15-$B$8,0),MAX($B$8-J15,0)) and copy to the range J35:J42						
30										
31										
32										
33										
34	**Put**	$13.49	$8.02	$3.72	$1.04	$0.02	$0.00	$0.00	$0.00	$0.00
35			$18.25	$11.76	$6.04	$1.92	$0.03	$0.00	$0.00	$0.00
36				$23.93	$16.74	$9.60	$3.56	$0.05	$0.00	$0.00
37					$30.25	$22.96	$14.84	$6.58	$0.10	$0.00
38						$36.69	$30.07	$22.00	$12.17	$0.19
39							$42.60	$37.18	$30.57	$22.50
40	(8) If Cell to the Right & Down One = Blank, Then Blank Else Set Option Price = Price of the Corresponding Replicating Portfolio = Number of Shares of Stock * Stock Price + Money Borrowed Enter =IF(C35="","",B50*B15+B61) and copy to the range B34:I41 Do NOT copy to column J, which contains the option payoffs at maturity						$47.51	$43.09	$37.68
41									$51.61	$48.01
42										$55.04
43										
44										
45										

We see that the Binomial Option Pricing model predicts an eight-period European put price of $13.49.

FIGURE 18.7 Binomial Option Pricing - Multi-Period - Put (Continued).

	A	B	C	D	E	F	G	H	I	J
1	**BINOMIAL OPTION PRICING**			**Multi-Period**			**Put**			
2										
3	Inputs	Option Type								
4	Option Type	○ Call ● Put	2							
5	Stock Price Now	$69.81	69		Outputs					
6	Standard Dev (Annual)	71.65%	71	Time / Period		0.072				
7	Riskfree Rate (Annual)	4.95%	49	Riskfree Rate / Period		0.36%				
8	Exercise Price	$70.00	70	Up Movement / Period		21.23%				
9	Time To Maturity (Years)	0.5777	5	Down Movement/Period		-17.51%				
10	Number of Periods	8								
11		**Now**								**Maturity**
12	Period	0	1	2	3	4	5	6	7	8
13	Time	0.000	0.072	0.144	0.217	0.289	0.361	0.433	0.505	0.578
46										
47	**Replicating Portfolio**									
48										
49	**Stock Shares Bought (Sold)**									
50		(0.378)	(0.245)	(0.126)	(0.040)	(0.001)	0.000	0.000	0.000	
51			(0.546)	(0.396)	(0.234)	(0.089)	(0.001)	0.000	0.000	
52				(0.734)	(0.599)	(0.417)	(0.199)	(0.003)	0.000	
53					(0.904)	(0.828)	(0.691)	(0.446)	(0.006)	
54						(1.000)	(1.000)	(1.000)	(1.000)	
55							(1.000)	(1.000)	(1.000)	
56								(1.000)	(1.000)	
57									(1.000)	

(6) If Corresponding Option Down Price = Blank, Then Blank
Else Hedge Ratio = (Option Up Price - Option Down Price)
/ (Stock Up Price - Stock Down Price)
Enter =IF(C35="","",(C34-C35)/(C15-C16)) and copy to the range B50:I57

	A	B	C	D	E	F	G	H	I
60	**Money Lent (Borrowed)**								
61		$39.89	$28.78	$16.61	$5.96	$0.09	$0.00	$0.00	$0.00
62			$49.67	$39.38	$25.85	$11.03	$0.17	$0.00	$0.00
63				$58.80	$51.23	$38.71	$20.39	$0.32	$0.00
64					$65.67	$62.29	$54.64	$37.72	$0.59
65						$69.01	$69.25	$69.50	$69.75
66							$69.25	$69.50	$69.75
67								$69.50	$69.75
68									$69.75

(7) If Corresponding Option Down Price = Blank, Then Blank
Else (Option Down Price - Hedge Ratio * Stock Down Price)
/ (1 + Riskfree Rate / Period)
Enter =IF(C35="","",(C35-B50*C16)/(1+$F$7)) and copy in range B61:I68

As in the single period case, replicating a Call option requires **Buying** Shares of Stock and **Borrowing** Money, whereas a Put option requires **Selling** Shares of Stock and **Lending** Money. Notice that the quantity of Money Borrowed or Lent and the quantity of Shares Bought or Sold changes over time and differs for up nodes vs. down nodes. This process of changing the replicating portfolio every period based on the realized up or down movement in the underlying stock price is called dynamic replication.

Price accuracy can be increased by subdividing the option's time to maturity into more periods (15, 30, etc.). Typically, from 50 to 100 periods are required in order to achieve price accuracy to the penny.

18.4 Risk Neutral

The previous Excel model, **Binomial Option Pricing Multi-Period**, determined the price of an option by constructing a replicating portfolio, which combines a stock and a bond to replicate the payoffs of the option. An alternative way to price an option is the Risk Neutral method. Both techniques give you the same answer. The main advantage of the Risk Neutral method is that it is faster and easier to implement. The Replicating Portfolio method required the construction of four trees (stock prices, shares of stock **bought (sold)**, money **lent (borrowed)**, and option prices). The Risk Neutral method will only require two trees (stock prices and option prices).

Problem. Same as before, except we will use the risk neutral method to evaluate it. At the close of trading on June 20, 2007, the stock price of Amazon.com was $69.81, the standard deviation of daily returns is 71.65%, the yield on a six-month U.S. Treasury Bill was 4.95%, the exercise price of a January 70 call on Amazon.com was $70.00, the exercise price of a January 70 put on Amazon.com was $70.00, and the time to maturity for both January 18, 2008 maturity options was 0.5777 years. What is the price of a January 70 call and a January 70 put on Amazon.com?

Solution Strategy. First, copy the binomial tree parameters, stock price tree, and option payoffs at maturity from the multi-period model. Second, calculate the risk neutral probability. Finally, build a option value tree using the risk neutral probability.

FIGURE 18.8 Binomial Option Pricing – Risk Neutral - Call.

	A	B	C	D	E	F	G	H	I	J
1	**BINOMIAL OPTION PRICING**			**Risk Neutral**			**Call**			
2										
3	**Inputs**	Option Type								
4	Option Type	◉ Call ○ Put	1			(1) Copy the Outputs column from the previous sheet				
5	Stock Price Now	$69.81	69		**Outputs**	Copy the range F6:F9 from the previous sheet to the range F6:F9 on this sheet				
6	Standard Dev (Annual)	71.65%	71	Time / Period		0.072				
7	Riskfree Rate (Annual)	4.95%	49	Riskfree Rate / Period		0.36%	(2) (Riskfree Rate / Period			
8	Exercise Price	$70.00	70	Up Movement / Period		21.23%	- Down Movement / Period) / (Up Movement / Period			
9	Time To Maturity (Years)	0.5777	5	Down Movement/Period		-17.51%	- Down Movement / Period) Enter =(F7-F9)/(F8-F9)			
10	Number of Periods	8		Risk Neutral Probability		46.13%				
11		**Now**								**Maturity**
12	**Period**	0	1	2	3	4	5	6	7	8
13	**Time**	0.000	0.072	0.144	0.217	0.289	0.361	0.433	0.505	0.578
14										
15	**Stock**	$69.81	$84.63	$102.60	$124.39	$150.80	$182.82	$221.63	$268.69	$325.74
16			$57.58	$69.81	$84.63	$102.60	$124.39	$150.80	$182.82	$221.63
17				$47.50	$57.58	$69.81	$84.63	$102.60	$124.39	$150.80
18	(3) Copy the Stock Price Tree from the previous sheet				$39.18	$47.50	$57.58	$69.81	$84.63	$102.60
19	Copy the range B15:J23 from the previous sheet					$32.32	$39.18	$47.50	$57.58	$69.81
20	to the range B15:J23 on this sheet						$26.66	$32.32	$39.18	$47.50
21								$21.99	$26.66	$32.32
22									$18.14	$21.99
23										$14.96
24										
25										
26										
27										
28										
29										
30						(4) Copy the Payoffs at Maturity from the previous sheet				
31						Copy the range J34:J42 from the previous sheet				
32						to the range J34:J42 on this sheet				
33										
34	**Call**	$15.27	$24.38	$37.81	$56.67	$81.81	$113.56	$152.13	$198.94	$255.74
35			$7.57	$13.06	$21.91	$35.52	$55.16	$81.30	$113.07	$151.63
36				$2.92	$5.56	$10.40	$18.94	$33.16	$54.64	$80.80
37					$0.67	$1.45	$3.17	$6.89	$14.98	$32.60
38						$0.00	$0.00	$0.00	$0.00	$0.00
39							$0.00	$0.00	$0.00	$0.00
40								$0.00	$0.00	$0.00
41									$0.00	$0.00
42										$0.00
43	(5) If Cell to the Right & Down One = Blank, Then Blank									
44	Else Expected Value of Option Price Next Period (using the Risk Neutral Probability)									
45	Discounted at the Riskfree Rate									
46	= [(Risk Neutral Probability) * (Stock Up Price) + (1 - Risk Neutral Probability) * (Stock Down Price)] / (1+ Riskfree Rate / Period)									
47	Enter =IF(C35="","",($F$10*C34+(1-$F$10)*C35)/(1+$F$7)) and copy to the range B34:I41									
48	Do NOT copy to column J, which contains the option payoffs at maturity									
49										

We see that the Risk Neutral method predicts an eight-period European call price of $15.27. This is identical to previous section's Replicating Portfolio Price. Now let's check the put.

FIGURE 18.9 Binomial Option Pricing – Risk Neutral - Put.

	A	B	C	D	E	F	G	H	I	J
1	**BINOMIAL OPTION PRICING**			**Risk Neutral**			**Put**			
2										
3	Inputs	Option Type								
4	Option Type	○ Call ● Put	2			(1) Copy the Outputs column from the previous sheet Copy the range F6:F9 from the previous sheet to the range F6:F9 on this sheet				
5	Stock Price Now	$69.81	69		Outputs					
6	Standard Dev (Annual)	71.65%	71		Time / Period	0.072				
7	Riskfree Rate (Annual)	4.95%	49	Riskfree Rate / Period	0.36%		(2) (Riskfree Rate / Period - Down Movement / Period) / (Up Movement / Period - Down Movement / Period) Enter =(F7-F9)/(F8-F9)			
8	Exercise Price	$70.00	70	Up Movement / Period	21.23%					
9	Time To Maturity (Years)	0.5777	5	Down Movement/Period	-17.51%					
10	Number of Periods	8		Risk Neutral Probability	46.13%					
11		Now								Maturity
12	Period	0	1	2	3	4	5	6	7	8
13	Time	0.000	0.072	0.144	0.217	0.289	0.361	0.433	0.505	0.578
14										
15	Stock	$69.81	$84.63	$102.60	$124.39	$150.80	$182.82	$221.63	$268.69	$325.74
16			$57.58	$69.81	$84.63	$102.60	$124.39	$150.80	$182.82	$221.63
17				$47.50	$57.58	$69.81	$84.63	$102.60	$124.39	$150.80
18	(3) Copy the Stock Price Tree from the previous sheet Copy the range B15:J23 from the previous sheet to the range B15:J23 on this sheet				$39.18	$47.50	$57.58	$69.81	$84.63	$102.60
19						$32.32	$39.18	$47.50	$57.58	$69.81
20							$26.66	$32.32	$39.18	$47.50
21								$21.99	$26.66	$32.32
22									$18.14	$21.99
23										$14.96
24										
25										
26										
27										
28										
29										
30							(4) Copy the Payoffs at Maturity from the previous sheet Copy the range J34:J42 from the previous sheet to the range J34:J42 on this sheet			
31										
32										
33										
34	Put	$13.49	$8.02	$3.72	$1.04	$0.02	$0.00	$0.00	$0.00	$0.00
35			$18.25	$11.76	$6.04	$1.92	$0.03	$0.00	$0.00	$0.00
36				$23.93	$16.74	$9.60	$3.56	$0.05	$0.00	$0.00
37					$30.25	$22.96	$14.84	$6.58	$0.10	$0.00
38						$36.69	$30.07	$22.00	$12.17	$0.19
39							$42.60	$37.18	$30.57	$22.50
40								$47.51	$43.09	$37.68
41									$51.61	$48.01
42										$55.04
43	(5) If Cell to the Right & Down One = Blank, Then Blank Else Expected Value of Option Price Next Period (using the Risk Neutral Probability) Discounted at the Riskfree Rate = [(Risk Neutral Probability) * (Stock Up Price) + (1 - Risk Neutral Probability) * (Stock Down Price)] / (1+ Riskfree Rate / Period) Enter =IF(C35="","",($F$10*C34+(1-$F$10)*C35)/(1+$F$7)) and copy to the range B34:I41 Do NOT copy to column J, which contains the option payoffs at maturity									

We see that the Risk Neutral method predicts an eight-period European put price of $13.49. This is identical to previous section's Replicating Portfolio Price. Again, we get the same answer either way. The advantage of the Risk Neutral method is that we only have to construct two trees, rather than four trees.

18.5 American With Discrete Dividends

Problem. Same as before, except we will value American options where the underlying stock pays dividends. At the close of trading on June 20, 2007, the stock price of Amazon.com was $69.81, the standard deviation of daily returns is 71.65%, the yield on a six-month U.S. Treasury Bill was 4.95%, the exercise price of an American January 70 call on Amazon.com was $70.00, the exercise price of an American January 70 put on Amazon.com was $70.00, and the time to maturity for both January 18, 2008 maturity options was 0.5777 years. Assume that Amazon.com pays certain, riskfree $4.00 dividends on the periods show below. What is the price of an American January 70 call and an American January 70 put on Amazon.com?

Solution Strategy. First, copy the binomial tree parameters, the risk neutral probability, stock price tree, and option payoffs at maturity from the risk neutral model. Second, calculate the total stock price as the sum of the risky stock price plus the discounted value of future dividends. Finally, build a option value tree using the risk neutral probability and accounting for optimal early exercise.

FIGURE 18.10 Excel Model of Binomial Option Pricing – American With Discrete Dividends – Call.

	A	B	C	D	E	F	G	H	I	J
1	**BINOMIAL OPTION PRICING**			**American With Discrete Dividends**						**Call**
2										
3	**Inputs**	Option Type				Early Exercise				
4	Option Type	● Call ○ Put	1		Early Exercise	○ European ● American	2			
5	Stock Price Now	$69.81	69		**Outputs**					
6	Standard Dev (Annual)	71.65%	71		Time / Period	0.072				
7	Riskfree Rate (Annual)	4.95%	49		Riskfree Rate / Period	0.36%				
8	Exercise Price	$70.00	70		Up Movement / Period	21.23%				
9	Time To Maturity (Years)	0.5777	5		Down Movement/Period	-17.51%				
10	Number of Periods	8			Risk Neutral Probability	46.13%				
11		**Now**								**Maturity**
12	**Period**	0	1	2	3	4	5	6	7	8
13	**Time**	0.000	0.072	0.144	0.217	0.289	0.361	0.433	0.505	0.578
14										
15	**Risky Part of the Stock**	$69.81	$84.63	$102.60	$124.39	$150.80	$182.82	$221.63	$268.69	$325.74
16			$57.58	$69.81	$84.63	$102.60	$124.39	$150.80	$182.82	$221.63
17				$47.50	$57.58	$69.81	$84.63	$102.60	$124.39	$150.80
18					$39.18	$47.50	$57.58	$69.81	$84.63	$102.60
19						$32.32	$39.18	$47.50	$57.58	$69.81
20							$26.66	$32.32	$39.18	$47.50
21								$21.99	$26.66	$32.32
22									$18.14	$21.99
23										$14.96
24										
25	**Riskfree Dividends**		$0.00	$0.00	$0.00	$4.00	$0.00	$0.00	$4.00	$0.00
26										
27	**Cum. Pres Value Factor**	100.00%	95.28%	90.79%	86.51%	82.43%	78.54%	74.84%	71.31%	67.94%
28										
29	**Total Stock Price**	$75.96	$91.09	$109.38	$131.50	$154.26	$186.45	$225.44	$268.69	$325.74
30			$64.04	$76.58	$91.74	$106.06	$128.02	$154.61	$182.82	$221.63
31				$54.27	$64.69	$73.27	$88.26	$106.41	$124.39	$150.80
32					$46.29	$50.96	$61.22	$73.62	$84.63	$102.60
33						$35.78	$42.81	$51.31	$57.58	$69.81
34							$30.29	$36.13	$39.18	$47.50
35								$25.80	$26.66	$32.32
36									$18.14	$21.99
37										$14.96

Callout boxes:

(1) Copy the Outputs column (including the Risk Neutral Probability) from the previous sheet Copy the range F6:F10 from the previous sheet to the range F6:F10 on this sheet

(2) Copy the Stock Price Tree from the previous sheet Copy the range B15:J23 from the previous sheet to the range B15:J23 on this sheet

(3) 1 / ((1 + (Riskfree Rate / Period)) ^ Period) Enter =1/((1+$B$7)^C12) and copy across

(4) If corresponding cell on Risky Part of Stock tree is blank, Then blank, Else Risky Part of Stock + SUMPRODUCT(Riskfree Dividends Range, Cum. Pres Value Factor Range) / (Cum. Pres Value Factor(t)) Enter =IF(B15="","",B15+SUMPRODUCT(C$25:$J$25, C$27:$J$27)/B$27) and copy to the range B29:I36 Do NOT copy to column J, which contains a different formula

(5) Risky Part of the Stock Tree Enter =J15 and copy down

FIGURE 18.11 Excel Model of Binomial Option Pricing – American With Discrete Dividends - Call.

	A	B	C	D	E	F	G	H	I	J
1	**BINOMIAL OPTION PRICING**			**American With Discrete Dividends**						**Call**
2										
3	Inputs	Option Type				Early Exercise				
4	Option Type	◉ Call ○ Put	1	Early Exercise		○ European ◉ American		2		
5	Stock Price Now	$69.81	69	Outputs						
6	Standard Dev (Annual)	71.65%	71	Time / Period		0.072				
7	Riskfree Rate (Annual)	4.95%	49	Riskfree Rate / Period		0.36%				
8	Exercise Price	$70.00	70	Up Movement / Period		21.23%				
9	Time To Maturity (Years)	0.5777	5	Down Movement/Period		-17.51%				
10	Number of Periods	8		Risk Neutral Probability		46.13%				
11		**Now**								**Maturity**
12	Period	0	1	2	3	4	5	6	7	8
13	Time	0.000	0.072	0.144	0.217	0.289	0.361	0.433	0.505	0.578
44						(6) Copy the Payoffs at Maturity from the previous sheet Copy the range J34:J42 from the previous sheet to the range J48:J56 on this sheet				
45										
46										
47										
48	**American Call**	$16.35	$26.20	$40.79	$61.50	$85.08	$116.86	$155.44	$198.94	$255.74
49			$8.02	$13.88	$23.34	$37.83	$58.43	$84.61	$113.07	$151.63
50				$3.06	$5.88	$11.09	$20.43	$36.41	$54.64	$80.80
51					$0.67	$1.45	$3.17	$6.89	$14.98	$32.60
52						$0.00	$0.00	$0.00	$0.00	$0.00
53						$0.00	$0.00	$0.00	$0.00	$0.00
54							$0.00	$0.00	$0.00	$0.00
55								$0.00	$0.00	$0.00
56										$0.00

(7) If Cell to the Right & Down One = Blank, Then Blank
    Else Max{ Not Exercised Value, Exercised Value}
where: Not Exercised Value = [(Risk Neutral Probability) * (Stock Up Price)
                        + (1 - Risk Neutral Probability) * (Stock Down Price)]
                        / (1+ Riskfree Rate / Period),
            Exercised Value = If Early Exercise = European, Then 0,
                        Else If (Option Type = Call, 1, -1)
                        * (Total Stock Price - Exercise Price) }
    Enter =IF(C49="","",MAX(($F$10*C48+(1-$F$10)*C49)/(1+$F$7),
                    IF($H$4=1,0,IF($C$4=1,1,-1)*(B29-$B$8))))

Optionally, use Conditional Formatting to highlight Early Exercise cells:
    click on Home | Styles | Conditional Formatting | New Rule
    click on "use a formula to determine which cells to format"
    enter the rule: =AND($H$4=2,B48=IF($C$4=1,1,-1)*(B29-$B$8))
    click on the Format button, click on the Fill tab,
    click on the color of your choice, click on OK, click on OK

Then copy to the range B48:I55
Do NOT copy to column J, which contains the option payoffs at maturity

The purple-shading highlights the periods and call prices where it is optimal to exercise the American call early. Notice that it is optimal to exercise an

American call early just before a dividend is paid, which will reduce the value of the underlying stock and thus reduce the value of an unexercised call option. We see that the model predicts an eight-period American call price of $16.35.

FIGURE 18.12 American With Discrete Dividends - Put.

	A	B	C	D	E	F	G	H	I	J
1	**BINOMIAL OPTION PRICING**			**American With Discrete Dividends**						**Put**
2										
3	Inputs	┌─ Option Type ─┐				┌─ Early Exercise ─┐				
4	Option Type	○ Call ◉ Put	2		Early Exercise	○ European ◉ American	2			
5	Stock Price Now	$69.81	69		Outputs					
6	Standard Dev (Annual)	71.65%	71		Time / Period	0.072				
7	Riskfree Rate (Annual)	4.95%	49		Riskfree Rate / Period	0.36%				
8	Exercise Price	$70.00	70		Up Movement / Period	21.23%				
9	Time To Maturity (Years)	0.5777	5		Down Movement/Period	-17.51%				
10	Number of Periods	8			Risk Neutral Probability	46.13%				
11		**Now**								**Maturity**
12	Period	0	1	2	3	4	5	6	7	8
13	Time	0.000	0.072	0.144	0.217	0.289	0.361	0.433	0.505	0.578

> (6) Copy the Payoffs at Maturity from the previous sheet
> Copy the range J34:J42 from the previous sheet
> to the range J48:J56 on this sheet

	A	B	C	D	E	F	G	H	I	J
48	**American Put**	$13.63	$8.12	$3.78	$1.06	$0.02	$0.00	$0.00	$0.00	$0.00
49			$18.43	$11.90	$6.13	$1.96	$0.03	$0.00	$0.00	$0.00
50				$24.14	$16.92	$9.74	$3.63	$0.05	$0.00	$0.00
51					$30.48	$23.19	$15.03	$6.71	$0.10	$0.00
52						$36.94	$30.32	$22.25	$12.42	$0.19
53							42.84	$37.43	$30.82	$22.50
54								$47.76	$43.34	$37.68
55									$51.86	$48.01
56										$55.04

> (7) If Cell to the Right & Down One = Blank, Then Blank
> Else Max{ Not Exercised Value, Exercised Value}
> where: Not Exercised Value = [(Risk Neutral Probability) * (Stock Up Price)
> + (1 - Risk Neutral Probability) * (Stock Down Price)]
> / (1+ Riskfree Rate / Period),
> Exercised Value = If Early Exercise = European, Then 0,
> Else If (Option Type = Call, 1, -1)
> * (Total Stock Price - Exercise Price) }
> Enter =IF(C49="","",MAX(($F$10*C48+(1-$F$10)*C49)/(1+$F$7),
> IF($H$4=1,0,IF($C$4=1,1,-1)*(B29-$B$8))))
>
> **Optionally, use Conditional Formatting to highlight Early Exercise cells:**
> click on Home | Styles | Conditional Formatting | New Rule
> click on "use a formula to determine which cells to format"
> enter the rule: =AND($H$4=2,B48=IF($C$4=1,1,-1)*(B29-$B$8))
> click on the Format button, click on the Fill tab,
> click on the color of your choice, click on OK, click on OK
>
> Then copy to the range B48:I55
> Do NOT copy to column J, which contains the option payoffs at maturity

The purple-shading highlights the periods and call prices where it is optimal to exercise the American put early. Notice that it is optimal to exercise an American put early just when a dividend is paid, which will reduce the value of the underlying stock and thus increases the value of the put option. We see that the model predicts an eight-period American put price of $13.63.

18.6 Full-Scale

Problem. Same as before, except we will use a fifty-period model to evaluate it in order to increase accuracy. At the close of trading on June 20, 2007, the stock price of Amazon.com was $69.81, the standard deviation of daily returns is 71.65%, the yield on a six-month U.S. Treasury Bill was 4.95%, the exercise price of an American January 70 call on Amazon.com was $70.00, the exercise price of an American January 70 put on Amazon.com was $70.00, and the time to maturity for both January 18, 2008 maturity options was 0.5777 years. Assume that Amazon.com pays certain, riskfree $5.00 dividends on the periods show below. What is the price of an American January 70 call and an American January 70 put on Amazon.com?

Solution Strategy. First, copy the binomial tree parameters, the risk neutral probability, stock price tree, and option payoffs at maturity from the risk neutral model. Second, calculate the total stock price as the sum of the risky stock price plus the discounted value of future dividends. Finally, build a option value tree using the risk neutral probability and accounting for optimal early exercise.

FIGURE 18.13 Binomial Option Pricing - Full-Scale Estimation - Call.

	A	B	C	D	E	F	G	H
1	**BINOMIAL OPTION PRICING**			**Full-Scale**			**American Call**	
2								
3	**Inputs**	Option Type				Early Exercise		
4	Option Type	● Call ○ Put	1	Early Exercise		○ European ● American		2
5	Risky Part of Stock Now	$69.81	69		Outputs			
6	Standard Dev (Annual)	71.65%	71	Time / Period		0.012		
7	Riskfree Rate (Annual)	4.95%	49	Riskfree Rate / Period		0.06%		
8	Exercise Price	$70.00	70	Up Movement / Period		8.01%		
9	Time To Maturity (Years)	0.5777	5	Down Movement/Period		-7.41%		
10	Number of Periods	50		Risk Neutral Probability		48.45%		
11		**Now**						
12	**Period**	**0**	**1**	**2**	**3**	**4**	**5**	**6**
13	**Time**	**0.000**	**0.012**	**0.023**	**0.035**	**0.046**	**0.058**	**0.069**
14								
15	**Risky Part of the Stock**	$69.81	$75.40	$81.44	$87.96	$95.00	$102.60	$110.82
16			$64.64	$69.81	$75.40	$81.44	$87.96	$95.00
17				$59.84	$64.64	$69.81	$75.40	$81.44
18	(1) Risky Part of Stock Now Enter =B5				$55.41	$59.84	$64.64	$69.81
19						$51.30	$55.41	$59.84
20							$47.50	$51.30
21	(2) Copy the Stock Price fomula from the previous sheet							$43.98
22	and expand it to a larger range							
23	Copy the cell C15 from the previous sheet							
24	to the range C15:AZ65 on this sheet							

The up movement / period and down movement / period are calibrated to correspond to the stock's annual standard deviation. It is not necessary to calibrate them to the stock's expected return.[5]

---

[5] At full-scale (50 periods), the binomial option price is very insensitive to the expected return of the stock. For example, suppose that you calibrated this Amazon.com case to an annual expected return of 10%. Just add **.1*F6** to the formulas for the up and down movements / period. So the up movement / period in cell **F8** would become **=EXP(.1*F6+B6*SQRT(F6))-1** and the down movement / period in cell **F9** would become **=EXP(.1*F6-B6*SQRT(F6))-1**. This changes the option price by less than 1/100th of one penny! In the (Black Scholes) limit as the number of (sub)periods goes to infinity, the option price becomes totally insensitive to the expected return of the stock. Because of this

FIGURE 18.14 Excel Model of Binomial Option Pricing - Full-Scale Estimation - Call Option (Continued).

	A	B	C	D	E	F	G	H
1	**BINOMIAL OPTION PRICING**			**Full-Scale**			**American Call**	
2								
3	Inputs	Option Type					Early Exercise	
4	Option Type	◉ Call ○ Put	1	Early Exercise		○ European ◉ American		2
5	Risky Part of Stock Now	$69.81	69	Outputs				
6	Standard Dev (Annual)	71.65%	71	Time / Period		0.012		
7	Riskfree Rate (Annual)	4.95%	49	Riskfree Rate / Period		0.06%		
8	Exercise Price	$70.00	70	Up Movement / Period		8.01%		
9	Time To Maturity (Years)	0.5777	5	Down Movement/Period		-7.41%		
10	Number of Periods	50		Risk Neutral Probability		48.45%		
11		**Now**						
12	**Period**	0	1	2	3	4	5	6
13	**Time**	0.000	0.012	0.023	0.035	0.046	0.058	0.069
62								
63	(3) (Cum. Pres Value Factor(t-1)) * EXP(- (Riskfree Rate / Period))							
64	Enter =B69*EXP(-$F$7)							
65	and copy across							
66								
67	**Riskfree Dividends**		$0.00	$0.00	$0.00	$0.00	$5.00	$0.00
68								
69	**Cum. Pres Value Factor**	100.000%	99.943%	99.886%	99.829%	99.771%	99.714%	99.657%
70								
71	**Total Stock Price**	$84.64	$90.24	$96.28	$102.81	$109.86	$112.47	$120.69
72			$79.47	$84.66	$90.25	$96.30	$97.83	$104.87
73				$74.69	$79.49	$84.67	$85.27	$91.31
74					$70.26	$74.71	$74.51	$79.69
75						$66.16	$65.28	$69.72
76	(4) If corresponding cell on Risky Part of Stock tree is blank,						$57.37	$61.18
77	Then blank,							$53.86
78	Else Risky Part of Stock							
79	+ SUMPRODUCT(Riskfree Dividends Range,							
80	Cum. Pres Value Factor Range)							
81	/ (Cum. Pres Value Factor(t))							
82	Enter =IF(B15="","",B15+SUMPRODUCT(C$67:$AZ$67,C$69:$AZ$69)/B$69)							
83	and copy to the range B71:AY120							
84	Do NOT copy to column AZ, which contains a different formula							

insensitivity, the conventions for calculating the up movement / period and down movement / period ignore the expected return of the stock.

FIGURE 18.15 Excel Model of Binomial Option Pricing - Full-Scale Estimation - Call Option (Continued).

	AT	AU	AV	AW	AX	AY	AZ
11							**Maturity**
12	**44**	**45**	**46**	**47**	**48**	**49**	**50**
13	**0.508**	**0.520**	**0.531**	**0.543**	**0.555**	**0.566**	**0.578**
63					$1.73	$1.87	$2.02
64						$1.60	$1.73
65							$1.48
66							
67	$0.00	$0.00	$0.00	$0.00	$0.00	$0.00	$0.00
68							
69	97.514%	97.458%	97.403%	97.347%	97.291%	97.236%	97.180%
70							
71	$2,068.32	$2,233.91	$2,412.76	$2,605.92	$2,814.55	$3,039.88	$3,283.25
72	$1,773.06	$1,915.01	$2,068.32	$2,233.91	$2,412.76	$2,605.92	$2,814.55
73	$1,519.94	$1,641.63	$1,773.06	$1,915.01	$2,068.32	$2,233.91	$2,412.76
74	$1,302.96	$1,407.28	$1,519.94	$1,641.63	$1,773.06	$1,915.01	$2,068.32

(5) Risky Part of the Stock Tree
Enter =AZ15 and copy down

FIGURE 18.16 Excel Model of Binomial Option Pricing - Full-Scale Estimation - Call Option (Continued).

	AR	AS	AT	AU	AV	AW	AX	AY	AZ
11									**Maturity**
12	**42**	**43**	**44**	**45**	**46**	**47**	**48**	**49**	**50**
13	**0.485**	**0.497**	**0.508**	**0.520**	**0.531**	**0.543**	**0.555**	**0.566**	**0.578**
119							$1.73	$1.87	$2.02
120								$1.60	$1.73
121									$1.48
122									
123									
124									
125	$1,703.38	$1,845.29	$1,998.56	$2,164.11	$2,342.92	$2,536.04	$2,744.63	$2,969.92	$3,213.25
126	$1,450.26	$1,571.91	$1,703.30	$1,845.21	$1,998.48	$2,164.03	$2,342.84	$2,535.96	$2,744.55
127	$1,233.28	$1,337.56	$1,450.18	$1,571.83	$1,703.22	$1,845.13	$1,998.40	$2,163.95	$2,342.76
128	$1,047.28	$1,136.66	$1,233.20	$1,337.48	$1,450.10	$1,571.75	$1,703.14	$1,845.05	$1,998.32
129	$887.82	$964.44	$1,047.20	$1,136.58	$1,233.12	$1,337.40	$1,450.02	$1,571.67	$1,703.06

(6) If Option Type = Call,
  Then Call Payoff at Maturity = Max (Stock Price at Maturity - Exercise Price, 0)
  Else Put Payoff at Maturity = Max (Exercise Price - Stock Price at Maturity, 0)
  Enter =IF($C$4=1,MAX(AZ71-$B$8,0),MAX($B$8-AZ71,0))
  and copy to the range AZ126:AZ175

FIGURE 18.17 Excel Model of Binomial Option Pricing - Full-Scale Estimation - Call Option (Continued).

	A	B	C	D	E	F	G	H	T	U
1	**BINOMIAL OPTION PRICING**			**Full-Scale**			**American Call**			
2										
3	**Inputs**	Option Type				Early Exercise				
4	Option Type	● Call ○ Put	1		Early Exercise	○ European ● American		2		
5	Risky Part of Stock Now	$69.81	69		**Outputs**					
6	Standard Dev (Annual)	71.65%	71		Time / Period	0.012				
7	Riskfree Rate (Annual)	4.95%	49	Riskfree Rate / Period	0.06%					
8	Exercise Price	$70.00	70	Up Movement / Period	8.01%					
9	Time To Maturity (Years)	0.5777	5	Down Movement/Period	-7.41%					
10	Number of Periods	50		Risk Neutral Probability	48.45%					
11		**Now**								
12	**Period**	0	1	2	3	4	5	6	18	19
13	**Time**	0.000	0.012	0.023	0.035	0.046	0.058	0.069	0.208	0.220
66										
67	**Riskfree Dividends**		$0.00	$0.00	$0.00	$0.00	$5.00	$0.00	$0.00	$0.00
68										
125	**American Call**	$17.55	$21.76	$26.82	$32.85	$39.86	$43.99	$51.71	$219.23	$241.55
126			$13.62	$17.03	$21.19	$26.30	$30.64	$36.77	$179.36	$198.49
127				$10.43	$13.14	$16.40	$20.31	$24.91	$145.19	$161.58
128					$7.90	$10.08	$12.75	$16.00	$115.90	$129.94
129						$5.86	$7.58	$9.72	$90.78	$102.82
130							$4.25	$5.58	$69.26	$79.57
131								$3.02	$50.80	$59.64
132									$34.98	$42.55
133									$22.05	$27.91
134									$13.01	$16.58
135									$7.37	$9.67
136									$3.85	$5.21
137									$1.84	$2.57
138									$0.80	$1.15
139									$0.31	$0.47
140									$0.11	$0.17
141									$0.03	$0.05
142									$0.01	$0.01
143									$0.00	$0.00
144										$0.00

(7) If Cell to the Right & Down One = Blank, Then Blank
Else Max{ Not Exercised Value, Exercised Value}
where: Not Exercised Value = [(Risk Neutral Probability) * (Stock Up Price)
+ (1 - Risk Neutral Probability) * (Stock Down Price)]
/ (1+ Riskfree Rate / Period),
Exercised Value = If Early Exercise = European, Then 0,
Else If (Option Type = Call, 1, -1)
* (Total Stock Price - Exercise Price) }
Enter =IF(C126="","",MAX(($F$10*C125+(1-$F$10)*C126)/(1+$F$7),
IF($H$4=1,0,IF($C$4=1,1,-1)*(B71-$B$8))))

Optionally, use Conditional Formatting to highlight Early Exercise cells:
click on Home | Styles | Conditional Formatting | New Rule
click on "use a formula to determine which cells to format"
enter the rule: =AND($H$4=2,B125=IF($C$4=1,1,-1)*(B71-$B$8))
click on the Format button, click on the Fill tab,
click on the color of your choice, click on OK, click on OK

Then copy to the range B125:AY174
Do NOT copy to column AZ, which contains the option payoffs at maturity

Again, optimal early exercise for an American call occurs just before a dividend is paid. We see that the Full-Scale model predicts an American call price of $17.55. Now let's check the put.

FIGURE 18.18 Excel Model of Binomial Option Pricing - Full-Scale Estimation - Put Option.

	A	B	C	D	E	F	G	H	AY	AZ
1	**BINOMIAL OPTION PRICING**			**Full-Scale**			**American Put**			
2										
3	**Inputs**	Option Type				Early Exercise				
4	Option Type	○ Call ◉ Put	2		Early Exercise	○ European ◉ American		2		
5	Risky Part of Stock Now	$69.81	69		**Outputs**					
6	Standard Dev (Annual)	71.65%	71		Time / Period	0.012				
7	Riskfree Rate (Annual)	4.95%	49	Riskfree Rate / Period		0.06%				
8	Exercise Price	$70.00	70	Up Movement / Period		8.01%				
9	Time To Maturity (Years)	0.5777	5	Down Movement/Period		-7.41%				
10	Number of Periods	50		Risk Neutral Probability		48.45%				
11		**Now**								**Maturity**
12	Period	0	1	2	3	4	5	6	49	50
13	Time	0.000	0.012	0.023	0.035	0.046	0.058	0.069	0.566	0.578
14										
15	**Risky Part of the Stock**	$69.81	$75.40	$81.44	$87.96	$95.00	$102.60	$110.82	$3,039.88	$3,283.25
16			$64.64	$69.81	$75.40	$81.44	$87.96	$95.00	$2,605.92	$2,814.55
17				$59.84	$64.64	$69.81	$75.40	$81.44	$2,233.91	$2,412.76
18					$55.41	$59.84	$64.64	$69.81	$1,915.01	$2,068.32
19						$51.30	$55.41	$59.84	$1,641.63	$1,773.06
20							$47.50	$51.30	$1,407.28	$1,519.94
21								$43.98	$1,206.38	$1,302.96
22									$1,034.16	$1,116.96
23									$886.53	$957.50
24									$759.97	$820.81
25									$651.48	$703.64
26									$558.48	$603.19
27									$478.75	$517.08
28									$410.41	$443.26
29									$351.82	$379.99

FIGURE 18.19 Excel Model of Binomial Option Pricing - Full-Scale Estimation - Put Option.

	A	B	C	D	E	F	G	H	AJ	AK
1	**BINOMIAL OPTION PRICING**			**Full-Scale**			**American Put**			
2										
3	**Inputs**	⌐ Option Type ⌐				⌐ Early Exercise				
4	Option Type	○ Call ◉ Put	2	Early Exercise		○ European ◉ American		2		
5	Risky Part of Stock Now	$69.81	69		**Outputs**					
6	Standard Dev (Annual)	71.65%	71	Time / Period		0.012				
7	Riskfree Rate (Annual)	4.95%	49	Riskfree Rate / Period		0.06%				
8	Exercise Price	$70.00	70	Up Movement / Period		8.01%				
9	Time To Maturity (Years)	0.5777	5	Down Movement/Period		-7.41%				
10	Number of Periods	50		Risk Neutral Probability		48.45%				
11		**Now**								
12	**Period**	**0**	**1**	**2**	**3**	**4**	**5**	**6**	**34**	**35**
13	**Time**	**0.000**	**0.012**	**0.023**	**0.035**	**0.046**	**0.058**	**0.069**	**0.393**	**0.404**
66										
67	**Riskfree Dividends**		$0.00	$0.00	$0.00	$0.00	$5.00	$0.00	$0.00	$5.00
68										
69	**Cum. Pres Value Factor**	100.000%	99.943%	99.886%	99.829%	99.771%	99.714%	99.657%	98.074%	98.018%
70										
71	**Total Stock Price**	$84.64	$90.24	$96.28	$102.81	$109.86	$112.47	$120.69	$962.50	$1,034.16
72			$79.47	$84.66	$90.25	$96.30	$97.83	$104.87	$825.81	$886.53
73				$74.69	$79.49	$84.67	$85.27	$91.31	$708.64	$759.97
74					$70.26	$74.71	$74.51	$79.69	$608.19	$651.48
75						$66.16	$65.28	$69.72	$522.08	$558.48
76							$57.37	$61.18	$448.26	$478.75
77								$53.86	$384.98	$410.41
78									$330.74	$351.82
79									$284.24	$301.60
80									$244.37	$258.54
81									$210.20	$221.63
82									$180.91	$189.99
83									$155.79	$162.87
84									$134.27	$139.62
85									$115.81	$119.69

FIGURE 18.20 Excel Model of Binomial Option Pricing - Full-Scale Estimation - Put Option (Continued).

	AI	AJ	AK	AL	AM	AN
11						
12	33	34	35	36	37	38
13	0.381	0.393	0.404	0.416	0.427	0.439
66						
67	$0.00	$0.00	$5.00	$0.00	$0.00	$0.00
68						
125	$0.00	$0.00	$0.00	$0.00	$0.00	$0.00
126	$0.00	$0.00	$0.00	$0.00	$0.00	$0.00
127	$0.00	$0.00	$0.00	$0.00	$0.00	$0.00
128	$0.00	$0.00	$0.00	$0.00	$0.00	$0.00
129	$0.00	$0.00	$0.00	$0.00	$0.00	$0.00
130	$0.00	$0.00	$0.00	$0.00	$0.00	$0.00
131	$0.00	$0.00	$0.00	$0.00	$0.00	$0.00
132	$0.00	$0.00	$0.00	$0.00	$0.00	$0.00
133	$0.00	$0.00	$0.00	$0.00	$0.00	$0.00
134	$0.00	$0.00	$0.00	$0.00	$0.00	$0.00
135	$0.00	$0.00	$0.00	$0.00	$0.00	$0.00
136	$0.02	$0.00	$0.00	$0.00	$0.00	$0.00
137	$0.11	$0.04	$0.01	$0.00	$0.00	$0.00
138	$0.43	$0.18	$0.06	$0.02	$0.00	$0.00
139	$1.30	$0.67	$0.30	$0.11	$0.03	$0.00
140	$3.15	$1.90	$1.02	$0.48	$0.18	$0.05
141	$6.35	$4.33	$2.72	$1.54	$0.76	$0.30
142	$10.99	$8.26	$5.84	$3.83	$2.27	$1.18
143	$16.76	$13.57	$10.53	$7.74	$5.30	$3.30
144	$23.07	$19.77	$16.45	$13.17	$10.04	$7.18
145	$29.30	$26.19	$22.92	$19.55	$16.13	$12.74
146	$35.02	$32.26	$29.29	$26.12	$22.78	$19.32
147	$40.00	$37.64	$35.09	$32.30	$29.28	$26.06
148	$44.27	$42.26	$40.08	$37.68	$35.09	$32.30
149	$47.93	$46.21	$44.35	$42.30	$40.08	$37.68
150	$51.07	$49.60	$48.01	$46.25	$44.35	$42.30
151	$53.76	$52.51	$51.15	$49.64	$48.01	$46.25
152	$56.07	$55.00	$53.84	$52.55	$51.15	$49.64
153	$58.05	$57.13	$56.15	$55.04	$53.84	$52.55
154	$59.74	$58.97	$58.13	$57.17	$56.15	$55.04
155	$61.19	$60.54	$59.82	$59.01	$58.13	$57.17
156	$62.44	$61.88	$61.27	$60.58	$59.82	$59.01
157	$63.51	$63.03	$62.52	$61.92	$61.27	$60.58
158	$64.42	$64.02	$63.59	$63.07	$62.52	$61.92
159		$64.87	$64.50	$64.06	$63.59	$63.07
160			$65.29	$64.91	$64.50	$64.06
161				$65.64	$65.29	$64.91
162					$65.96	$65.64
163						$66.26

Optimal early exercise for an American put often occurs on the date that the dividend is paid. More generally, it is optimal to exercise an American put option when the underlying stock price is very low for a given amount of time to maturity.

FIGURE 18.21 Excel Model of Binomial Option Pricing - Full-Scale Estimation - Put Option (Continued).

	A	B	C	D	E	F	G	H	AJ	AK
1	**BINOMIAL OPTION PRICING**			**Full-Scale**			**American Put**			
2										
3	**Inputs**	⌐ Option Type ¬				⌐ Early Exercise				
4	Option Type	○ Call ● Put	2		Early Exercise	○ European ● American		2		
5	Risky Part of Stock Now	$69.81	69		**Outputs**					
6	Standard Dev (Annual)	71.65%	71		Time / Period	0.012				
7	Riskfree Rate (Annual)	4.95%	49		Riskfree Rate / Period	0.06%				
8	Exercise Price	$70.00	70		Up Movement / Period	8.01%				
9	Time To Maturity (Years)	0.5777	5		Down Movement/Period	-7.41%				
10	Number of Periods	50			Risk Neutral Probability	48.45%				
11		**Now**								
12	**Period**	**0**	**1**	**2**	**3**	**4**	**5**	**6**	**34**	**35**
13	**Time**	**0.000**	**0.012**	**0.023**	**0.035**	**0.046**	**0.058**	**0.069**	**0.393**	**0.404**
66										
67	**Riskfree Dividends**		$0.00	$0.00	$0.00	$0.00	$5.00	$0.00	$0.00	$5.00
68										
125	**American Put**	$14.02	$11.92	$9.96	$8.18	$6.58	$5.17	$3.97	$0.00	$0.00
126			$16.02	$13.77	$11.66	$9.69	$7.90	$6.31	$0.00	$0.00
127				$18.14	$15.78	$13.52	$11.38	$9.41	$0.00	$0.00
128					$20.38	$17.92	$15.53	$13.25	$0.00	$0.00
129						$22.72	$20.19	$17.70	$0.00	$0.00
130							$25.12	$22.55	$0.00	$0.00
131								$27.56	$0.00	$0.00
132									$0.00	$0.00
133									$0.00	$0.00
134									$0.00	$0.00

We see that the Full-Scale model predicts an American put price of $14.02.

Problems

1. Download three months of daily stock price for any stock that has listed options on it. What is the annual standard deviation of your stock based on continuous returns?

2. Lookup the current stock price of your stock, use the standard deviation of daily returns you computed, lookup the yield on a six-month U.S. Treasury Bill, lookup the exercise price of a call on your stock that matures in

approximately six months, lookup the exercise price of a put on your stock that matures in approximately six months, and compute the time to maturity for both options in fractions of a year. For the call and put that you identified on your stock, determine the replicating portfolio and the price of the call and put using a single-period, replicating portfolio model.

3. For the same inputs as problem 2, determine the replicating portfolio and the price of the call and put using an eight-period, replicating portfolio model.

4. For the same inputs as problem 3, determine the price of the call and put using an eight-period, risk neutral model.

5. Use the same inputs as problem 4. Further, forecast the dividends that you stock pays or make an assumption about the dividends that your stock pays. What is the price of an American call and an American put using an eight-period, risk neutral model of American options with discrete dividends?

6. For the same inputs as problem 5, determine the price of an American call and an American put using a fifty-period, risk neutral model of American options with discrete dividends?

5. Extend the Binomial Option Pricing model to analyze Digital Options. The only thing which needs to be changed is the option's payoff at maturity.
   (a.) For a Digital Call, the Payoff At Maturity
       = $1.00 When Stock Price At Mat > Exercise Price
       Or $0.00 Otherwise.
   (b.) For a Digital Put, the Payoff At Maturity
       = $1.00 When Stock Price At Mat < Exercise Price
       Or $0.00 Otherwise.

6. Extend the **Binomial Option Pricing – Full-Scale Estimation** model to determine how fast the binomial option price converges to the price in the **Black Scholes Option Pricing – Basics** model. Reduce the Full-Scale model to a 10 period model and to a 20 period model. Increase the 50 period model to a 100 period model. Then for the same inputs, compare call and put prices of the 10 period, 20 period, 50 period, 100 period, and Black-Scholes models.

7. Extend the **Binomial Option Pricing – Full-Scale Estimation** model to determine how fast the binomial option price with averaging of adjacent odd and even numbers of periods converges to the price in the **Black Scholes Option Pricing – Basics** model. As you increase the number of periods in the binomial model, it oscillates between overshooting and undershooting the true price. A simple technique to increase price efficiency is to average adjacent odd and even numbers of periods. For example, average the 10 period call price and the 11 period call price. Reduce the Full-Scale model to a 10 period, 11 period, 20 period, and 21 period model. Increase the 50 period model to a 51 period, 100 period, and 101 period model. Then for the same inputs, compare call and put prices of the average of the 10 and 11 period models, 20 and 21 period models, 50 and 51 period models, 100 and 101 period models, and Black-Scholes model.

Chapter 19 Real Options

19.1 NPV Correctly vs. NPV Ignoring Option

Problem. You have the opportunity to purchase a piece of land for $0.4 million which has known reserves of 200,000 barrels of oil. The reserves are worth $5.3 million based on the current crude oil price. The cost of building the plant and equipment to develop the oil is $5.7 million, so it is not profitable to develop these reserves right now. However, development may become profitable in the future if the price of crude oil goes up. For simplicity, assume there is a single date in 1.0 years when you can decide whether to develop the oil or not. Further assume that all of the oil can be produced immediately. Using historical data on crude oil prices, you determine that the mean value of the reserves is $6.0 million based on a mean value of the one-year ahead oil prices and the standard deviation is 30.0%. The riskfree rate is 6.0% and cost of capital for a project of this type is 13.80%. What is the project's NPV when correctly calculated as an option to develop the oil only if it is profitable? What would the NPV be if you committed to develop it today no matter what and thus, (incorrectly) ignored the option feature?

Solution Strategy. One year from now, you will develop the oil if it is profitable and won't develop it if it is not. Thus, the payoff is Max (Value of the Reserves - Cost of Development, 0). This is identical to the payoff of a call option, where the Cost of Development is the Exercise Price and the Value of the Reserves Now is the Asset Price Now. This call option can be valued using the Binomial Option Pricing model. Open the Excel model that you created for Binomial Option Pricing - Risk Neutral. Calculate the NPV Using Binomial by taking the Binomial Option Value and subtracting the cost of the option (i.e., cost of the land). Calculate the NPV Ignoring Option projecting expected cash flows from developing the oil no matter whether it is profitable or not and discounting these expected cash flows back to the present.

FIGURE 19.1 Real Options – NPV Correctly vs. NPV Ignoring Option.

	A	B	C	D	E	F	G	H	I	J
1	REAL OPTIONS	NPV Correctly vs. NPV Ignoring Option					Call			
2					Land Cost = Cost of Real Option	$0.40	4			
3	Inputs				Date 1 Expected Asset Value	$6.00	60			
4	Option Type	Option Type ● Call ○ Put	1		Discount Rate	13.80%	138			
5	Asset Value Now	$5.30	53		Outputs					
6	Asset Value Standard Dev (Ann.)	30.00%	30		Time / Period	0.125				
7	Riskfree Rate (Annual)	6.00%	60		Riskfree Rate / Period	0.75%				
8	Exercise Price	$5.70	57		Up Movement / Period	11.19%				
9	Time To Maturity (Years)	1.00	10		Down Movement/Period	-10.06%				
10	Number of Periods	8			Risk Neutral Probability	50.89%				
11		Now								Maturity
12	Period	0	1	2	3	4	5	6	7	8
13	Time	0.000	0.125	0.250	0.375	0.500	0.625	0.750	0.875	1.000
14										
15	Stock	$5.30	$5.89	$6.55	$7.29	$8.10	$9.01	$10.02	$11.14	$12.38
16			$4.77	$5.30	$5.89	$6.55	$7.29	$8.10	$9.01	$10.02
17				$4.29	$4.77	$5.30	$5.89	$6.55	$7.29	$8.10
18					$3.86	$4.29	$4.77	$5.30	$5.89	$6.55
19						$3.47	$3.86	$4.29	$4.77	$5.30
20							$3.12	$3.47	$3.86	$4.29
21								$2.80	$3.12	$3.47
22									$2.52	$2.80
23										$2.27
24										
25										
26										
27										
28										
29										
30										
31										
32										
33										
34	Call	$0.62	$0.92	$1.34	$1.89	$2.59	$3.43	$4.40	$5.48	$6.68
35			$0.31	$0.50	$0.78	$1.19	$1.76	$2.49	$3.35	$4.32
36				$0.12	$0.21	$0.37	$0.63	$1.03	$1.63	$2.40
37					$0.03	$0.06	$0.11	$0.22	$0.43	$0.85
38						$0.00	$0.00	$0.00	$0.00	$0.00
39							$0.00	$0.00	$0.00	$0.00
40								$0.00	$0.00	$0.00
41									$0.00	$0.00
42										$0.00

(1) Copy the Outputs column (including the Risk Neutral Probability) from Binomial Option Pricing - Risk Neutral model Copy the range F6:F10 from Binomial Option Pricing - Risk Neutral model to the range F6:F10 on this sheet

(2) Copy the Stock and Option Price Trees from Binomial Option Pricing - Risk Neutral model Copy the range B15:J42 from Binomial Option Pricing - Risk Neutral model to the range B15:J42 on this sheet

FIGURE 19.2 Real Options – NPV Correctly vs. NPV Ignoring Option.

	A	B	C	D	E	F	G	H	I	J
1	**REAL OPTIONS**	**NPV Correctly vs. NPV Ignoring Option**					**Call**			
2					Land Cost = Cost of Real Option	$0.40	4			
3	**Inputs**				Date 1 Expected Asset Value	$6.00	60			
4	Option Type	Option Type · Call ○ Put	1		Discount Rate	13.80%	138			
5	Asset Value Now	$5.30	53		**Outputs**					
6	Asset Value Standard Dev (Ann.)	30.00%	30		Time / Period	0.125				
7	Riskfree Rate (Annual)	6.00%	60		Riskfree Rate / Period	0.75%				
8	Exercise Price	$5.70	57		Up Movement / Period	11.19%				
9	Time To Maturity (Years)	1.00	10		Down Movement/Period	-10.06%				
10	Number of Periods	8			Risk Neutral Probability	50.89%				
11		**Now**								**Maturity**
12	Period	0	1	2	3	4	5	6	7	8
13	Time	0.000	0.125	0.250	0.375	0.500	0.625	0.750	0.875	1.000
37					$0.03	$0.06	$0.11	$0.22	$0.43	$0.85
38						$0.00	$0.00	$0.00	$0.00	$0.00
39							$0.00	$0.00	$0.00	$0.00
40								$0.00	$0.00	$0.00
41									$0.00	$0.00
42										$0.00
43										
44	**NPV Correctly**	$0.22								
45										
46	**NPV Ignoring Option**									
47	Date	0.00	1.00							
48	Expected Cash Flows ($ Millions)	($0.40)	$0.30							
49	Present Value of Exp Cash Flows	($0.40)	$0.26							
50	NPV Ignoring Option	($0.14)								
51										
52										
53										
54										
55										

(3) Call Value - Land Cost Enter =B34-F2

(4) -(Land Cost) Enter =-F2

(5) Date 1 Expected Asset Value - Exercise Price Enter =F3-B8

(6) (Expected Cash Flow) / ((1 + Discount Rate) ^ Date Number) Enter =B48/((1+$F$4)^B47) and copy across

(7) Sum of all of the Present Value of Expected Cash Flows Enter =SUM(B49:C49)

We obtain opposite results from the two approaches. The NPV Using Black-Scholes is positive $0.22 million, whereas the Ignore Option NPV is negative ($0.14) million. NPV Ignoring Option incorrectly concludes that the project should be rejected. This mistake happened precisely because it ignores the option to develop oil only when profitable and avoid the cost of development when it is not. NPV Using Black-Scholes correctly demonstrates that the project should be accepted. This is because the *value of the option* to develop the oil when profitable is greater than the *cost of the option* (i.e., the cost of the land).

Problems

1. You have the opportunity to purchase a piece of land for $0.7 million which has known reserves of 375,000 barrels of oil. The reserves are worth $12.6 million based on the current crude oil price of $33.60 per barrel. The cost of building the plant and equipment to develop the oil is $4.5 million, so it is not profitable to develop these reserves right now. However, development may become profitable in the future if the price of crude oil goes up. For simplicity, assume there is a single date in 1.4 years when you can decide whether to develop the oil or not. Further assume that all of the oil can be produced immediately. Using historical data on crude oil prices, you determine that the mean value of the reserves is $13.4 million based on a mean value of the one-year ahead oil price of $35.73 per barrel and the standard deviation 30.0%. The riskfree rate is 4.7% and cost of capital for a project of this type is 12.15%. What is the project's NPV using the binomial model? What would the NPV be if you committed to develop it today no matter what and thus, (incorrectly) ignored the option to develop the oil only if it is profitable?

Chapter 20 Black Scholes Option Pricing

20.1 Basics

Problem. At the close of trading on June 20, 2007, the stock price of Amazon.com was $69.81, the standard deviation of daily returns was 71.65%, the yield on a six-month U.S. Treasury Bill was 4.95%, the exercise price of a January 70 call on Amazon.com was $70.00, the exercise price of a January 70 put on Amazon.com was $70.00, and the time to maturity for both January 18, 2008 maturity options was 0.5777 years. What is the price of a January 70 call and a January 70 put on Amazon.com?

FIGURE 20.1 Excel Model for Black Scholes Option Pricing - Basics.

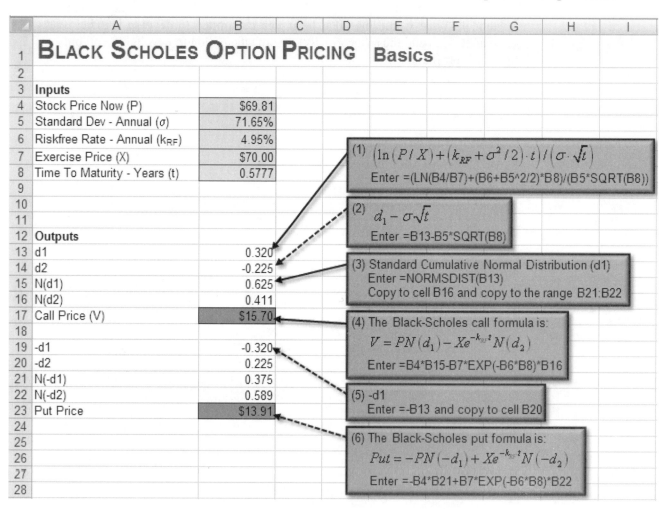

The Black-Scholes model predicts a call price of $15.70. This is seven cents different that what the Binominal Option Pricing - Full-Scale Estimation model predicts for a European call with identical inputs (including no dividends). The Black-Scholes model predicts a put price of $13.91. This is six cents different that what the Binominal Option Pricing - Full-Scale Estimation model predicts for a European put with identical inputs (including no dividends).. The advantage of the Black Scholes model and its natural analytic extensions is they are quick and easy to calculate. The disadvantage is that they are limited to a narrow range of derivatives (such as European options only, etc.).

20.2 Continuous Dividend

Problem. Suppose that Amazon.com paid dividends in tiny amounts on a continuous basis throughout the year at a 1.0% / year rate. What would be the new price of the call and put?

Solution Strategy. Modify the basic Black Scholes formulas from above to include the continuous dividend.

FIGURE 20.2 Excel Model for Black Scholes Option Pricing - Contin Div.

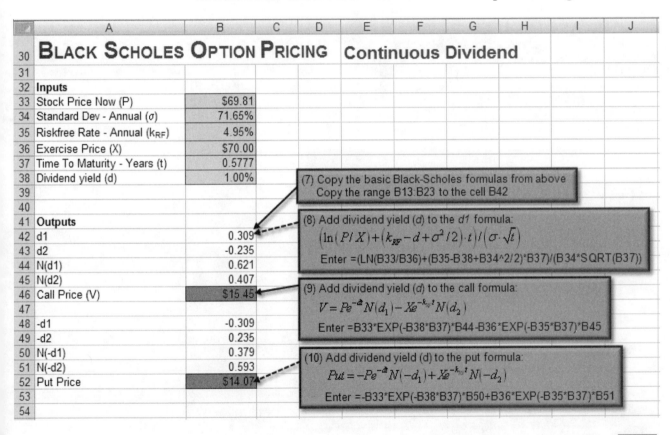

We see that the continuous dividend model predicts a call price of $15.45. This is a drop of 25 cents from the no dividend version. The continuous dividend model predicts a put price of $14.07. This is a rise of 16 cents from the no dividend version.

20.3 Dynamic Chart

If you increased the standard deviation of the stock, what would happen to the price of the call option? If you increased the time to maturity, what would happen to the price of the call? You can answer these questions and more by creating a *Dynamic Chart* using spin buttons. Spin buttons are up-arrow / down-arrow buttons that allow you to easily change the inputs to the model with the click of a mouse. Then Excel recalculates the model and instantly redraws the model outputs on the graph.

FIGURE 20.3 Black Scholes Option Pricing - Dynamic Chart - Call Option.

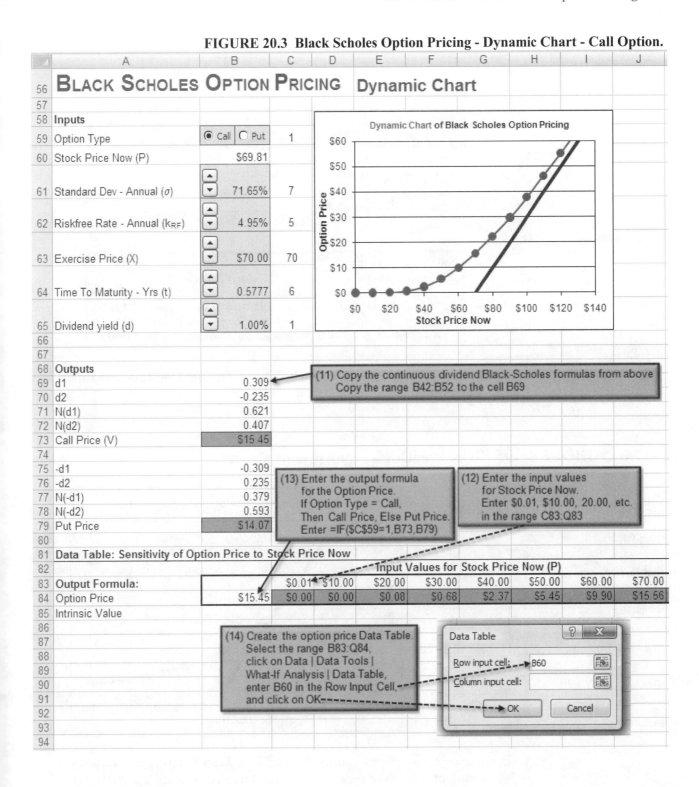

FIGURE 20.4 Option Price and Intrinsic Value.

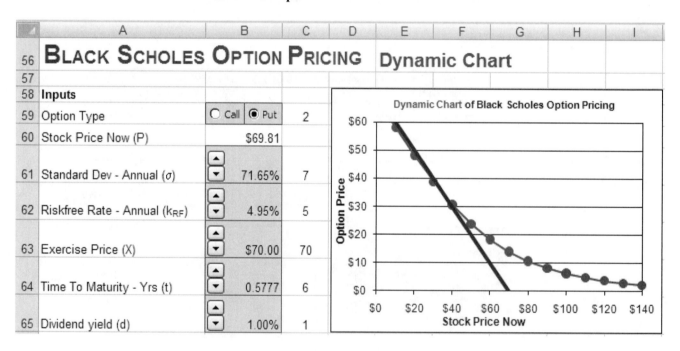

	O	P	Q	R	S	T	U
78							
79	(15) Lowest X-Axis Price, Exercise Price, Highest X-Axis Price						
80	Enter $0.01 in R83, =B63 in S83, $140.00 in T83						
81							
82							
83	$120.00	$130.00	$140.00	$0.01	$70.00	$140.00	
84	$55.04	$64.14	$73.45				
85				$0.00	$0.00	$70.00	
86							
87							
88	(16) If Option Type = Call,						
89	Then Max(Stock Price Now - Exercise Price, 0)						
90	Else Max(Exercise Price - Stock Price Now, 0)						
91	Enter =IF($C$59=1,MAX(R83-$B$63,0),MAX($B$63-R83,0))						
92	and copy across						

FIGURE 20.5 Excel Model for Black Scholes Option Pricing - Dynamic Chart - Put Option.

Your *Dynamic Chart* allows you to change Black-Scholes inputs and instantly see the impact on a graph of the option price and intrinsic value. This allows you to perform instant experiments on the Black-Scholes option pricing model. Below is a list of experiments that you might want to perform:

- What happens when the standard deviation is increased?
- What happens when the time to maturity is increased?
- What happens when the exercise price is increased?

- What happens when the riskfree rate is increased?
- What happens when the dividend yield is increased?
- What happens when the standard deviation is really close to zero?
- What happens when the time to maturity is really close to zero?

Notice that the Black-Scholes option price is usually greater than the payoff you would obtain if the option was maturing today (the "intrinsic value"). This extra value is called the "Time Value" of the option. Given your result in the last experiment above, can you explain *why* the extra value is called the "Time Value"?

20.4 Implied Volatility

Problem. In the afternoon of June 20, 2007, SPX, a security based on the S&P 500 index, traded at 1,512.84. European call and put options on SPX with the exercise prices show below traded for the following prices:

Exercise price	1,450	1,500	1,520	1,540	1,600
Call price	$105.60	$63.40	$45.50	$40.00	$14.50
Put price	$17.70	$32.40	$39.50	$42.00	$76.50

These call options mature on September 17, 2007, which is in 0.2416 years. The S&P 500 portfolio pays a continuous dividend yield of 1.62% per year and the annual yield on a Treasury Bill which matures on September 13th is 4.62% per year. What is the implied volatility of each of these calls and puts? What pattern do these implied volatilities follow across exercise prices and between calls vs. puts?

Solution Strategy. Calculate the difference between the observed option price and the option price predicted by the continuous dividend yield version of the Black-Scholes model using a dummy value for the stock volatility. Have the Excel Solver tool adjust the stock volatility by trial and error until the difference between the observed price and the model price is equal to zero (within a very small error tolerance).

FIGURE 20.6 Graph of the "Scowl" Pattern of Implied Volatilities.

	A	B	C	D	E	F	G	H	I	J	K
96	**BLACK SCHOLES OPTION PRICING**				Implied Volatility						
97											
98				(17) Copy the dynamic chart Black-Scholes formulas from above Copy the range B69:B79 to the range B110:K120							
99	**Inputs**										
100	Option Type: 1=Call, 2=Put	1	1	1	1	1	2	2	2	2	2
101	Stock Price Now (P)	$1,513	$1,513	$1,513	$1,513	$1,513	$1,513	$1,513	$1,513	$1,513	$1,513
102	Standard Dev - Annual (σ)	21.66%	17.31%	14.77%	16.01%	13.81%	15.66%	14.73%	14.02%	11.25%	6.31%
103	Riskfree Rate - Annual (k_{RF})	4.62%	4.62%	4.62%	4.62%	4.62%	4.62%	4.62%	4.62%	4.62%	4.62%
104	Exercise Price (X)	$1,450	$1,500	$1,520	$1,540	$1,600	$1,450	$1,500	$1,520	$1,540	$1,600
105	Time To Maturity - Yrs (t)	0.2416	0.2416	0.2416	0.2416	0.2416	0.2416	0.2416	0.2416	0.2416	0.2416
106	Dividend yield (d)	1.62%	1.62%	1.62%	1.62%	1.62%	1.62%	1.62%	1.62%	1.62%	1.62%
107	Observed Option Price	$105.60	$63.40	$45.50	$40.00	$14.50	$17.70	$32.40	$39.50	$42.00	$76.50
108											
109	**Outputs**										
110	d1	0.520	0.228	0.071	-0.095	-0.685	0.684	0.254	0.071	-0.163	-1.556
111	d2	0.413	0.143	-0.001	-0.173	-0.753	0.607	0.182	0.002	-0.218	-1.587
112	N(d1)	0.698	0.590	0.528	0.462	0.247	0.753	0.600	0.528	0.435	0.060
113	N(d2)	0.660	0.557	0.499	0.431	0.226	0.728	0.572	0.501	0.414	0.056
114	Model Call Price (V)	$105.60	$63.40	$45.50	$40.00	$14.50	$90.73	$55.98	$43.30	$26.02	$1.19
115											
116	-d1	-0.520	-0.228	-0.071	0.095	0.685	-0.684	-0.254	-0.071	0.163	1.556
117	-d2	-0.413	-0.143	0.001	0.173	0.753	-0.607	-0.182	-0.002	0.218	1.587
118	N(-d1)	0.302	0.410	0.472	0.538	0.753	0.247	0.400	0.472	0.565	0.940
119	N(-d2)	0.340	0.443	0.501	0.569	0.774	0.272	0.428	0.499	0.586	0.944
120	Model Put Price	$32.57	$39.82	$41.70	$55.98	$89.81	$17.70	$32.40	$39.50	$42.00	$76.50
121											
122	**Solver**										
123	Difference (observed - model)	4E-07	7.2E-08	4E-08	9.5E-07	2.2E-07	9.6E-07	4.8E-07	-3.2E-07	7.2E-08	8.0E-07

(18) If Option Type = Call,
   Then Observed Option Price - Model Call Price
   Else Observed Option Price - Model Put Price
   Enter =IF(B100=1,B107-B114,B107-B120)

(19) Use Solver to determine the
   Implied Volatility.
      * Click on Data | Analysis | Solver,
      * enter B123 in Set Target Cell,
      * click on the Value Of button,
      * enter 0 in the adjacent box,
      * enter B102 in By Changing Cells,
      * and click on Solve.
   When Solver finds a solution,
      * click on the Keep Solver Solution
      button
      * and click on OK.
   Repeat using Solver to determine
   the implied volatility for column C.
   Repeat for column D, ..., column K.

Solver Parameters

Set Target Cell: $B$123

Equal To: Max   Min   Value of: 0

By Changing Cells:
$B$102

Subject to the Constraints:

[Solve] [Close] [Guess] [Options] [Add] [Change] [Delete] [Reset All] [Help]

Solver Results

Solver found a solution. All constraints and optimality conditions are satisfied.

Reports: Answer, Sensitivity, Limits

● Keep Solver Solution
○ Restore Original Values

[OK] [Cancel] [Save Scenario...] [Help]

Excel 2003 Equivalent

To install Solver in Excel 2003, click on **Tools**, **Add-Ins**, check the **Solver** checkbox on the Add-Ins dialog box, and click on **OK**.

If you don't see **Solver** on the **Data** Tab in the **Analysis** Group, then you need to install the Solver. To install the Solver, click on the **Office** button, click on the Excel Options button at the bottom of the drop-down window, click on **Add-Ins**, highlight **Solver** in the list of Inactive Applications, click on **Go**, check **Solver**, and click on **OK**.

FIGURE 20.7 Graph of the "Scowl" Pattern of Implied Volatilities.

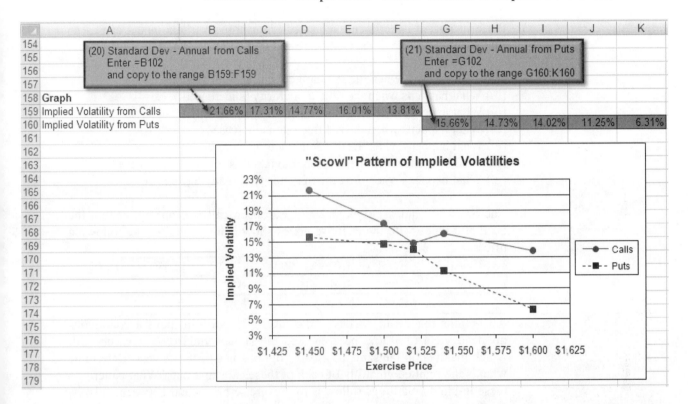

If the market's beliefs about the distribution of returns of the S&P 500 Index matched the theoretical distribution of returns assumed by the Black-Scholes model, then all of the implied volatilities would be the same. From the graph we see this is not the case. The implied volatility pattern declines sharply with the exercise price and puts have lower implied volatilities than calls. In the '70s and '80s, the typical implied volatility pattern was a U-shaped, "Smile" pattern. In the '90s and 2000s, it is more typical to see a downward-sloping, "Scowl" pattern.

Problems

1. Download three months of daily stock price for any stock that has listed options on it and compute the standard deviation of daily returns. Lookup the current stock price of your stock, use the standard deviation of daily returns you just computed, lookup the yield on a six-month U.S. Treasury Bill, lookup the exercise price of a call on your stock that matures in approximately six months, lookup the exercise price of a put on your stock that matures in approximately six months, and compute the time to maturity

for both options in fractions of a year. For the call and put that you identified on your stock, determine the price of the call and put using the Black-Scholes basics model.

2. Use the same inputs as problem 1. Forecast the continuous dividend that your stock pays or make an assumption about the continuous dividend that your stock pays. Determine the price of the call and put using the Black-Scholes continuous dividend model.

3. Perform instant experiments on whether changing various inputs causes an increase or decrease in the Call Price and in the Put Price and by how much.

(a.) What happens when the standard deviation is increased?
(b.) What happens when the time to maturity is increased?
(c.) What happens when the exercise price is increased?
(d.) What happens when the riskfree rate is increased?
(e.) What happens when the dividend yield is increased?
(f.) What happens when the standard deviation is really close to zero?
(g.) What happens when the time to maturity is really close to zero?

4. The S&P 500 index closes at 2000. European call and put options on the S&P 500 index with the exercise prices show below trade for the following prices:

Exercise price	1,950	1,975	2,000	2,025	2,050
Call price	$88	$66	$47	$33	$21
Put price	$25	$26	$32	$44	$58

All options mature in 88 days. The S&P 500 portfolio pays a continuous dividend yield of 1.56% per year and the annual yield on a Treasury Bill which matures on the same day as the options is 4.63% per year. Determine what is the implied volatility of each of these calls and puts. What pattern do these implied volatilities follow across exercise prices and between calls vs. puts?

Chapter 21 Debt And Equity Valuation

21.1 Two Methods

Problem. The Value of the Firm (V) is $340 million, the Face Value of the Debt (B) is $160 million, the time to maturity of the debt (t) is 2.00 years, the riskfree rate (k_{RF}) is 5.0%, and the standard deviation of the return on the firm's assets (σ) is 50.0%. There are two different methods for valuing the firm's equity and risky debt based in an option pricing framework. Using both methods, what the firm's Equity Value (E) and Risky Debt Value (D)? Do both methods produce the same result?

Solution Strategy. In the first method, equity is considered to be a call option. Thus, E = Call Price. For this call option, the underlying asset is the Value of the Firm (V) and the exercise price is the face value of the debt (B). Hence, the call price is calculated from the Black-Scholes call formula by substituting V for P and B for X. The rational is that if V > B, then the equityholders gain the net profit V-B. However, if V < B, then the equityholders avoid the loss by declaring bankruptcy, turning V over to the debtholders, and walking away with zero rather than owing money. Thus, the payoff to equityholders is Max (V - B, 0), which has the same payoff form as a call option. Further, we can use the fact that Debt plus Equity equals Total Value of Firm (D + E = V) and obtain the value of debt D = V - E = V - Call.

In the second method, Risky Debt is considered to be Riskfree Debt minus a Put option. Thus, D = Riskfree Debt - Put. For this put option, the underlying asset is also the Value of the Firm (V) and the exercise price is also the face value of the debt (B). Hence, the put price is calculated from the Black-Scholes put formula by substituting V for P and B for X. The rational is that the put option is a *Guarantee* against default in repaying the face value of the debt (B). Specifically, if V > B, then the equityholders repay the face value B in full and the value of the guarantee is zero. However, if V < B, then the equityholders only pay V and default on the rest, so the guarantee must pay the balance B - V. Thus, the payoff on the guarantee is Max (B - V, 0), which has the same payoff form as a put option. Further, we can use the fact that Debt plus Equity equals Total Value of Firm (D + E = V) and obtain E = V - Risky Debt = V - (Riskfree Debt - Put).

FIGURE 21.1 Excel Model for Stocks and Risky Bonds.

	A	B	C	D	E	F	G	H	I	J
1	**DEBT AND EQUITY VALUATION**				**Two Methods**					
2										
3	Inputs				Analogous Inputs for a Black-Scholes Call Option on a Stock					
4	Value of Firm (V)	$340.00			Stock Price					
5	Firm Asset Std Dev (σ)	50.0%			Stock Std Dev					
6	Risk-free Rate (k_RF)	5.0%			Risk-free Rate					
7	Face Value of Debt (B)	$160.00			Exercise Price					
8	Time to Maturity (t)	2.00			Time to Maturity					
9										
10	Outputs									
11	**Black-Scholes Option Pricing**									
12	d1	1.561								
13	d2	0.854								
14	N(d1)	0.941								
15	N(d2)	0.803			(1) (Face Value of Debt) * Exp[- (Risk-free Rate) * (Time to Maturity)]					
16	Call Price	$203.54			Enter =B7*EXP(-B6*B8)					
17										
18	-d1	-1.561			(2) Call Price					
19	-d2	-0.854			Enter =B16					
20	N(-d1)	0.059								
21	N(-d2)	0.197			(3) V - Call Price					
22	Put Price	$8.31			Enter =B4-B16					
23										
24	**Corporate Finance Applications**				(4) Equity + Risky Debt					
25	Riskfree Debt Value	$144.77			Enter =C30+C32					
26										
27			Method One:		Method Two (equivalent by Put-Call Parity):					
28			Equity is a Call		Risky Debt is Riskfree Debt minus Put					
29										
30	Equity Value (E)	= Call	$203.54		= V - Riskfree Debt + Put	$203.54	(5) V - Riskfree Debt Value + Put Price			
31							Enter =B4-B25+B22			
32	Risky Debt Value (D)	= V - Call	$136.46		= Riskfree Debt - Put	$136.46	(6) Riskfree Debt Value - Put Price			
33							Enter =B25-B22			
34	Total Value of Firm (V)	= V	$340.00		= V	$340.00	(7) Equity + Risky Debt			
35							Enter =F30+F32			
36										
37										

Both methods of doing the calculation find that the Equity Value (E) = $203.54 and the Risky Debt Value (D) = $136.46. We can verify that both methods should always generate the same results. Consider what we get if we equate the Method One and Method Two expressions for the Equity Value (E): **Call Price = V – Riskfree Bond Value + Put Price**. You may recognize this as an alternative version of Put-Call Parity. The standard version of Put-Call Parity is: **Call Price = Stock Price - Bond Price + Put Price**. To get the alternative version, just substitute V for the Stock Price and substitute the Riskfree Bond Value for the Bond Price. Consider what we get if we equate the Method One and Method Two expressions for the Risky Debt Value (D): **V - Call Price = Riskfree Bond - Put Price**. This is simply a rearrangement of the alternative version of Put-Call Parity. Since Put-Call Parity is always true, then both methods of valuing debt and equity will always yield the same results!

21.2 Impact of Risk

Problem. What impact does the firm's risk have upon the firm's Debt and Equity valuation? Specifically, if you increased Firm Asset Standard Deviation, then what would happen to the firm's Equity Value and Risky Debt Value?

Solution Strategy. Create a **Data Table** of Equity Value and Risky Debt Value for different input values for the Firm's Asset Standard Deviation. Then graph the results and interpret it.

FIGURE 21.2 Excel Model of the Sensitivity of Equity Value and Risky Debt Value.

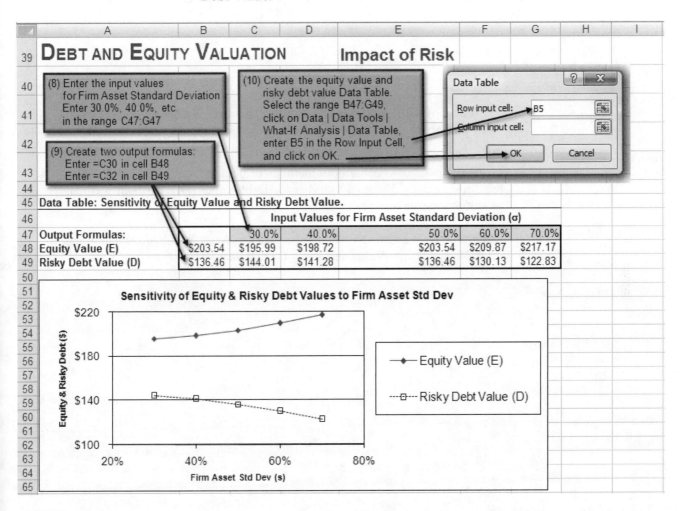

Excel 2003 Equivalent

To call up a Data Table in Excel 2003, click on **Data | Table**

Looking at the chart, we see that increasing the firm's asset standard deviation causes a wealth transfer from debtholders to equityholders. This may seem surprising, but this is a direct consequence equity being a call option and debt being V *minus* a call option. We know that increasing the standard deviation makes a call more valuable, so equivalently increases the firm's asset standard deviation makes the firm's Equity Value more valuable and reduces the Risky Debt Value by the same amount.

The intuitive rational for this is that an increase in standard deviation allows equityholders to benefit from more frequent and bigger increases in V, while not being hurt by more frequent and bigger decreases in V. In the later case, the equityholders are going to declare bankruptcy anyway so they don't care how much V drops. Debtholders are the mirror image. They do *not* benefit from more frequent and bigger increases in V since repayment is capped at B, but they are *hurt* by more frequent and bigger decreases in V. In the latter case, the size of the repayment default (B – V) increases as V drops more.

The possibility of transferring wealth from debtholders to equityholders (or visa versa) illustrates the potential for conflict between equityholders and debtholders. Equityholders would like the firm to take on riskier projects, but debtholders would like the firm to focus on safer projects. Whether the firm ultimately decides to take on risky or safe projects will determine how wealth is divided between the two groups.

Problems

1. The Value of the Firm (V) is $780 million, the Face Value of the Debt (B) is $410 million, the time to maturity of the debt (t) is 1.37 years, the riskfree rate (k_{RF}) is 3.2%, and the standard deviation of the return on the firm's assets (σ) is 43.0%. Using both methods of debt and equity valuation, what the firm's Equity Value (E) and Risky Debt Value (D)? Do both methods produce the same result?

2. Determine what impact an increase in the Firm Asset Standard Deviation has on the firm's Equity Value and Risky Debt Value.

Chapter 22 International Parity

22.1 System of Four Parity Conditions

Problem. Suppose the Euro/Dollar Exchange Rate is €1 = \$1.3640, the annual US riskfree rate is 4.47%, the US inflation rate is 2.69%, and the annual Eurozone riskfree rate is 4.27%. What is the one-year Forward Euro/Dollar Exchange Rate, the one-year ahead Expected Spot Euro/Dollar Exchange Rate, and Eurozone inflation rate? What is the Percent Difference in:

- the Eurozone Riskfree Rate vs. US Riskfree Rate,
- the Forward Euro/Dollar Exchange Rate vs. the Spot Rate,
- the Expected Spot Euro/Dollar Exchange Rate vs. the Spot Rate, and
- the Eurozone Inflation Rate vs. the US Inflation Rate?

Solution Strategy. Use Interest Rate Parity to determine the one-year Forward Euro/Dollar Exchange Rate. Then use the Expectations Theory of Exchange Rates to determine the one-year ahead Expected Spot Euro/Dollar Exchange Rate. Then use Purchase Power Parity to determine the Eurozone inflation rate. Finally, the International Fisher Effect to confirm the Eurozone riskfree rate. Compute the four percent differences. Under the four international parity condition, the four percent differences should be identical.

FIGURE 22.1 International Parity – System of Four Parity Conditions.

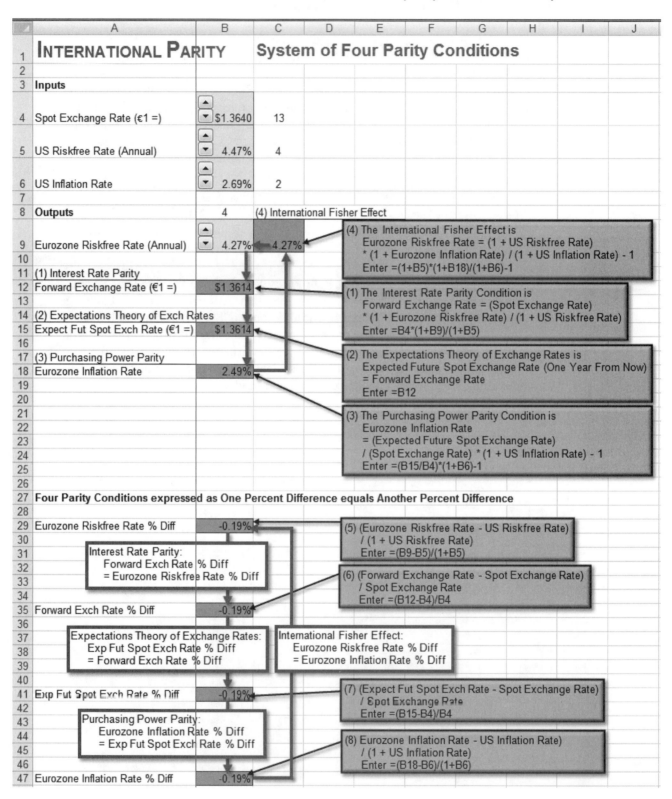

In theory, the four international parity conditions are tightly connected to each other.

22.2 Estimating Future Exchange Rates

Problem. Suppose the Euro/Dollar Exchange Rate is €1 = $1.3640, the annual US riskfree rate is 4.47%, the US inflation rate is 2.69%, the annual Eurozone riskfree rate is 4.27%, the Eurozone inflation rate is 1.90%, and the one-year Forward Euro/Dollar Exchange Rate is €1 = $1.3739. What will the Euro/Dollar Exchange Rate be in one-year, two-years, three-years, four-years, and five-years?
Solution. Use three different methods for forecast future exchange rates: (1) Purchasing Power Parity, (2) Interest Rate Parity + Expectations Theory of Exchange Rates, (3) Only the Expectations Theory of Exchange Rates.

FIGURE 22.2 International Parity – Estimating Future Exchange Rates.

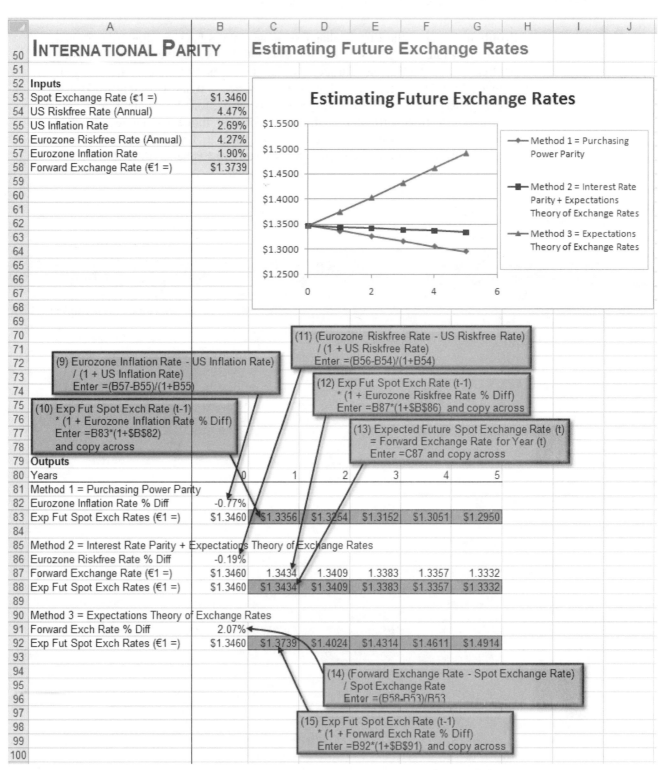

In practice, when you use real data, the various international parity conditions yield very different forecasts of future exchange rates.

Problems

1. Suppose the Euro/Dollar Exchange Rate is €1 = $1.283, the annual US riskfree rate is 3.61%, the US inflation rate is 2.69%, and the annual Eurozone riskfree rate is 5.39%. What is the one-year Forward Euro/Dollar Exchange Rate, the one-year ahead Expected Spot Euro/Dollar Exchange Rate, and Eurozone inflation rate? What is the Percent Difference in:
   - the Eurozone Riskfree Rate vs. US Riskfree Rate,
   - the Forward Euro/Dollar Exchange Rate vs. the Spot Rate,
   - the Expected Spot Euro/Dollar Exchange Rate vs. the Spot Rate, and
   - the Eurozone Inflation Rate vs. the US Inflation Rate?

2. Suppose the Euro/Dollar Exchange Rate is €1 = $1.7271, the annual US riskfree rate is 6.31%, the US inflation rate is 4.52%, the annual Eurozone riskfree rate is 3.15%, the Eurozone inflation rate is 3.15%, and the one-year Forward Euro/Dollar Exchange Rate is €1 = $1.8241. What will the Euro/Dollar Exchange Rate be in one-year, two-years, three-years, four-years, and five-years under three forecast methods: (1) purchasing power parity, (2) interest rate parity + expectations theory of exchange rates, and (3) using just the expectations theory of exchange rates?

PART 6 EXCEL SKILLS

Chapter 23 Useful Excel Tricks

23.1 Quickly Delete The Instructions and Arrows

Task. Quickly get rid of all of the instruction boxes and arrows after you are done building the Excel model/estimation.

How To. All of the instruction boxes and arrows are *objects* and there is an easy way to select all of them at once. Click on **Home | Editing | Find & Select down-arrow | Select Objects.** This causes the cursor to become a pointer. Then point to a **location above and to the left** of the instruction boxes and arrows, continue to hold down the left mouse button while you drag the pointer to a **location below and to the right** of the instruction boxes and arrows, and then let go of the left mouse button. This selects *all* of the instruction boxes and arrows (see example below). Then just press the **Delete** key and they are all gone!

Excel 2003 Equivalent

To get the Select Objects cursor in Excel 2003, click on the **Drawing** icon on the Standard toolbar and then click on the **Select Objects** icon (which looks like pointer) on the Drawing toolbar in the lower-left corner of the screen.

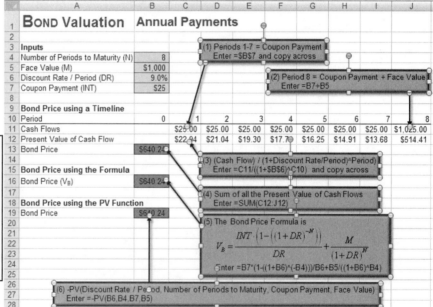

23.2 Freeze Panes

Task. Freeze column titles at the top of the columns and/or freeze row titles on the left side of the rows. This is especially useful for large spreadsheets.

How To. In the example below, suppose you want to freeze the column titles from row 8 and above (freezing Barrick over column B, Hanson over column C, etc.) and you want to freeze the row titles in column A. Select cell **B9** (as shown), because cell **B9** this is just below row 8 that want to freeze and just to the right of column A that you want to freeze.

	A	B	C	D	E	F	G	H
1	COST OF CAPITAL		Static CAPM Using Fama-MacBeth Method					
2								
3	Inputs							
4	Market Portfolio Benchmark	Market Portfolio Benchmark ○ SPDR ETF ● CRSP VWMR ○ DJ World Stock			2			
5	Asset Type	Asset Type ○ Stock ● US Port ○ Country Port			2			
6								
7		Stock	Stock	Stock	Stock	Stock	Stock	US Portfolio
8		Barrick	Hanson	IBM	Nokia	Telefonos	YPF	Small-Growth
9	Monthly Returns							
10	Dec 2006	-3.50%	-0.24%	2.06%	8.76%	8.63%	0.50%	-0.59%
11	Nov 2006	-2.37%	4.88%	5.69%	0.51%	9.01%	-0.95%	2.58%
12	Oct 2006	1.79%	3.78%	-0.12%	1.70%	-1.08%	3.49%	5.87%
13	Sep 2006	0.92%	-3.49%	12.69%	0.93%	3.14%	7.02%	1.09%
14	Aug 2006	-8.23%	14.36%	1.20%	-5.68%	6.76%	-3.83%	3.22%

Then click on **View | Window | Freeze Panes down-arrow | Freeze Panes**.

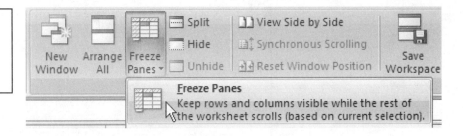

23.3 Spin Buttons and the Developer Tab

Task. Add a spin button to make an input interactive.

How To. Spin buttons and other so-called "form controls" are located on the Developer tab Developer . If you don't see a Developer tab, then you need to take a simple step to make it visible. Click on the **Office** button , click on the **Excel Options** button at the bottom of the drop-down window, in the section **Top options for working with Excel** check the **Show Developer tab in the Ribbon** checkbox ☑ Show Developer tab in the Ribbon ⓘ , and click **OK**.

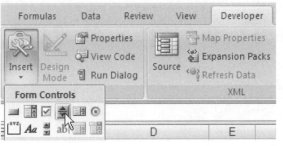

Then click on **Developer | Controls | Insert down-arrow | Form Controls | Spin Button**.

Then point the cursor crosshairs to the upper-left corner of where you want the spin button to be, click and drag to the lower-right corner, and release. You get a

spin button 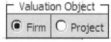. Now place the cursor over the top of the spin button, right-click, and select **Format Control** from the pop-up menu. On the **Control** tab of the **Format Control** dialog box, enter **C4** in the **Cell Link** entry box, and click **OK**.

Now when you spin button, the value in cell **C4** will increase or decrease by 1. For convenience, I scale the spin button output to appropriate scale of the input. For example, in the spreadsheet below the spin button in cell **B6** is linked to the cell **C6** and creates the integer value **5**. The formula in cell B6 is **=C6/100** and this create the value **5.0%** for the riskfree rate.

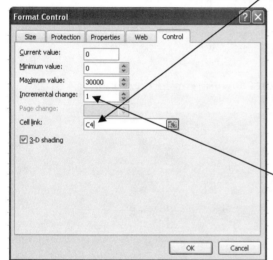

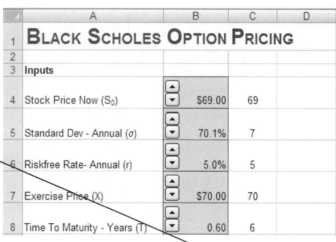

	A	B	C	D
1	**BLACK SCHOLES OPTION PRICING**			
2				
3	**Inputs**			
4	Stock Price Now (S$_0$)	$69.00	69	
5	Standard Dev - Annual (σ)	70.1%	7	
6	Riskfree Rate- Annual (r)	5.0%	5	
7	Exercise Price (X)	$70.00	70	
8	Time To Maturity - Years (T)	0.60	6	

Unfortunately, Spin Buttons are only allowed to have **Incremental Changes** that are integers (1, 2, 3, etc.). It would be convenient if they could have **Incremental Changes** of any value, such as .01 or -.0043.

23.4 Option Buttons and Group Boxes

Task. Add option buttons to allow input choices.

How To. Option buttons and other so-called "form controls" are located on the Developer tab . If you don't see a Developer tab, then you need to take a simple step to make it visible (see the section above).

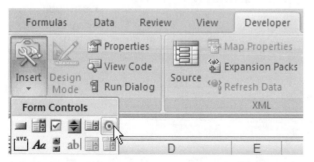

Then click on **Developer | Controls | Insert down-arrow | Form Controls | Option Button**.

Then point the cursor crosshairs to the upper-left corner of where you want the option button to be, click and drag to the lower-right corner, and release. You get a option button 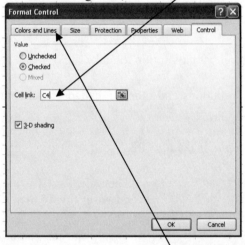. Repeat this process to get more option buttons.

Now place the cursor over the top of the first option button, right-click, then click over the blank text area, click a second time over the blank text area, delete any unwanted text (e.g., "Option Button1"), enter a text description of the choice (e.g., "Firm"), and then click outside the option button to finish ⊙ Firm. Repeat this process for the other option buttons (e.g., "Project") ⊙ Project.

Now place the cursor over the top of the first option button, right-click, and select **Format Control** from the pop-up menu. On the **Control** tab of the **Format Control** dialog box, enter **C4** in the **Cell Link** entry box, and click **OK**.

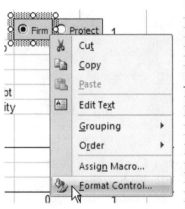

Now when the first option button is clicked, then the cell **C4** will show a **1**, and when the second option button is clicked, then the cell **C4** will show a **2**. Optionally, you click on the **Colors and Lines** tab of **Format Control** dialog box and specify the option button's fill color, line color, etc.

If you just want to have *one set* of option buttons on a spreadsheet, then you are done. However, if you want to have two or more sets of option buttons (see example below), then you need to use **Group Boxes** to indicate which option buttons belong to which set.

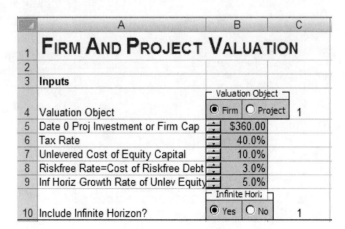

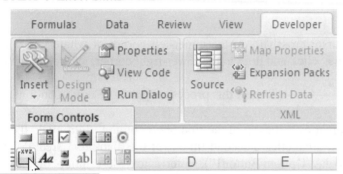

Click on **Developer | Controls | Insert down-arrow | Form Controls | Group Box**.

Then point the cursor crosshairs above and left of the first option button, click and drag to below and right of the second option button (or last option button in the set), and release. A Group Box is created which surrounds the option buttons. Click on the title of the Group Box, delete any unwanted text (e.g., "Group Box 1"), enter a text description (e.g., "Valuation Object"). Now when you click on the Firm or Project option button in cell **B4** of the example above, then the linked cell **C4** changes to 1 or 2. Repeat the process of creating option buttons and surrounding them by group boxes to create all of the sets of option buttons that you want.

Excel 2003 Equivalent

To insert a Group Box in Excel 2003, click on **View | Toolbars | Forms**. Then click on the **Group Box** icon on the Forms Toolbar.

23.5 Scroll Bar

Excel 2003 Equivalent

To insert a Scroll Bar in Excel 2003, click on **View | Toolbars | Forms**. Then click on the **Scroll Bar** icon on the Forms Toolbar.

Task. Add a scroll bar call option to make big or small changes to an input.

How To. Option buttons and other so-called "form controls" are located on the Developer tab ⟨Developer⟩. If you don't see a Developer tab, then you need to take a simple step to make it visible (see two sections above).

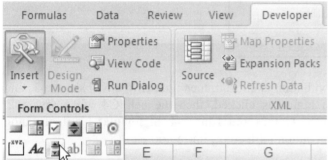

Then click on **Developer | Controls | Insert down-arrow | Form Controls | Scroll Bar**.

Then point the cursor crosshairs to the upper-left corner of where you want the option button to be, click and drag to the lower-right corner, and release. You get a scroll bar ⟨ scroll bar ⟩.

Now place the cursor over the top of the scroll bar, right-click, and select **Format Control** from the pop-up menu. On the **Control** tab of the **Format Control** dialog box, enter **I7** in the **Cell Link** entry box, and click **OK**. Optionally, you can specify the **Page Change** amount, which is the change in the cell link when you click on the white space of the scroll bar. In this example, a Page Change of 12 months jumps a year ahead.

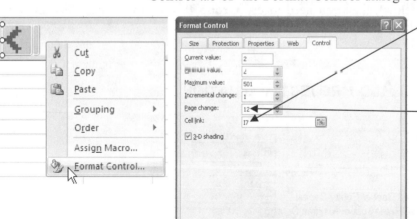

The advantage of a scroll bar is that you can make big or small changes (see example below). Clicking on the left or right arrow, lowers or raises the value in cell **I7** by 1. Clicking on the white space of the scroll bar, lowers or raises the value in cell **I7** by 12 (the Page Change). Sliding the position bar allows you to rapidly scroll through the entire range of values.

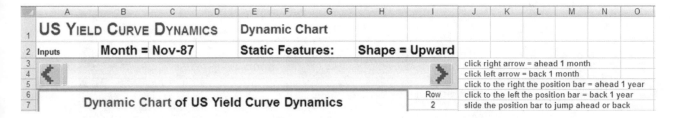

23.6 Install Solver or the Analysis ToolPak

Task. Install Solver or the Analysis ToolPak.

How To. Excel provides several special tools, such as Solver and the Analysis ToolPak, which need to be separately installed. Solver is a sophisticated, yet easy to use optimizer. The Analysis ToolPak contains advanced statistical programs and advanced functions.

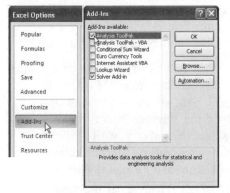

To install the Analysis ToolPak, click on the **Office** button , click on the **Excel Options** button at the bottom of the drop-down window, click on **Add-Ins**, highlight the **Analysis ToolPak** Analysis ToolPak in the list of Inactive Applications, click on **Go** Go... near the bottom of the dialog box, check the **Analysis ToolPak**, and click on **OK**.

To install Solver, do the same steps except substitute **Solver** in place of **Analysis ToolPak** along the way.

23.7 Format Painter

Task. Apply formatting from one cell to other cells.

How To. Select the cell(s) whose format you want to copy (e.g., select **D5:E5** in the example below). Then click on **Home | Clipboard | Format Painter** Format Painter. The cursor now includes a paint brush. Then select the range that you want to apply the formatting to (e.g., range **D6:E17** in the example below). Notice that Format Painter copies all of the formatting, including number type (percentage), number of decimals, background color, and border color.

Before

	A	B	C	D	E
1	THE YIELD CURVE	Obtaining and Using It			
2		Maturity	Time To	Yield To	Forward
3	Yield Curve Inputs	Date	Maturity	Maturity	Rates
4	Today's Date	5/22/2007			
5	One Month Treasury Bill	6/22/2007	0.08	4.90%	4.90%
6	Three Month Treasury Bill	8/22/2007	0.25	0.0477	0.0471
7	Six Month Treasury Bill	11/22/2007	0.50	0.0481	0.0485
8	One Year Treasury Strip	5/15/2008	0.98	0.0489	0.0497
9	Two Year Treasury Strip	8/15/2009	2.23	0.0482	0.0477
10	Three Year Treasury Strip	8/15/2010	3.23	0.0474	0.0456
11	Four Year Treasury Strip	8/15/2011	4.23	0.0472	0.0466
12	Five Year Treasury Strip	8/15/2012	5.23	0.0471	0.0467
13	Ten Year Treasury Strip	8/15/2017	10.23	0.0493	0.0516
14	Fifteen Year Treasury Bond	8/15/2022	15.23	0.0514	0.0557
15	Twenty Year Treasury Bond	8/15/2027	20.23	0.0511	0.0502
16	Twenty Five Year Treasury Bond	8/15/2032	25.23	0.0497	0.0441
17	Thirty Year Treasury Bond	2/15/2037	29.73	0.0495	0.0484

After

	A	B	C	D	E
1	THE YIELD CURVE	Obtaining and Using It			
2		Maturity	Time To	Yield To	Forward
3	Yield Curve Inputs	Date	Maturity	Maturity	Rates
4	Today's Date	5/22/2007			
5	One Month Treasury Bill	6/22/2007	0.08	4.90%	4.90%
6	Three Month Treasury Bill	8/22/2007	0.25	4.77%	4.71%
7	Six Month Treasury Bill	11/22/2007	0.50	4.81%	4.85%
8	One Year Treasury Strip	5/15/2008	0.98	4.89%	4.97%
9	Two Year Treasury Strip	8/15/2009	2.23	4.82%	4.77%
10	Three Year Treasury Strip	8/15/2010	3.23	4.74%	4.56%
11	Four Year Treasury Strip	8/15/2011	4.23	4.72%	4.66%
12	Five Year Treasury Strip	8/15/2012	5.23	4.71%	4.67%
13	Ten Year Treasury Strip	8/15/2017	10.23	4.93%	5.16%
14	Fifteen Year Treasury Bond	8/15/2022	15.23	5.14%	5.57%
15	Twenty Year Treasury Bond	8/15/2027	20.23	5.11%	5.02%
16	Twenty Five Year Treasury Bond	8/15/2032	25.23	4.97%	4.41%
17	Thirty Year Treasury Bond	2/15/2037	29.73	4.95%	4.84%

23.8 Conditional Formatting

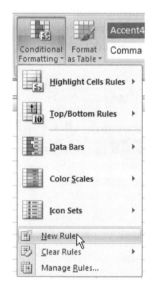

Task. Conditionally format a cell. This allows the displayed format to change based upon the results of a formula calculation.

How To. Suppose you want to use special formatting to highlight the best portfolio in constrained portfolio optimization (see example below). Select cell M166. Click on **Home | Styles | Conditional Formatting down-arrow | New Rule**. Then click on Use a formula to determine which cells to format

► Use a formula to determine which cells to format

. In the text entry box, enter **=M166=1**. This checks whether the value of cell M166 is equal to one. Formulas for conditional fomatting must begin with an equal sign, so oddly you end up with two equal signs in the formula. Then click on the **Format** button. In the **Format Cells** dialog box, click on the **Fill** tab, select the **color** you like, click **OK**, and then click **OK** again. Finally, copy this new conditional format down the column using Format Painter. Click on **Home | Clipboard | Format Painter**

Format Painter

. The cursor now includes a paint brush. Then select the range **M167:M181**. In this example, the cell **M173** turns orange because it is the highest ranking (#1) portfolio. If you changed one of the problem inputs, then a different portfolio might be ranked #1 and the cell corresponding to the new #1 would be highlighted in orange.

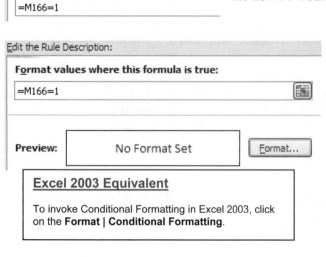

Edit the Rule Description:

Format values where this formula is true:

=M166=1

Edit the Rule Description:

Format values where this formula is true:

=M166=1

Preview: No Format Set   **Format...**

Excel 2003 Equivalent

To invoke Conditional Formatting in Excel 2003, click on the **Format | Conditional Formatting**.

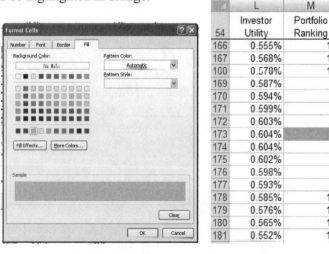

	L	M
54	Investor Utility	Portfolio Ranking
166	0.555%	15
167	0.568%	13
100	0.570%	11
169	0.587%	9
170	0.594%	7
171	0.599%	5
172	0.603%	3
173	0.604%	1
174	0.604%	2
175	0.602%	4
176	0.598%	6
177	0.593%	8
178	0.585%	10
179	0.576%	12
180	0.565%	14
181	0.552%	16

23.9 Fill Handle

Task. Fill in row 10 with integers from 0 to 8 to create the timeline (see example below). This fill technique works for wide range of patterns.

How To. Enter **0** in cell **B10** and **1** in cell **C10**. Select the range **B10:C10**, then hover the cursor over the fill handle ▬▮ (the square in the lower-right corner) of cell **C10** and the cursor turns to a plus symbol ╈. Click, drag the plus symbol to cell **J10**, and release. The range fills up with the rest the pattern from 2 to 8.

Before

	A	B	C	D	E	F	G	H	I	J
1	Bᴏɴᴅ Valuation	Annual Payments								
2										
3	Inputs									
4	Number of Periods to Maturity (N)	8								
5	Face Value (M)	$1,000								
6	Discount Rate / Period (DR)	9.0%								
7	Coupon Payment (INT)	$25								
8										
9	Bond Price using a Timeline									
10	Period	0	1							
11	Cash Flows		$25.00	$25.00	$25.00	$25.00	$25.00	$25.00	$25.00	$1,025.00
12	Present Value of Cash Flow		$22.94	$25.00	$25.00	$25.00	$25.00	$25.00	$25.00	$1,025.00
13	Bond Price	########								

After

	A	B	C	D	E	F	G	H	I	J
1	Bᴏɴᴅ Valuation	Annual Payments								
2										
3	Inputs									
4	Number of Periods to Maturity (N)	8								
5	Face Value (M)	$1,000								
6	Discount Rate / Period (DR)	9.0%								
7	Coupon Payment (INT)	$25								
8										
9	Bond Price using a Timeline									
10	Period	0	1	2	3	4	5	6	7	8
11	Cash Flows		$25.00	$25.00	$25.00	$25.00	$25.00	$25.00	$25.00	$1,025.00
12	Present Value of Cash Flow		$22.94	$21.04	$19.30	$17.71	$16.25	$14.91	$13.68	$514.41
13	Bond Price	$640.24								

23.10 2-D Scatter Chart

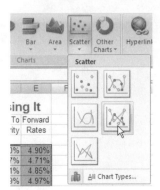

Task. Create a two-dimensional Scatter Chart.

How To. Select the range that has the data you wish to graph (e.g., select **C5:E17** in the example below). Click on **Insert | Charts | Scatter down-arrow | Scatter with Straight Lines and Markers**.

> **Excel 2003 Equivalent**
>
> To insert a 2-D Scatter Chart in Excel 2003, click on the **Insert | Chart | XY (Scatter) | Scatter with data points connected by lines**.

	A	B	C	D	E
1	THE YIELD CURVE	Obtaining and Using It			
2		Maturity	Time To	Yield To	Forward
3	**Yield Curve Inputs**	Date	Maturity	Maturity	Rates
4	Today's Date	5/22/2007			
5	One Month Treasury Bill	6/22/2007	0.08	4.90%	4.90%
6	Three Month Treasury Bill	8/22/2007	0.25	4.77%	4.71%
7	Six Month Treasury Bill	11/22/2007	0.50	4.81%	4.85%
8	One Year Treasury Strip	5/15/2008	0.98	4.89%	4.97%
9	Two Year Treasury Strip	8/15/2009	2.23	4.82%	4.77%
10	Three Year Treasury Strip	8/15/2010	3.23	4.74%	4.56%
11	Four Year Treasury Strip	8/15/2011	4.23	4.72%	4.66%
12	Five Year Treasury Strip	8/15/2012	5.23	4.71%	4.67%
13	Ten Year Treasury Strip	8/15/2017	10.23	4.93%	5.16%
14	Fifteen Year Treasury Bond	8/15/2022	15.23	5.14%	5.57%
15	Twenty Year Treasury Bond	8/15/2027	20.23	5.11%	5.02%
16	Twenty Five Year Treasury Bond	8/15/2032	25.23	4.97%	4.41%
17	Thirty Year Treasury Bond	2/15/2037	29.73	4.95%	4.84%

A rough version of the 2-D Scatter Chart appears.

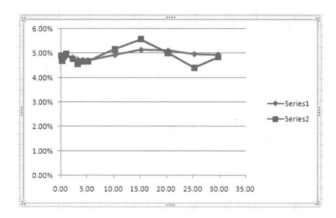

As long as the Chart is selected, three new tabs appear that provide lots of chart options for Design, Layout, and Formatting.

Chart Tools

Design   Layout   Format

Alternatively, you can right-click on parts of the chart to get pop-up menus with formatting choices. Here is what a fully-formatted 2-D Scatter Chart looks like.

23.11 3-D Surface Chart

Task. Create a three-dimensional Surface Chart.

How To. Select the range that has the data you wish to graph (e.g., select **C94:G98** in the example below). Click on **Insert | Charts | Other Charts down-arrow | Surface | 3-D Surface**.

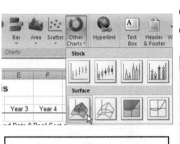

Excel 2003 Equivalent

To insert a 3-D Surface Chart in Excel 2003, click on the **Insert | Chart | Surface | 3-D Surface**.

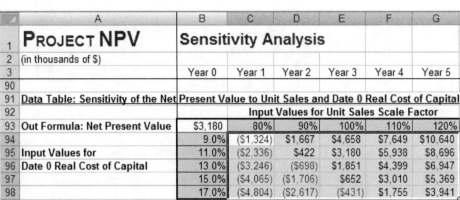

	A	B	C	D	E	F	G
1	**PROJECT NPV**	**Sensitivity Analysis**					
2	(in thousands of $)						
3		Year 0	Year 1	Year 2	Year 3	Year 4	Year 5
90							
91	Data Table: Sensitivity of the Net Present Value to Unit Sales and Date 0 Real Cost of Capital						
92			Input Values for Unit Sales Scale Factor				
93	Out Formula: Net Present Value	$3,180	80%	90%	100%	110%	120%
94		9.0%	($1,324)	$1,667	$4,658	$7,649	$10,640
95	Input Values for	11.0%	($2,336)	$422	$3,180	$5,938	$8,696
96	Date 0 Real Cost of Capital	13.0%	($3,246)	($698)	$1,851	$4,399	$6,947
97		15.0%	($4,065)	($1,706)	$652	$3,010	$5,369
98		17.0%	($4,804)	($2,617)	($431)	$1,755	$3,941

A rough version of the 3-D Surface Chart appears.

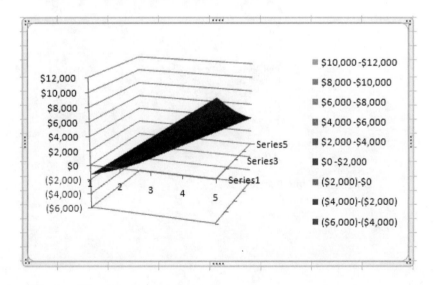

As long as the Chart is selected, three new tabs appear that provide lots of chart options for Design, Layout, and Formatting.

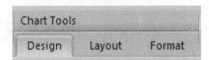

Alternatively, you can right-click on parts of the chart to get pop-up menus with formatting choices.

It is often useful to rotate a 3-D chart. To do this, click on **Layout | Background | 3-D Rotation**. 3-D Rotation provides the ability to rotate the surface in the X-axis direction, Y-axis direction, or Z-axis direction.

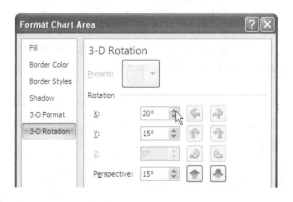

Here is what a fully-formatted 3-D Surface Chart looks like.

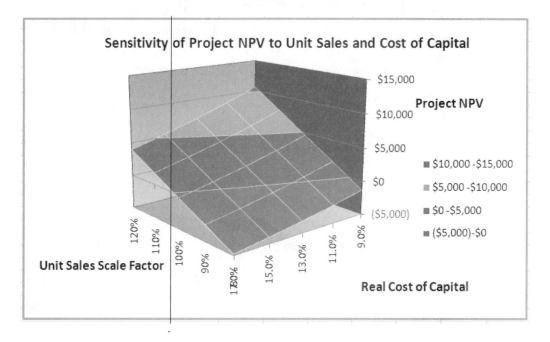

READ THIS LICENSE CAREFULLY BEFORE OPENING THIS PACKAGE. BY OPENING THIS PACKAGE, YOU ARE AGREEING TO THE TERMS AND CONDITIONS OF THIS LICENSE. IF YOU DO NOT AGREE, DO NOT OPEN THE PACKAGE. PROMPTLY RETURN THE UNOPENED PACKAGE AND ALL ACCOMPANYING ITEMS TO THE PLACE YOU OBTAINED THEM FOR A FULL REFUND OF ANY SUMS YOU HAVE PAID FOR THE SOFTWARE. *THESE TERMS APPLY TO ALL LICENSED SOFTWARE ON THE DISK EXCEPT THAT THE TERMS FOR USE OF ANY SHAREWARE OR FREEWARE ON THE DISKETTES ARE AS SET FORTH IN THE ELECTRONIC LICENSE LOCATED ON THE CD-ROM:*

1.   GRANT OF LICENSE and OWNERSHIP: The enclosed computer programs and data ("Software") are licensed, not sold, to you by Pearson Education, Inc. publishing as Prentice-Hall, Inc. ("We" or the "Company") and in consideration of your purchase or adoption of the accompanying Company textbooks and/or other materials, and your agreement to these terms. We reserve any rights not granted to you. You own only the disk(s) but we and/or our licensors own the Software itself. This license allows you to use and display your copy of the Software on a single computer (i.e., with a single CPU) at a single location for <u>academic</u> use only, so long as you comply with the terms of this Agreement. You may make one copy for back up, or transfer your copy to another CPU, provided that the Software is usable on only one computer.

2.   RESTRICTIONS: You may <u>not</u> transfer or distribute the Software or documentation to anyone else. Except for backup, you may <u>not</u> copy the documentation or the Software. You may <u>not</u> network the Software or otherwise use it on more than one computer or computer terminal at the same time. You may <u>not</u> reverse engineer, disassemble, decompile, modify, adapt, translate, or create derivative works based on the Software or the Documentation. You may be held legally responsible for any copying or copyright infringement that is caused by your failure to abide by the terms of these restrictions.

3.   TERMINATION: This license is effective until terminated. This license will terminate automatically without notice from the Company if you fail to comply with any provisions or limitations of this license. Upon termination, you shall destroy the Documentation and all copies of the Software. All provisions of this Agreement as to limitation and disclaimer of warranties, limitation of liability, remedies or damages, and our ownership rights shall survive termination.

4.   LIMITED WARRANTY AND DISCLAIMER OF WARRANTY: Company warrants that for a period of 60 days from the date you purchase this SOFTWARE (or purchase or adopt the accompanying textbook), the Software, when properly installed and used in accordance with the Documentation, will operate in substantial conformity with the description of the Software set forth in the Documentation, and that for a period of 30 days the disk(s) on which the Software is delivered shall be free from defects in materials and workmanship under normal use. The Company does <u>not</u> warrant that the Software will meet your requirements or that the operation of the Software will be uninterrupted or error-free. Your only remedy and the Company's only obligation under these limited warranties is, at the Company's option, return of the disk for a refund of any amounts paid for it by you or replacement of the disk. THIS LIMITED WARRANTY IS THE ONLY WARRANTY PROVIDED BY THE COMPANY AND ITS LICENSORS, AND THE COMPANY AND ITS LICENSORS DISCLAIM ALL OTHER WARRANTIES, EXPRESS OR IMPLIED, INCLUDING WITHOUT LIMITATION, THE IMPLIED WARRANTIES OF MERCHANTABILITY AND FITNESS FOR A PARTICULAR PURPOSE. THE COMPANY DOES NOT WARRANT, GUARANTEE OR MAKE ANY REPRESENTATION REGARDING THE ACCURACY, RELIABILITY, CURRENTNESS, USE, OR RESULTS OF USE, OF THE SOFTWARE.

5.   LIMITATION OF REMEDIES AND DAMAGES: IN NO EVENT, SHALL THE COMPANY OR ITS EMPLOYEES, AGENTS, LICENSORS, OR CONTRACTORS BE LIABLE FOR ANY INCIDENTAL, INDIRECT, SPECIAL, OR CONSEQUENTIAL DAMAGES ARISING OUT OF OR IN CONNECTION WITH THIS LICENSE OR THE SOFTWARE, INCLUDING FOR LOSS OF USE, LOSS OF DATA, LOSS OF INCOME OR PROFIT, OR OTHER LOSSES, SUSTAINED AS A RESULT OF INJURY TO ANY PERSON, OR LOSS OF OR DAMAGE TO PROPERTY, OR CLAIMS OF THIRD PARTIES, EVEN IF THE COMPANY OR AN AUTHORIZED REPRESENTATIVE OF THE COMPANY HAS BEEN ADVISED OF THE POSSIBILITY OF SUCH DAMAGES. IN NO EVENT SHALL THE LIABILITY OF THE COMPANY FOR DAMAGES WITH RESPECT TO THE SOFTWARE EXCEED THE AMOUNTS ACTUALLY PAID BY YOU, IF ANY, FOR THE SOFTWARE OR THE ACCOMPANYING TEXTBOOK. BECAUSE SOME JURISDICTIONS DO NOT ALLOW THE LIMITATION OF LIABILITY IN CERTAIN CIRCUMSTANCES, THE ABOVE LIMITATIONS MAY NOT ALWAYS APPLY TO YOU.

6.   GENERAL: THIS AGREEMENT SHALL BE CONSTRUED IN ACCORDANCE WITH THE LAWS OF THE UNITED STATES OF AMERICA AND THE STATE OF NEW YORK, APPLICABLE TO CONTRACTS MADE IN NEW YORK, AND SHALL BENEFIT THE COMPANY, ITS AFFILIATES AND ASSIGNEES. HIS AGREEMENT IS THE COMPLETE AND EXCLUSIVE STATEMENT OF THE AGREEMENT BETWEEN YOU AND THE COMPANY AND SUPERSEDES ALL PROPOSALS OR PRIOR AGREEMENTS, ORAL, OR WRITTEN, AND ANY OTHER COMMUNICATIONS BETWEEN YOU AND THE COMPANY OR ANY REPRESENTATIVE OF THE COMPANY RELATING TO THE SUBJECT MATTER OF THIS AGREEMENT. If you are a U.S. Government user, this Software is licensed with "restricted rights" as set forth in subparagraphs (a)-(d) of the Commercial Computer-Restricted Rights clause at FAR 52.227-19 or in subparagraphs (c)(1)(ii) of the Rights in Technical Data and Computer Software clause at DFARS 252.227-7013, and similar clauses, as applicable.

Should you have any questions concerning this agreement or if you wish to contact the Company for any reason, please contact in writing: Director of New Media, Higher Education Division, Prentice Hall, Inc., Upper Saddle River, NJ 07458